PROCEEDINGS

OF THE

SOCIETY OF ANTIQUARIES

OF LONDON

27TH NOVEMBER 1913 TO 25TH JUNE 1914

SECOND SERIES, VOL. XXVI

PRINTED AT OXFORD BY HORACE HART FOR

THE SOCIETY OF ANTIQUARIES

BURLINGTON HOUSE, LONDON

LIST OF ILLUSTRATIONS

PROCEEDINGS

OF THE

SOCIETY OF ANTIQUARIES

OF LONDON

SESSION 1913—1914.

THURSDAY, 27th NOVEMBER, 1913.

Sir CHARLES HERCULES READ, Knt., LL.D., President,
in the Chair.

The following gifts were announced, and thanks for the same
ordered to be returned to the donors :

From the Rev. Professor Bonney, F.S.A. :—Inscriptions from Swiss
chalets. By Walter Larden. 8vo. Oxford, 1913.

From the Author :—Notes on the history of the Armourers' and Brasiers'
Company. By E. J. Barron, F.S.A. 8vo. London, 1913.

From the Author :—The Hospital and Chapel of St. Mary Roncevall at
Charing Cross. By James Galloway, M.D. 8vo. London, 1913.

From the Author :—Esher Place, and its associations with Cardinal
Wolsey and the Spanish Armada. By the Rev. J. K. Floyer, F.S.A.
8vo. n.p. n.d.

From the Author, W. H. St. John Hope, Esq., Litt.D., D.C.L. :
1. A grammar of heraldry. 12mo. Cambridge, 1913.
2. Heraldry for craftsmen and designers. 8vo. London, 1913.

From J. H. C. Evelyn, Esq. :—The churches of Wotton, Abinger, and
Oakwood. By F. R. Fairbank. Privately printed. 8vo. Guildford, 1911.

From the Author :—Cellæ Trichoræ and other Christian antiquities in
the Byzantine Provinces of Sicily with Calabria and North Africa,
including Sardinia. Vol. i. By E. H. Freshfield, F.S.A. 8vo. n.p.
1913.

From the Editor :—Syrian anatomy, pathology, and therapeutics, or
'The Book of Medicines'. 2 vols. Edited by E. A. W. Budge,
F.S.A. London, 1913.

From Rev G W. W. Minns, F.S A.:—Scythians and Greeks A survey of ancient history and archaeology on the north coast of the Euxine from the Danube to the Caucasus By E H Minns. 4to   Cambridge, 1913.

From the Earl of Crawford and Balcarres, LL D., V -P S A —Bibliotheca Lindesiana   Vol viii. Handlist of Proclamations, 1714–1910. fol. Wigan, 1913

From the Author —Barnwell Castle, Northamptonshire. By C. A. Markham, F S.A. 8vo. n p. 1913.

From the Author:—Robert and Andrew Foulis and the Glasgow press, with some account of the Glasgow Academy of Fine Arts   By David Murray, LL D , F.S A. 8vo. Glasgow, 1913

From Harold Sands, Esq , F S A. —Cliff castles and cave dwellings of Europe. By S Baring-Gould 8vo. London, 1911

From Rev. Canon Barwell, F S A.:—Vincentio Saviolo his Practise.   In two Bookes The first intreating of the use of the Rapier and Dagger. The second of Honor and honorable Quarrels 4to. London, 1595.

From the Author, L. F. Salzmann, Esq., B A., F.S.A.:
1 Mediaeval byways. 8vo. London, 1913
2. English industries of the Middle Ages. 8vo London, 1913.

From the Editor —A handbook for Birmingham and the neighbourhood, prepared for the meeting of the British Association, 1913 Edited by G A. Auden, M D , F.S.A 8vo. Birmingham, 1913

From William H Whitehead, Esq .—Retrospections. By Sir Charles Whitehead, F S A 8vo. . Maidstone, n p.

From the Author—Ashby-de-la-Zouch Castle, Leicestershire, historic and descriptive. By Thomas H. Fosbrooke. 4to   n.p. n.d.

From the Delegates of the Clarendon Press.—The archaeology of the Anglo-Saxon settlements. By E. Thurlow Leeds, F.S.A. 8vo. Oxford, 1913.

From the Author:—Sussex church plate By J. E Couchman. 8vo. Brighton, 1913.

From the Author —The ancient earthworks of Cranborne Chase By Heywood Sumner, F.S A. 8vo London, 1913.

From Rev. William Hudson, F S A.:—Register or memorial of Ewell, Surrey. Edited by Cecil Deedes, M A 8vo London, 1913.

From the Author :—English historical literature in the fifteenth century. By C. L. Kingsford, F.S.A 8vo. Oxford, 1913

From the Author:—The royal manor and park of Shotwick in Cheshire. By R. Stewart-Brown, F.S.A. 8vo n p. 1912.

From the Author, J. W. Willis-Bund, Esq , F S A :
1. The battle of Worcester 12mo. Worcester, 1913 , and
2. The legendary lore of Worcestershire. 8vo. Lincoln. n.d.

From the Author :—Notes on pre-conquest church architecture in Hampshire and Surrey. By Colonel H. L. Jessep. 8vo. Winchester, 1913.

Fig. 1.   CROSS AND BASE : ST. SAMPSON'S, GUERNSEY $(\frac{1}{5})$

From the Author:—The China Collector. A guide to the porcelain of the English factories. By H. W. Lewer. 12mo. London. n.d.

From the Author:—Historic Darlington. By Edward Wooler, F.S.A. 8vo. London, 1913.

From the Royal Society :—The celebration of the two hundred and fiftieth anniversary of the Royal Society of London, July 15-19, 1912. 4to. London, 1913.

From the Author :—The Bretts of Rotherby. By Rev. W. D. Bushell, F.S.A. 8vo. n.p. n.d.

From the Vice-Chairman and Board of the National Portrait Gallery :— Portrait medal of Viscount Dillon, D.C.L., F.S.A. 1913.

From W. H. Quarrell, Esq., F.S.A.:—Portrait of Richard Warren, M.D., F.R.S., F.S.A., from a picture by G. Stuart, engraved by G. Bartolozzi.

The President announced that the late Canon Barwell, F.S.A., had bequeathed to the Society any of his books which the President chose to select, and that in consequence some fifty volumes would be added to the Society's Library.

The President also announced that under the Ancient Monuments Act the Council had nominated the Earl of Crawford and Balcarres to be the representative of the Society on the Advisory Board for England and that he himself had been appointed by the Trustees to represent the British Museum on the Board.

The President further drew attention to the improvements which had been made in lighting the meeting room.

Walter Knight, Earl Ferrers, was admitted a Fellow.

The Rev. William Taylor, Rector of St. Sampson's, Guernsey, sent for exhibition a number of latten objects lately discovered in St. Sampson's Church, on which the Secretary made the following remarks :

"We have to thank our local Secretary, Dr. Marett, for the opportunity of seeing the very interesting group of latten objects exhibited here to-night by the Rev. William Taylor, Rector of St. Sampson's, Guernsey.

They were found under the following circumstances on 20th June, 1913. It had become necessary to rehang the bell; and the plan adopted was to erect a steel frame whose footings should be on a level, or thereabouts, with the crown of the stone vault of the tower, the ground floor of which is used as a baptistery. The haunches of the vault were found to be filled in with rubbly soil nearly to the underside of the wooden floor of the bell-chamber, and this soil was being cleared away, in order to put in concrete footings for the bell-frame, when a loose stone was noticed in the south wall of the tower. Its removal disclosed the entrance to a small chamber in the wall, and in this chamber were found the objects you now see.

They consist of a cross, part of a censer, two standing candle-sticks, part of a triple candlestick intended to be set in a socket, four branches, and a loose bowl and pricket.

The cross (fig. 1) is of a type with which the Society is familiar, and the example in our own collection is shown for comparison.

It is provided with a socketed base, in which it stood on the altar, but when occasion required it could be taken off its base

Fig. 2.   BOWL OF CENSER, ST. SAMPSON'S, GUERNSEY ($\frac{1}{2}$).

and used as a processional cross, set on a long staff. Compared with the Society's specimen, it will be seen that it is not its equal in workmanship, and is moreover, except that it retains its base, less perfect, having lost the lozenge at the foot of the cross and the sockets which carried the brackets on which stood the figures of our Lady and St. John. The three remaining lozenges, at the ends of the arms, are engraved with the IHS, instead of the evangelistic symbols as on our specimen ; and at the back have a design of four leaves, instead of suns. The stem and arms have a running leaf pattern on both faces and plain bevelled edges from which spring foliate crockets. The figure of our Lord is in good preservation, and the three nails fastening it to the cross are still in their places. The knop at the foot of the cross is hexagonal, the faces of the bosses being engraved with four-leaved flowers, and alternating with the bosses are leaf-shaped raised figures above and below, with a tracery pattern on them. The socketed circular base is domed,

Fig. 3. STANDING CANDLESTICK: ST. SAMPSON'S, GUERNSEY ($\frac{1}{3}$)

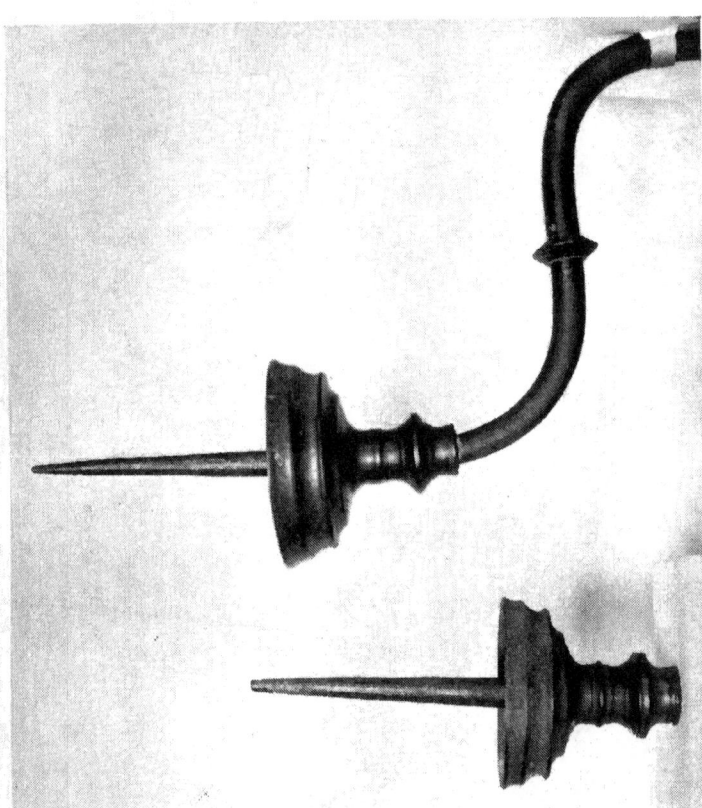

Fig. 6. BRANCH AND SOCKET OF CANDLESTICK (⅓)
ST. SAMPSON'S, GUERNSEY

Fig. 4. STANDING CANDLESTICK (⅓)

Fig. 5.   TRIPLE CANDLESTICK (ONE BRANCH MISSING): ST. SAMPSON'S, GUERNSEY ($\frac{1}{3}$)

To face page 4

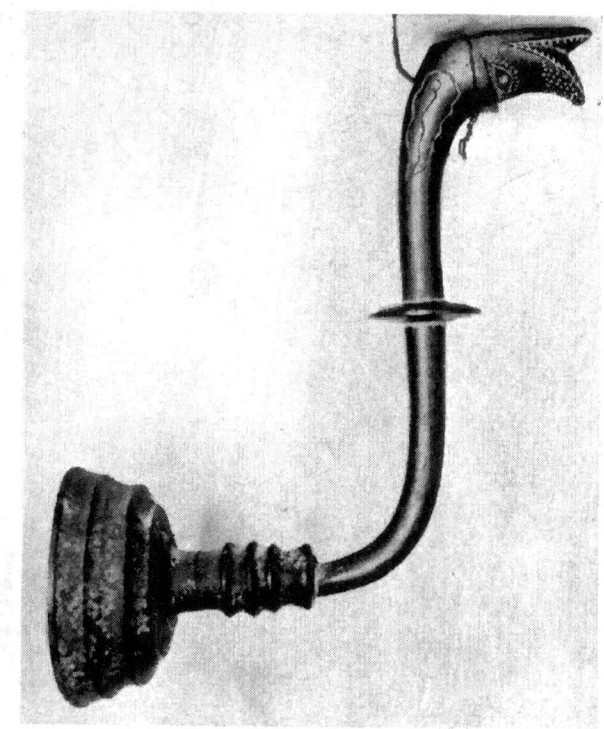
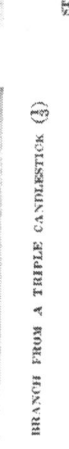

Fig. 7. BRANCH FROM A TRIPLE CANDLESTICK ($\frac{1}{3}$)

Fig. 8. BRANCH CANDLESTICK ($\frac{1}{3}$)

ST. SAMPSON'S, GUERNSEY

with a gadroon ornament issuing from beneath a projecting ring with an open cresting of crosses and fleurs-de-lis, from which in turn rises the cylindrical socket over which the socket of the cross fits. It has a six-lobed foot to steady it, engraved with a hatched zigzag pattern.

The lower half of a censer (fig. 2) is of a very simple form, such ornament as it had being doubtless reserved for the upper half, which is unfortunately missing. The bowl is circular, and the foot worked into an octagon; there are remains of what looks like incense in the bowl.

The larger standing candlestick (fig. 3) is 12 in. high to the top of the cup and 18½ in. high to the top of the pricket. The cup and foot are circular, with simple mouldings, and there are rings at the middle and both ends of the stem. The second standing candlestick (fig. 4) is of a more elaborate kind, having an embattled bowl, and a base raised on three lion's feet. It is 9¼ in. high to the top of the bowl, 12½ in. to the top of the pricket. The triple candlestick (fig. 5), retaining unfortunately only two of its holders, has a pinhole through its stem at the level of the sockets for its two branches, showing that it was thus fastened to some form of holder or stem. The sockets are marked for fitting with one and two grooves respectively, and the remaining branch has a single groove to identify it as belonging to the single-grooved socket. The four branches are all odd pieces; two (figs. 6 and 7) have fitted into ring sockets like that last described, a third (fig. 8) which ends in a beast's head, has been fastened by something like the hanging hook of a door, and the fourth (fig. 9), a remarkable specimen in the form of a dragon-like beast with a curved horn and a long whip-like tail, and having a shield fastened to his lower jaw, has two lugs pierced to fit over a vertical pin.

It will be well now, before going further, to quote two English inventories dealing with similar objects.

The first is that of Long Melford Church, Suffolk, 1529:

Two great candlesticks.
Two second candlesticks, lately bought, which are called Secondans.
Two small candlesticks to the high altar.
Two small candlesticks to Jesus altar, both of Lattyn.
A candlestick of Lattin, with ten branches, standing before the image of Jesus.
A candlestick.
A candlestick, ten branches, before St. Ann.
A candlestick, with three branches, belonging to the Trinity; and now the said candlestick standeth before the image of St. Nicholas.
A candlestick with ten branches, standing before the high altar.
Two little pretty candlesticks of Lattin, belonging to John Hill's altar.
A candlestick of Lattin, with ten branches, now in the vestry.
A candlestick of Lattin, with three branches, now in the vestry.

The second is of St. Mary's Guild, Boston, 1534:

Two great candelstickes of latten
Two secondary candelstickes of latten
Two lesser candelstickes of latten standing at the altar ende.
A litill candelstick of latten standyng of three lions
An other lesse candelstyk standynge afore owr lady.
Two litill candillstickes of latten standynge on the high altar of owr lady.
A candelstick of latten w^t two flowres for the morow masse
An other litill candelstik of latten w^t two flowres for one of the side altars
Two other litill candelstickes of latten w^t two pynnes
Two laten candelstickes standinge uppon the altar

These are the outfits of a well-appointed church and a wealthy guild, and are on a more lavish scale than St. Sampson's could probably attain to The first three items in each inventory are similar, and refer to the lights near the high altar, namely, two great candlesticks or standards, two lesser candlesticks or secondars, and two small candlesticks standing at the altar end, not on the altar, but probably on the iron rod from which the costers or riddels hung , and from the St Mary's Guild inventory it is also clear that there were two little candlesticks standing on the high altar also The branched candlesticks, of ten or three branches, stood before various images, but one is said to stand before the high altar.

We may therefore consider that the candlesticks exhibited may be described as belonging to a set of latten, and to consist of one secondan which could also be carried in procession, one altar candlestick, and remains of several sets of branched candlesticks The triple candlestick may be another form of a three-branched candlestick, but it may also be for the Judas candle or candles used in the Easter Even service. This was properly a taper made of three candles twisted together into one at the bottom and separating above into three, fastened to a staff for carrying them. As a substitute for this triple candle three separate candles were sometimes fixed on to a frame.

Their use was to carry the new fire into the choir for lighting the great paschal candle.

The remaining branches may have been part either of standing candlesticks, like those in the inventories, an elaborate development of which may be seen in the drawing of Abbot Islip's hearse at Westminster, [1] or they may have been attached to wall sconces. The dragon candlestick and that ending in a beast's head are perhaps in the second category, and fitted into sconces, the other two being parts of standing candlesticks

We know nothing of the history of these objects beyond what has been already said, but a few suggestions are possible.

[1] *Vetusta Monumenta,* vol. vii

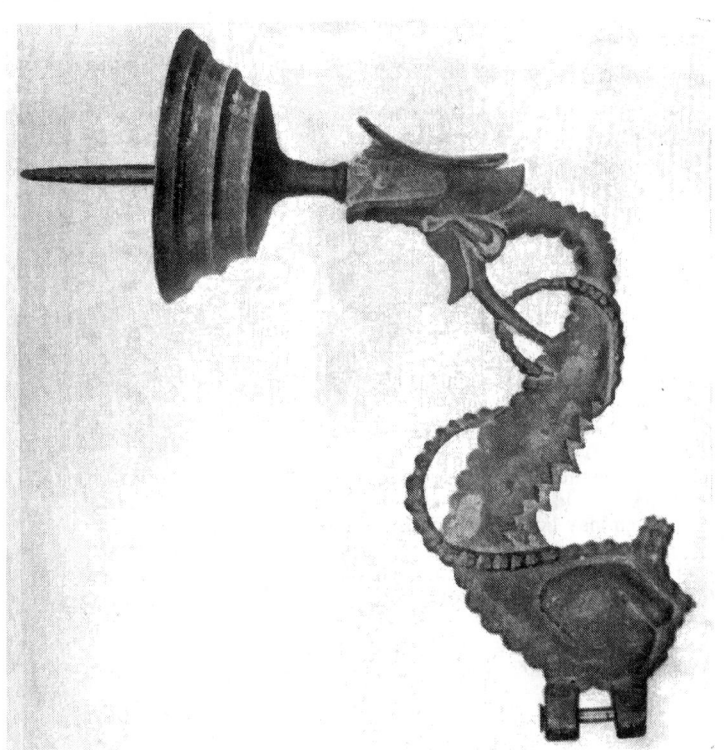

Fig. 9. BRANCH CANDLESTICK, SIDE AND FRONT VIEWS : ST. SAMPSON'S, GUERNSEY ($\frac{1}{3}$)

In the first place, the date of all is approximately the same, namely, 1500 to 1520. From the circumstances of their finding they were evidently intentionally hidden, probably with a view to their re-use if ever, as Mr. Roger Martin of Long Melford said in 1580, the time should serve.

The inference is, also, that they belonged to St. Sampson's Church, though of course this cannot definitely be stated. The Channel Islands being more remote in the sixteenth century than now, the changes of the Reformation were somewhat slow in taking effect, and indeed can hardly be said to have made themselves a dominant factor till 1565, when Guernsey was transferred from the diocese of Coutances to that of Winchester. This may suggest a date for the disuse and concealment of such church fittings, and the excellent condition of all is a further proof that they never fell into unsympathetic hands. The gilding of the cross, particularly of the base, is so complete, allowing for the natural tarnishing due to over three centuries of disuse, that it seems likely that the cross was in use up to the moment of its removal to the safe hiding-place in the haunch of the tower vault.

The last observation which I should wish to make is that the cross, on the analogy of other examples, has every appearance of being English work, nor is there anything in the other pieces to suggest a different origin.

We may therefore conclude, with due reservations, that we have here the remains of an English-made service of latten, acquired by St. Sampson's early in the sixteenth century, hidden about 1565 by an adherent of the old faith, and fortunately preserved intact till our own days, in which we may hope that their safety is definitely assured."

Mr. CRACE asked whether any other pockets of the vaulting had been examined for relics of the same kind.

Mr. HOPE remarked that the series was curiously made up of odd pieces, as if they had been preserved from spoliation in the hope of completing the sets later. The work was almost certainly English, the crown on the foot of the cross, for instance, having alternate crosses and fleurs-de-lis, as on the candle-bracket in front of the grate of Henry VII's chapel at Westminster (formerly at Windsor).

Mr. BARRON agreed as to the provenance of the exhibit. He was familiar with the products of Dinant-sur-Meuse, but recognized something different in the Guernsey specimens, which were

inferior to Dinanderie properly so called. They could not have
been made at Dinant, as that town had been previously sacked
by Charles the Bold.

Mr VALLANCE noted a resemblance in the foot of the crucifix
to one from Stoke Poges illustrated in *Proceedings*, xxiii. 49,
but did not feel sure that the foot exhibited originally belonged
to the crucifix. Three lumps round the foot-rim would be
visible if the candlesticks had ever had feet. The bowl of a
censer was rarely found, covers being comparatively common.
The branches suggested that the candles were placed in front of
consecration crosses. Outside Salisbury Cathedral Church there
were ten (out of twelve) discs 2½ ft. in diameter, each with a
small hole 2½ in. below for fixing a candle.

The PRESIDENT had no doubt about the English origin of the
exhibit, which had a general resemblance to Dinanderie, but by
a process of elimination could be narrowed down to England
Church goods would at that date have been more naturally
supplied from France, but they would in that case have been of
superior workmanship. In the absence of proof to the contrary
that type of cross might be considered English, and several
examples were known. The thanks of the Society were due to
the vicar and churchwardens for a most interesting and unusual
exhibition.

O. M DALTON, Esq, M.A., F.S.A., read the following paper
on medieval objects in the Borradaile Collection

"The medieval objects which Mr. Charles Borradaile has
deposited in the British Museum during the present year include works of so fine a quality that it is desirable to draw
special attention to their merits. They are not numerous—less
than a dozen in all;[1] but as selected examples acquired by a
discerning collector they attain a remarkably high level, and,
since they belong to classes which have almost ceased to appear
in the auction-rooms, their addition to the medieval series in
the museum is a matter for special congratulation. They fall
into two almost equal groups, ivory carvings and metal-work,
of which the former may be first described
The first object to be noticed, the ivory horn,[2] (fig. 1) fills a

---

[1] It may be mentioned that Mr Borradaile at the same time deposited
a number of rare and important pieces of English porcelain.
[2] Acquired at the Magniac sale in 1892, lot 251. Length, 22 inches.
Probably the horn exhibited by Mr Magniac at the special exhibition of

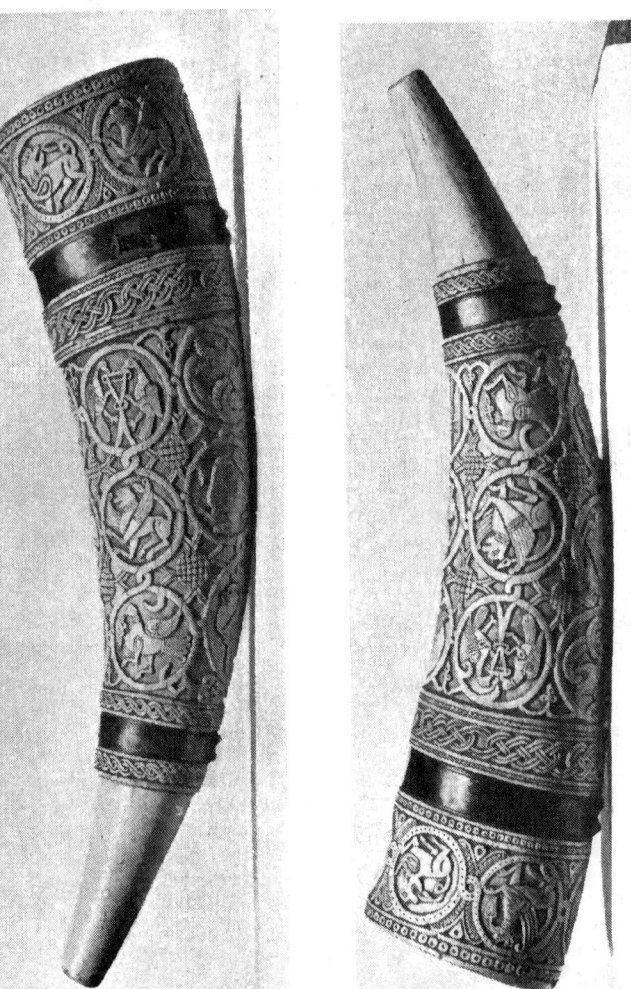

Fig. 1. IVORY HORN : BORRADAILE COLLECTION

gap in the collection which bade fair to remain in perpetuity; for while South Kensington possesses good examples, at Bloomsbury the type was unrepresented. These
horns, or oliphants,[1] are difficult to date or place with any
precision. It is only certain that they were produced between the ninth and thirteenth centuries, and that all but a few
show direct or indirect oriental influence. Nor is their destination always clear. Most of them were undoubtedly made as
war- or hunting-horns; but a few, to which we shall revert
later, may have had some connexion with the hippodrome; while
another small group, carved with sacred subjects, was from the
first associated with churches or monasteries, in early days perhaps employed to summon worshippers, command silence, or to
awaken the monks, in later times to contain relics; for the latter
purpose, indeed, any kind of oliphant might in course of time be
adopted. There are further instances in which the oliphant
served as a legal symbol, as in the case of the interesting horn
at York, through which Ulph delivered the seisin of certain
lands to St. Peter's.[2]

The present specimen was probably made for hunting, and is
ornamented in a style analogous to that of other known examples. A network of interlacing circles containing beasts and
monsters covers the body; a zone of similar circles runs round
the mouth; while bands of interlacing, zigzag, guilloche, and
pierced discs separate and enclose the several parts. On the
body of the horn, the spaces between the circles are filled by
formal designs possibly derived from bunches of grapes, a supposition perhaps confirmed by the appearance round the mouth
of intermediate foliage, recalling vine-leaves, on the two external
rows in the main diaper, of projecting tendrils and leaves, and,
pendent from one of the circles round the mouth, quite unmistak-
able grapes. The whole framework of the animals would thus
suggest a schematized vine. The general idea of the interlacing
circles is common to early mosaics, textiles, and other objects,
chiefly East-Roman and oriental, and numerous examples of its

works of art of the medieval, Renaissance, and more recent periods,
South Kensington, 1862. (Catalogue, edited by J. C. Robinson, no. 213,
p. 18.)

[1] For oliphants see E. Molinier, *Ivoires*, p. 93, and Musée national du
Louvre, *Cat. des ivoires*, 1896, pp. 63-4; C. Cahier, *Nouveaux mélanges
d'archéologie*, ii, 1874, p. 35; F. Bock, *Ueber den Gebrauch der Hörner im
Alterthum*, etc., in *Mittelalterliche Kunstdenkmale des österreichischen
Kaiserstaates*, edited by J. Heider and R. Eitelberger, 1862, vol. ii, pp.
126 ff.; J. Hampel, *Alterthümer des frühen Mittelalters in Ungarn*, ii,
pp. 888 ff., and various references there given.

[2] Reproduced in Poole and Hugall's guide to York Cathedral; cf. also
Archaeologia, i, 187.

employment survive.[1] The beasts [2] in their turn are conventionalized, the treatment of the joints and the wings being probably in origin Eastern, while there are points, such as the rounded and upturned tails of the birds, which nearly recall the tails of the well-known Sassanian 'gryphon'; but features of this kind became so early a common artistic heritage, that they do not in themselves entitle us to ascribe the horn to the East. The eagles stand in the Byzantine attitude, with the legs side by side before the depending tail; [3] the birds with the vase represent a motive which may have entered Christian art from the East, but soon became one of its favourite ornamental designs; [4] the 'dragons' with knotted bodies (fig 2) are perhaps, though not certainly, of European invention.[5] The decoration of the horn is

[1] Cf. O von Falke, *Kunstgeschichte der Seidenweberei*, 1913, i, p. 18. In addition to the antique mosaic pavements, North Italian examples of the eleventh century may be compared. Cf. especially that of the cathedral of Cremona, E. Aus'm Weerth, *Der Mosaikboden in St. Gereon zu Coln*, pl. vi.

[2] Round the mouth, the order is as follows eagle, lion, gryphon, large bird, gryphon, lion; the eagle forming the mid-point, and flanked by the lions and gryphons, which face towards it

On the body of the horn, beginning nearest the broad end, we have, in the first row a cock, flanked on each side by the familiar device of confronted birds drinking from a vase, beyond which are two contiguous circles, each containing a dragon with interlaced body biting its own tail, while a smaller subsidiary head, which goes off at a tangent, bites a tendril of the vine The second or middle row contains a gryphon, flanked by two winged lions, beyond which are two circles, each with a regardant bird. In the third row, at the narrow end, an eagle is flanked by two birds, while behind, in a circle of greater diameter than any other, are two confronted lions rampant and regardant, two paws raised high over their heads, two crossed below their breasts (fig 2)

In the treatment of many of the beasts there is an element of the grotesque; the tails are foliated and bitten by their owners, and in some cases twisted Both quadrupeds and birds frequently carry leaves in their mouths It may be noted that the cock appears on the horn at Angers (Cahier, as above, p 35) and is found on early Persian textiles

[3] Von Falke, as above, ii, p. 16.

[4] Lasting in Italy into the high Middle Ages. Cf H. von der Gabelentz, *Mittelalterliche Plastik von Venedig*, 1903, p. 71 The birds are generally peacocks, but in the present case lack the usual crests

[5] Quite a near parallel to the dragons on the horn occurs on the cross from Gosforth in Cumberland, assigned to the beginning of the eleventh century, or even earlier (Collingwood in *Victoria County History, Cumberland*, vol i, p 263; *Mémoires de la Société des Antiquaires du Nord*, 1884-1889, p. 17; cast in the Victoria and Albert Museum) Cf also the font at Chaddesley-Corbett (F. Bond, *Fonts and Font-covers*, p 53.) The appearance of these knotted dragons upon the oliphant makes us instinctively think of Scandinavia; the invention of such devices should not, however, be ascribed to Northern art without further investigation It is probable that interlacings as a whole were first borrowed from the South by the barbaric tribes at the time of the great migrations (Von der Gabelentz, as above, pp. 77 ff , 89), and that some of the grotesque features in beast-ornament, such as the knotting of the body, multiplication of heads, etc.,

To face page 10

Fig. 2. DETAILS OF ORNAMENT ON IVORY HORN ; BORRADAILE COLLECTION

in fact due to what has been described as 'the great international culture of the earlier Middle Ages'; and this cosmopolitan character is responsible for the difficulty of finding a place of origin for objects of the kind.[1] When from Mesopotamia to the British Isles, from Egypt to Denmark, there appear on every hand beasts and monsters of one family and distinguished only in the mannerisms imposed on them by different peoples, it is clear that the task of locating specimens in which mannerism is not conspicuous must often be a matter of perplexity. Almost identical designs may appear at opposite ends of Europe. The analogy between the knotted dragons of this horn and those at Gosforth has been already noticed; the confronted lions are in conception akin to a similar motive on a seventh-century cross-shaft at Collingham, Yorkshire,[2] and to a version of the same subject on an early Romanesque capital in France.[3] There is nothing national in these designs; if the use of a long word may be pardoned, they are ecumenical, common to most countries of the known inhabited world.[4] To what country, then, is the present oliphant to be attributed? There is fortunately a clue which suggests an approximate, if not a certain, answer: it has direct and close points of resemblance to another horn on which much has been written—the oliphant of Jasz Berény in Hungary; it

were introduced by peoples in more immediate contact with late-Roman and Byzantine civilization than the Scandinavians ever were. A monster with a knotted body is carved on a capital in the atrium of S. Ambrogio at Milan (F. de Dartein, *Étude sur l'architecture lombarde*, Atlas, pl. xliii), which some consider as early as the ninth century, though others put rather later (Cattaneo, *Architecture in Italy*, English edition, 1896, p. 247); and on the gold crosses found in Lombard graves the interlacings sometimes end in beast-heads (Von der Gabelentz, p. 78). When we find dragons with interlaced bodies in the Mohammedan art of the twelfth century and a little later (Van Berchem and Strzygowski, *Amida*, pp. 83–4 and figs. 30–4: reliefs on Aleppo gate of Diarbekr, citadel gate of Aleppo, coins of Qara Arslan), on copper coins of Mohammed II of Turkey, and in medieval MSS. from Servia, Bulgaria, and Bohemia (V. Stassoff, *L'Ornement-Slav*, pl. vi, viii, xxii, etc.), it becomes probable that this style of ornament did not start in the north of Europe but in some more central region.

[1] After the fall of the Empire in the West, Graeco-Roman art rapidly lost the ground which it still held, and the popular beast-ornament, already existing but not officially recognized, broke loose and ultimately covered half the world. With the more decided trend to orientalism in Byzantine art which iconoclasm encouraged, a new impetus was given to a movement destined to continue until the rise of Gothic art.

[2] W. G. Collingwood, in *V. C. H. Yorkshire*, vol. ii, p. 111. At present no photographic illustration of this cross is published.

[3] On a capital in Ste-Radegonde at Poitiers (Vitry and Brière, *Documents de sculpture française du Moyen Age*, pl. xxix, fig. 2).

[4] Thus practically the same design may be found on Coptic and Sassanian reliefs or stuffs, on Byzantine objects of the middle period, in 'Saracenic' art, in early-medieval sculpture, mosaic-pavements and minor works of art, in Northern Italy, France, Spain, Germany, Scandinavia, and the British Isles.

has also points of analogy with two other horns in the cathedral of Prague.[1] Several of the beasts are almost repetitions of those round the mouth of the Jasz Berény horn,[2] and the foliate ornament in the spandrels between the circles is also identical. Further, a similar border of pierced discs is also seen on one of the Prague oliphants. Now both these horns of the east of Europe have on the body scenes from the amphitheatre or circus, in one case jugglers and acrobats, in the other, four-horse chariot-races It is argued that in the tenth or eleventh century, to which date they are assigned, such subjects should relate to the hippodrome at Constantinople; and therefore the two horns have been generally accepted as Byzantine. If that is so, Mr Borradaile's oliphant, though without the circus-subjects, may also be Byzantine. we have already noticed the Byzantine type of the eagle, and there is perhaps no feature of which we can definitely say that it could not be the work of a Byzantine ivory-carver, since at this period beast-ornament was very general in the East-Roman Empire There remains, however, the possibility of an origin in North Italy, where Byzantine models were closely copied, or perhaps even in some East European country where the influences of Constantinople were predominant. The horn may well belong to the tenth century, and is not likely to be later than the eleventh

Of two characteristic Byzantine ivories, one, a panel with the subject known as the *Deesis*, i e. our Lord between the Virgin and St. John the Baptist, beneath a pierced canopy, dates perhaps from the early twelfth century It is a good example of a style which does not aim at extreme finish, and is represented in various collections, but hitherto imperfectly in the Museum.[3]

---

[1] Both horns are described and reproduced by Hampel, as above, vol ii, pp 889 ff, and in plates, 532 ff

[2] The birds, both in type and in the manner in which they hold leaves in their mouths, recall those on the early cedar chest at Terracina, an object which some are inclined to place as early as the eighth or ninth century, and for which an oriental origin is probable (J Strzygowski, *Das orientalische Italien*, in *Monatshefte für Kunstwissenschaft*, vol 1, Leipzig, figs. 8–10; A Muñoz, *L'Art byzantin a l'exposition de Grottaferrata*, p 181 (1906), A Venturi, *Storia dell' arte italiana*, ii, figs. 83–5). It is interesting to note that points of resemblance exist between this coffer and the Jasz Berény horn, while at the same time it suggests affinities with the Franks casket in the British Museum (*Catalogue of Ivory Carvings*, no 30). A further analogy to the beasts of pre-Carolingian illuminated manuscripts should be noted. Lions with twisted tails which they bite, very similar to those on the horn, are to be seen in an Augustine on the Heptateuch, formerly at Corbie, and dating from the eighth century (Comte A de Bastard, *Peintures et ornements des manuscrits*, etc., abbreviated edition, pl. 21) The same manuscript has beasts holding leaves in their mouths

[3] The panel, which is 6 in high, was in the Keele Hall Collection and exhibited at Manchester in 1857 and Leeds in 1868. An example of

Fig. 3.   IVORY TRIPTYCH (CLOSED) :   BORRADAILE COLLECTION

The second, a large triptych 10¾ in. high, is here reproduced (figs. 3 and 4): it may be rather earlier, and of the eleventh century. In the middle is the Crucifixion between the Virgin and St. John, with half-figures of the archangels above, all accompanied by descriptive legends. On the two leaves are half-figures of SS. Cyrus and John, and the following saints in pairs : SS. George and Theodore Stratelates ; Eustathius and Clement of Ancyra ; Menas and Procopius ; Stephen and Cyrion. On the outside of the leaves are two ornate crosses, each having at the intersection of the limbs a medallion with a bust, one of St. Joachim, the other of St. Anna. Above and below the crosses are four medallions with busts of SS. Basil, James the Persian, Barbara, and Thekla.[1] All the saints have their names carved beside them in the usual manner. This diptych has unfortunately no pedigree ;[2] and it has been objected to it that the cutting of the central panel is suspiciously sharp, while this panel also differs from the leaves and colour. But the sharpness of execution occurs in other triptychs, of which the authenticity has never been questioned ; and is perhaps the natural condition of an interior which is not exposed to rubbing.

The difference in colour would seem to be rather in favour of genuineness than against it. The tinting of ivories being to-day a fine art, a forger would be more likely to harmonize his tones than to leave a visible contrast between them ; it must also be remembered that the centre and the leaves may be derived from different tusks.[3] There is another point which is also worthy

a similar style is the panel from a triptych with the Virgin and Child in the Stroganoff Collection at Rome (H. Graeven, *Elfenbeinwerke in photographischer Nachbildung*, Italian Series, no. 68). The *Deesis* occurs on other Byzantine ivories at Berlin, Liverpool, in the Vatican, etc.

[1] Of the well-known saints it is unnecessary to say anything here. SS. Cyrus and John were martyred in Egypt, and are usually represented together (see *Acta Sanctorum*, Jan. 31): their day is January 31. St. Cyrion belongs to a group of martyrs who suffered at Alexandria on February 14 ; he is described as a priest. St. Barbara is not commonly found in minor Byzantine works of art : in this sphere her popularity may not have equalled that attained in the West in the fifteenth century ; but she is a saint of oriental origin, her legend was widely diffused in Syria and in other parts of the East, and she occurs in the Menologium of Basil II (fol. 224), as well as in monumental art, e. g. in the mosaics of the Monastery of St. Luke of Stiris in Phocis (Schultz and Barnsley, p. 50). St. James the Persian is seen on the Harbaville triptych (E. Molinier, *Ivoires*, p. 100) on the exterior of the right leaf.

[2] It was acquired by Mr. Borradaile in 1905-6, the story being that it came from a convent at Reims.

[3] Another feature which might at first sight be urged against the triptych is that the leaves are fastened by hinges, instead of by pins working in cavities in projecting ledges of the central panel—the usual Byzantine method. But if this point were made a test of falsity, the 'Triptych d'Harbaville' in Paris, the classical example of the Byzantine ivory-carver's

of mention In the bottom right-hand corner of one leaf there is a rare saint, Cyrion, and above his halo a very curious hood-like projection, which I am unable to explain. Here again, it seems unlikely that a forger would leave the safe beaten track to attempt an originality generally avoided in his profession. But apart from all this, the triptych is homogeneous in style and treatment, and consistent with the period to which it is assigned. The lettering is good, and the iconography apparently correct in its details. While duly observing, therefore, the caution now imperative in the case of every object without a history, we may leave the *onus probandi* to those who may feel suspicious. Meanwhile, the triptych may be regarded as an interesting addition to the Byzantine ivories in this country, and Mr. Borradaile may be congratulated on his courage in making an acquisition of which he knew the risks.

The charming French polyptych next illustrated,[1] (fig 5) dating from the first half of the fourteenth century, compels its own recognition, and may be left to speak for itself. The arrangement of the subjects follows a widely accepted scheme, exemplified, among others, by a fine larger polyptych in the Victoria and Albert Museum.[2] Upon the leaves are the Annunciation and Adoration of the Magi, the Nativity and Presentation in the Temple. The Virgin with the Child in the middle of the composition is a figure of admirable grace and delicacy.[3]

The diptych[4] next illustrated (fig. 6) is not the least remarkable among a group of pierced ivories which have given rise to a great deal of discussion.[5] They differ widely in execution and in merit, but points of analogy in execution and conception are always apt to occur between them ; for instance, a certain rather unintelligent type of head, especially noticeable in the bearded male figures, and a tendency to affected dramatic pose and to intensity of facial expression. The architecture is generally elaborate—this part of the work giving the carver obvious scope for display of his dexterity: architectural features are, however, not always the same in different examples. If we allow for a fanciful treatment, they represent a period comprising

art, would also be false The existing hinges, as well as the silver pin fastening the leaves when closed, are modern.

[1] Magniac Collection, lot 257 Height, 6¾ in

[2] For these devotional tabernacles, or *tableaux cloans*, as a class, see R. Koechlin in A Michel's *Histoire de l'art*, ii, p. 475

[3] Iconographically this Virgin and Child are regarded as forming part of the Adoration scene, the kings alone appearing on the leaf.

[4] The diptych, which is 4¾ in. high, does not seem to have formed part of any large collection.

[5] For this group, see British Museum *Catalogue of Ivory Carvings*, pp. xlv, xlvi

Fig. 5. FRENCH POLYPTYCH: BORRADAILE COLLECTION

Fig. 6. IVORY DIPTYCH: BORRADAILE COLLECTION

the close of the fourteenth and the beginning of the fifteenth
century; they render structural features not as they really
were, but as they existed in the mind's eye of the artist, and as they
are depicted in contemporary illuminated manuscripts.   To this
period these ivories are considered to belong, while they are commonly described as of North French or Flemish origin; both date
and local attribution appear to be supported by the manuscripts,
where a similar realistic treatment of the human figure, and,
one may add, a similar frequency of rather stupid-looking types,
may be found.   The iconography of these ivories, so far as I
was able to test it while preparing the Catalogue of Ivory Carvings in the British Museum, is correct, and agrees with that
of the illuminations, whether we examine the finer books, such
as the Bedford Hours, or the humbler work of the second or third
order, of which so much remains and so little is known.   The
ivories follow the manuscripts in this marked difference in quality.
Some are far better than others; and this fact favours the conclusion that, like the manuscripts, they represent the general style of
a period translated by hands of varying skill.   It seems more
reasonable to accept this view than to suppose them the work
of a forger, or small group of forgers, working in the first half
of the nineteenth century.   That date is the latest which the
sceptical could assign them, because several examples were known
to exist in collections before that time.[1]   The present diptych
must take rank with the best that was done in this style, and
probably no other example is more elaborate; the figures are
actually in the round, and the tracery is executed with a dexterity
which is almost Chinese.   The leaf on the spectator's left contains scenes from the history of the Virgin; that on the right,
scenes from the life of our Lord.   On the left we see, at the
bottom, the Nativity and Adoration of the Magi; above this,
the Death of the Virgin; at the top, the Virgin's soul received
by the Almighty, her Assumption, and (in the middle) her Coronation.   Under the intervening canopies are small figures of
angels with musical instruments, a motive which occurs in the
pierced panels at South Kensington, and those of the same set
formerly in the Carmichael Collection.   On the right leaf, we see,
at the bottom, the Holy Women with vessels of ointment, ap-
proaching the figure of our Lord, behind whom is Hell-Mouth,
with souls issuing from it, so that the Descent into Hell com-
bines with the other scene.   Above are the Annunciation, the
Crucifixion, and (in the middle), the Resurrection; at the top,
the Agony in the Garden and the Last Judgement, St. Michael
weighing the souls (the *psychostasis*) appearing on the left.   On

---

[1] e. g. those in the Debruge Dumenil and Maskell Collections.

this leaf the small figures under the intervening canopies are shown in the attitude of adoration.

The first of the objects in metal-work is a chrismatory of gilt copper on a high foot dating from about A.D. 1200[1] (fig. 7). In general structure it resembles other medieval chrismatories for the three oils. The body has three cylindrical compartments in filigree, between which are narrow bands of similar filigree, with coloured stones and pastes in plain settings. The hinged lid is of architectural design, with three bell-shaped pinnacles terminating in spheres, and surrounding a dome with high pierced drum, surmounted by a modern cross · between the pinnacles and the drum are three gables. The foot is of round section, with a lobed knop and expanding circular base, round which is engraved a Lombardic inscription with abbreviations, reading:

HIC E' INTVS   DE OLEO · BEATA MARIA · ET · DE
FASSTIONENTA · ET · DE OLEO · SCA R̄ DE OLEO SCA N.

On the edge of the foot, in similar characters, are the words :

✠ MEMENTOTE CORRADI

The foot and body appear to be of separate origins, and are rather clumsily joined · at present they are held together by a long metal rod of modern date. They are, however, of much the same period; and both appear to be genuine work of the close of the twelfth century or the beginning of the thirteenth. The three compartments of the body are now filled by modern cylinders, between which is a plate engraved with the initial letters IOC [2] a larger plate at the base of the lid is also modern, and there is a great deal of modern gilding.

The inscription on the foot gives in full the name of but one saint, only the initials of the other two appearing. There would seem to be little doubt, in spite of the faulty grammar of the engraver, that the K and N represent SS. Catharine and Nicholas; and an entry in the list of relics once belonging to the shrine of

[1] 9½ in. high. From the Keele Hall Collection Shown at the Art Treasures Exhibition, Manchester, in 1857 (figured by J B Waring, *Art Treasures of the United Kingdom*, 1858, *Plates*, Metal-work, pl 1, no. 2), and at the Loan Exhibition at South Kensington in 1862 (*Catalogue*, as above, no 1009, p 57)

[2] The initials stand for [*Oleum*] *Infirmorum, Oleum* [*catechumenorum*], and *Chrisma* These indicatory letters are subject to some variation The oil of the infirm is constant as I or OI. But that of the Catechumens may be rendered by S, because it is also described as *oleum sacrum* ; while the Chrism may be indicated by SC (*Sanctum Chrisma*). See G Hellepitte, *Revue de l'art chrétien*, 1884, p. 147

St. Cuthbert at Durham, quoted by Mr. Assheton Pownall in volume v of *Proceedings*,[1] seems to show that the St. Mary here mentioned must be St. Mary of Sardinia, since her balm or oil is recorded as kept at Durham in the same ivory casket as that of SS. Catharine and Nicholas. The oil of St. Catharine was perhaps the most famous of the healing oils, and, as is well known, is mentioned by Sir John Mandeville in his account of Mount Sinai.

The fact that the word *Vestimenta* is spelled with an F instead of a V suggests a Teutonic hand; the name Conrad is German; and it seems probable that this object was made somewhere on the Rhine. Filigree in this style, with scrolls and pellets, is common in the second half of the twelfth century, extending into the thirteenth; while the lettering on the foot should not take us far from the year 1200.[2]

The slender parcel-gilt silver tabernacle (fig. 8) is again one of those things which require no advertisement beyond their own obvious excellence.[3] Its only fault lies in the crucifix at the top, which is of more recent date than the rest.[4] The

Fig. 7.   COPPER-GILT CHRISMATORY :
BORRADAILE COLLECTION.

---

[1] p. 119.

[2] The date suggested in the Loan Exhibition Catalogue, viz. second half of the thirteenth century, appears to be too late. Similar filigree on a reliquary at Quedlinburg is dated to the period 1184–1203 (J. Marquet de Vasselot, *Monuments Piot*, vi, 1889, 183).

[3] Magniac Sale Catalogue, no. 792, exhibited at the Burlington Fine Arts Club in 1901 and at the Royal Academy Winter Exhibition, 1896. Formerly Leben Collection, Cologne.

[4] This part may be compared with the top of a fourteenth-century ciborium at Aix-la-Chapelle (E. Aus'm Weerth, *Kunstdenkmäler des christlichen Mittelalters in den Rheinlanden*, Album, pl. 38, fig. 5).

proportions of the tabernacle itself are exceedingly elegant, and the small group of the Virgin and Child fills its allotted place in a manner which leaves nothing to be desired This graceful object, which should be French, and be not later than the middle of the fourteenth century, has the greatest possible refinement and distinction.

The next object (fig. 9), also silver-gilt, is of rather later date, and from the same country. This too is a Magniac piece.[1] Mr. Middleton, describing it in the sale catalogue, said, with some truth, that it might almost serve as a model for a turret in stone. On the rim of the lower part is one of the silversmiths' marks with the letters fû underneath (fig. 10), and to the right a more modern control mark, a boar's head. Here again the destination is not very easy to determine. There is a foot, which appears to be part of the original design ; but at the sides there are two tubes for suspending cords. Clearly it was intended to stand on a flat surface, but also to be carried on occasion. It has been called a chrismatory, in which case it would be one of the single receptacles for the *Oleum Infirmorum*, of which examples are preserved.[2] But it differs from these in having a detachable instead of a hinged lid ; and in the possession of the arrangement for suspension. Again, it is rather narrow and deep for this purpose. Other suggestions are that it contained a relic, or that it served as a penner.

Fig. 10.

The sceptre or baton (figs. 11 and 12) also purchased by Mr Borradaile at the Magniac sale,[3] has a history which can be traced with certainty as far as the second half of the eighteenth century. It was lot seventy-three of the fifteenth day at the Strawberry Hill sale,[4] where it was described as having been given to Horace Walpole by his niece, Lady Temple. But before

---

[1] No. 787. Reproduced by P. de la Motte, *Choice Examples of Art Workmanship Selected from the Exhibition of Ancient and Mediaeval Art at the Society of Arts*, London, 1851.

[2] *Revue de l'art chrétien*, as above, p. 152, where examples are reproduced ; see also p 454 ff. A good illustration of a priest using a single chrismatory for extreme unction occurs in an early Netherlandish drawing in the manner of Rogier van der Weyden in the Ashmolean Museum at Oxford (*Burlington Magazine*, xxiv, plate opp. p. 224, B. January 1914)

[3] Magniac Collection, no 644, shown at the South Kensington Loan Exhibition in 1862 (*Catalogue*, as above, no. 1064, p. 68) In the Magniac Catalogue, Mr. Middleton suggests about 1520 as the date, while Mr Robinson in the Loan Catalogue gives the period from 1500–40.

[4] 'An exceedingly beautiful crystal sceptre, richly set in gold with pearls, and enamelled. A very curious and interesting relic from Lady Elizabeth Germain's Collection, and presented to Horace Walpole by his niece, Lady Temple.'

Fig. 11   Fig. 9   Fig. 8

Fig. 8.   PARCEL-GILT SILVER TABERNACLE
Fig. 9.   SILVER-GILT CHRISMATORY (?)
Fig. 11.   ROCK-CRYSTAL BATON

BORRADAILE COLLECTION

that, as the catalogue also stated, it had been in the collection of Lady Elizabeth [Betty] Germain, and appears in the catalogue of her sale in 1770, when it fetched £4 14s. 6d.[1]

Fig. 12.   DETAIL OF END OF BATON: BORRADAILE COLLECTION.

Lady Elizabeth collected works of art herself, and may have acquired this beautiful object by purchase, but it is just possible that it was once the property of the Second Earl of Arundel, a part of whose collections[2] came to her on her husband's death.

The baton is a rod of rock crystal, octagonal in transverse section, having at each end a silver-gilt mount (the early catalogues say 'gold') in a transitional Gothic style, the two mounts being identical in design though differing in size. Round the lower part of each is a band of pearls fixed by pins; above this, the metal is unornamented until we come to a series of mouldings; above these is a projecting octagonal gallery with balusters at the angles, and with a roof sloping up from each face, upon which are set more pearls. From this roof rises a smaller pierced octagonal gallery with a crenelated cresting, surmounted by a pyramidal

[1] *Catalogue of the noble collection of pictures, etc., of the Right Hon. Lady Eliz. Germain.* Langford's, Wednesday, March 7, 1770:

'Lot 53. A chrystal sceptre enriched with pearls, enamellings, etc.'

[2] Lady Elizabeth was born in 1680 and died in 1769. She was the second daughter of Charles, Earl of Berkeley, and married Sir John Germain, whose first wife had been Duchess of Norfolk. It was this lady who possessed the collection of gems made by Thomas Howard, second Earl of Arundel (1585-1646), the great collector of pictures, antiquities, and other works of art, which on her death passed to her second husband. Sir John left it to Lady Betty, and she presented the greater part to Lady Mary Beauclerk, her great-niece, who married Lord Charles Spencer, brother of the third Duke of Marlborough. The Arundel gems ultimately came into the possession of the Dukes of Marlborough and were sold in 1899.

ιoof of eight faces enamelled alternately in translucent blue and green. This ends in a collar of pearls, and an enamelled ball with a ring for suspension. There is a ring or loop at each end.

This very graceful work of the silversmith's art can hardly be older than the latter part of the fifteenth century on account of the baluster pinnacles, which are transitional to a Renaissance style : but for this feature, it might well be dated a hundred years earlier. Mr. Middleton, in the catalogue of the Magniac Collection, suggested an English origin; but though one would like to claim so beautiful a thing for our country, I think it more probable that we must seek its home in quite a different region. Unless Flanders can produce something similar, Western Europe as a whole seems excluded, for the work is not accepted as French, and does not appear to be either German or Spanish. The south-east of the Continent seems at present a more probable locality. Translucent enamels, and a lavish use of pearls, on an object of which the structural forms combine Gothic and Renaissance features, point to a region where a North Italian or 'Adriatic' influence prevailed, but, at the same time, a conservative use of Gothic. The Venetian area was such a region in the late fourteenth century and, in the fifteenth and early sixteenth centuries, Hungary. In the last-named country we find a late persistence of Gothic with intrusive Renaissance detail, upon numerous chalices and other examples of the goldsmith's art.[1] We also know that King Matthias Corvinus (d. 1490) patronized a number of Italian artists, whose names are recorded by Vasari.[2] In Hungary, therefore, we have the union of conditions required to explain an object of this sort, at once so splendid and so refined. Until it is shown that the baton must really come from some other part of Europe, it may be suggested that it was made by an Italian silversmith for a Hungarian patron. Even this much being admittedly conjectural, it would be too venturesome to go further, and associate it with Matthias Corvinus himself, supposing it to have been directly produced for him, like the well-known 'Calvary' at Gran, which bears his arms.[3] Yet the richness of the object tempts us to connect it with some prince or exalted

[1] Cf. Pulszky, Radisics, and Molinier, *Chefs-d'œuvre d'orfèvrerie ayant figuré à l'exposition de Budapest*, i, pp. 89, 139, ii, pl. 69, 87. *Die historischen Denkmäler Ungarns*, ii, p 234

[2] Among these names occur those of two natives of Trau in Dalmatia, Giovanni Dalmata and Jacopo Statilic. Cf. *Die historischen Denkmäler Ungarns*, ii, pp 291 ff.

[3] Pulszky, Radisics, and Molinier, as above, ii, p. 134 ; *Die historischen Denkmäler Ungarns*, ii, p. 209. The Calvary shows a similar juxtaposition of Gothic and Renaissance features, as does the well-known cross at Florence made by Pollaiuolo and Betto for the Baptistery of that city.

personage, and we not unnaturally think of the great Hungarian
patron of the arts. The destination of the baton is not more
certain than its place of origin. It is not easy to assign it an
ecclesiastical use;[1] nor is the task much simplified if we suppose
it secular. It bears no symbol which might justify us in regarding it as a royal sceptre; and the loops at the two ends
would, on this supposition, be unusual. For a marshal's baton
it seems altogether too delicate, though it may have served as
the insignia of some high court official.[2] For the present, perhaps, this small problem must remain unsolved.

The list closes with a silver processional cross, Italian of the
late fourteenth century, ornamented with Sienese translucent
enamels, some of which are of great charm.[3] The illustrations
will suffice to prove the importance of Mr. Borradaile's medieval
objects to the Museum, and the high quality of individual specimens, to which allusion was made at the beginning of these
notes."

The PRESIDENT fully approved of the conditions under which
the works of art described by Mr. Dalton were deposited in the
British Museum, and thought Mr. Borradaile displayed a rare
generosity in parting with them during his lifetime. The
owner's personal qualities led him to express the hope that the
series would not become national property for many years to
come.

H. CLIFFORD SMITH, Esq., M.A., F.S.A., exhibited an Heraldic
'Puzzle Table' on which he read the following note:

"This heraldic 'puzzle table' consists of a low four-legged
stool of beech-wood, into the top of which are fitted by pegs small
painted wooden blocks forming a coat of arms. The top
measures $15\frac{3}{4}$ in. by $11\frac{1}{4}$ in. The height is 8 in.

This curious and probably unique specimen of English woodwork was found by its owner, Mr. M. F. Codner, near Edenbridge
in Kent, in the possession of an old village carpenter who said that
he had removed it many years before from a house in the neighbourhood, where it had been used in the nursery as a children's
toy, and he further stated that it was supposed to have come
from Sterborough Castle in the same locality.

The arms, quarterly, 1 Howard, 2 Thomas of Brotherton,

[1] For a Cantor's baton it would be too short, as these objects appear to
have been several feet in length.
[2] Cf. Victor Gay, *Glossaire archéologique du Moyen Age et de la Renaissance*,
s.v. BÂTON D'OFFICES.
[3] Formerly in the Spitzer Collection (*La Collection Spitzer*, vol. i, p. 121,
no. 79). The cross shows signs of restoration.

3 Warenne, 4 Mowbray, form the insignia of Howard Duke of Norfolk, while the label of three points over all and the earl's coronet here unite in indicating an exemplification of the eldest son of the house, normally an Earl of Surrey or Arundel. The rendering of the arms is summary; and it is peculiar that the upper quarterings (1, 2) are in reversed order—facing to the sinister direction instead of to the dexter, though the lower quarterings (3, 4) come in their actual places, but the lion in 4 is turned to the sinister.

An heraldic puzzle based upon the ducal armorials and forming a practical introduction to the composing of a coat of arms, if (as I consider it to be) a toy, is one which might well be expected to have figured in the nursery of the Norfolk Howards; while the label which here differences the coat indicates the idea of the heraldic training of a young Earl of Surrey; and one may perhaps imagine an infant Earl of Surrey of the seventeenth century in his nursery taking to pieces and reconstructing this precursor of the modern and popular block puzzle forming his own heraldic achievement. It would be too much to assert that toys of the kind never formed a part of old English nursery furniture except in this instance; but it would be no easy matter to prove the contrary. Moreover the Howards of Norfolk stand alone in this connexion: that since 1672 continuously (earlier grants from 1483 onwards were forfeited by Howard attainders) the Dukes of Norfolk have held the office of Earl Marshal, while their heirs apparent as Earls of Surrey or Arundel have been called upon occasionally to act as 'deputy' Earls Marshal.[1] "

Mr. EVERARD GREEN, Somerset Herald, noticed that the arms were reversed and that the lions of England were missing from the second quarter. It seemed to him quite a juvenile attempt at heraldry.

Mr. BARRON thought such a contrivance would afford very questionable instruction in heraldry. Several details were missing, and it seemed more to the point to compare the table with the picture puzzles of modern times.

Lord FERRERS suggested that the exhibit was intended to cast copies of the arms.

Rev. E. E. DORLING thought the date suggested was too early, that form of coronet not occurring till towards the end of the seventeenth century.

[1] G. E. C[okayne], *Complete Peerage*, vol. v, pp. 263–6.

AN HERALDIC 'PUZZLE TABLE', TOP AND SIDE VIEWS ($\frac{1}{4}$)

The PRESIDENT suggested that if different coloured inks were applied in turn to the loose pieces, prints could be made of the arms in the proper tints; but its use for woodcuts was anything but certain. It was conceivable that certain cloths required this mark or ornament, and the process would be similar to calico-printing by hand at the present day.

Thanks were ordered to be returned for these communications.

THURSDAY, 4th DECEMBER, 1913.

Sir CHARLES HERCULES READ, Knt., LL.D., President,
in the Chair.

The following gifts were announced, and thanks for the same ordered to be returned to the donors.

From Sir Charles Hercules Read, President:
1. Cylinders and other ancient oriental seals in the Library of J. Pierpont Morgan. Catalogued by W. H Ward. Privately printed. 4to. New York, 1909.
2. Babylonian Records in the Library of J. Pierpont Morgan. Parts I and II. Edited by A. T. Clay. Privately printed. 4to. New York, 1912-13.

From E. Neil Baynes, Esq., F.S.A ·—Y Cymmrodor. Eleven parts helping to complete the copy in the Society's Library, also Transactions of the Honourable Society of Cymmrodorion, 1899-1900.

From the Author :—Ludlow in bye-gone days. By H. T. Weyman, F.S.A. 8vo. Ludlow, 1913.

The following were admitted Fellows:

The Rev. John Frederick Chanter, M.A.
Captain John Edward Acland, M.A.

Sir ARTHUR EVANS, D.Litt., F.S.A., read a paper on (1) The Pillar Rooms and Ritual Vessels of the 'Little Palace' at Knossos, and (2) The Tomb of the Double Axes, with associated group.

(1) It was shown that the 'Little Palace' now fully excavated west of the great building at Knossos and connected with it by a paved way was, like the Palace itself, largely devoted to cult purposes In the first excavated part was a shrine with fetish figures belonging to the last Minoan Period (L.M III). In the more recently excavated parts had come to light a series of

'Pillar Rooms', apparently the crypts of shrines above. Associated with one of these had been found a remarkable 'rhyton' or libation vessel in the form of a bull's head. It was formed of black steatite with shell inlays, and the eye-balls were of crystal with the pupils painted underneath. Near this was found part of a stepped steatite socket such as were used to insert the shafts of the sacred double axes of Minoan cult. Other ritual vessels of painted clay, including another bull's head rhyton, were found near.

The association of other pillar rooms with cult objects was pointed out and comparative examples were given of 'rhytons' in the form of animals' heads, including a fine marble example in the shape of a lioness's head from a shrine of the great Palace at Knossos. Of special interest was the fact that part of a similar stone vessel, evidently of Cretan fabric, was found at Delphi, thus identifying the Delphic and Minoan cults in the fifth century B.C.

(2) The discovery of the 'Royal Tomb' at Isopata on a hill north of the site of Knossos had an important sequel. About a quarter of a mile north of this, further Minoan tombs came to light, some of great interest. They belong to the last Palace Age of Knossos and the first discovered was a built tomb with remains of keel-shaped vault like that of the Royal Tomb. In this chamber was found a gold ring with a representation of a ritual dance. The furniture of some of these graves was characterized by the appearance of a new class of vessels decorated in red, black, and kyanos blue. The colours on these were imperfectly fixed, the brilliant decoration being specially designed for the use of the dead. In one of the tombs, the 'Mace-bearer's', was found a faceted stone mace of beautifully variegated marble and evidently of ceremonial use.

The most important of all the tombs was that to which the name of the 'Tomb of the Double Axes' has been given. It consisted of a rock-cut vault divided into two sections—on one side was a small chamber with a stone bench round, on the other a raised rock dais in which was sunk the burial cist. At the back of the chamber was a projecting pier of rock on which was cut a column in low relief. On the floor of the chamber stood a magnificent set of painted vases in the 'Palace style'. Near the projecting pier and column and at the back of the cist were remains of ritual vessels including a bull's head 'rhyton' of steatite, of the same class as that found in the 'Little Palace', and with them two bronze double axes of the thin 'votive' kind associated with shrines. What is specially remarkable, however, as indicating the influence of religious symbolism, the sepulchral cist itself was carefully cut out of the virgin rock in the outline of the sacred double axe. The tomb here was at the same time a shrine.

Elaborate plans and sections of the 'Little Palace' and tombs were exhibited, the results of very careful measurements executed on the spot by the architect, Mr. Christian Doll.

Mr. HOGARTH was not prepared to criticize the work done by an excavator of such eminence and authority as Sir Arthur Evans. The antiquities recovered under his able direction could not easily be compared with any from other places, the Minoan civilization having in some curious way developed in isolation. Crete was the Mediterranean Japan, and in spite of its relations with Egypt and less definite relations with Babylonia, it preserved its individuality. Its civilization owed very little to outside influences, but when in decay it spread in many directions and had been traced in Spain, Britain, Ireland, and Scandinavia. The illustrations showed how the rosette followed on the spiral curves of the lilies, and the Asiatic rosette could thus be traced to Crete. It was now said that the Cretan palaces were as much shrines of the divinity as residences of the living ; but were they divided up for their different functions ? The idea of having a separate house for the god did not develop at all, and the space allotted for divine occupation was very small when compared with the extent of the buildings. The palaces were domestic buildings of royalty in which the king and god, in some respects identical, lived together. He had come to listen and admire, and would express his own gratitude, and no doubt that of the meeting also, for a feast of rare and beautiful works of art.

Mr. H. R. HALL had derived much pleasure from the series of lantern-slides and referred more especially to excavations in Egypt that revealed a connexion with Crete. The cruciform mark on the dapple of the bull's head recalled the markings on the head of Hathor, where the same dappling was seen. On the other hand, in Crete the palace and temple were identical, in Egypt the temple was the greater building and quite apart from the palace, which was mud-built, gaily painted but very perishable. Possibly parallels for the combination of temple and palace would some day be found in Anatolia. The re-opening of Minoan tombs for religious purposes corresponded to that of the offering chamber in Egyptian tombs, which may even have remained open for some time. Inscriptions showed that the re-opening in Egypt was to enable the descendants to make offerings.

Mr. LEONARD KING confined his remarks to the novel features

of arrangement in the palace and their bearing on the possibility of an Oriental strain in Minoan culture. The suggestion had been made, for example, though he believed it had never been accepted in responsible quarters in this country, that in the drainage system of the main palace at Knossos we might perhaps see evidence of remote cultural contact with Chaldea. Such suggestions were rendered still less probable by the new facts ascertained in the course of the work upon the smaller palace. For the combination of palace and shrine, which Sir Arthur Evans had there clearly demonstrated, was quite contrary to Chaldean ideals.

Sir ARTHUR EVANS in reply expressed his agreement with Mr. Hall with regard to a connexion with Egypt, and was prepared to believe that the cult of Hathor reached Crete. The island was not compelled, as Palestine was, to take the impress of one or other of its neighbours, but held the alien at arm's length and borrowed at her own discretion. Some older Egyptian element had probably permeated Crete, as there were early stone vases in the island resembling those of predynastic Egypt, not to mention designs on seals and amulets. Nor was it possible to dispute an Egyptian influence in the Cretan hieroglyphic script. The west quarter of the palace at Knossos was, to judge from the basement, given over to business and other functions. It contained more small shrines than there were outside, but he quite agreed that it was difficult to separate divine and royal functions in such a case. The very name Minos was, like that of other early kings, supposed to be divine, and the Cretan kings were at the same time divinities themselves, priests of the divinity and rulers of men. Anatolia was a great centre of such priest-kings, who took the name of a divinity and regarded themselves as such. Though Cretan civilization was in a way isolated, in one form or another it spread as far as Spain, Italy, and Central Europe, and so far lost its insularity. It was at an early date bound to Egypt, and Greek culture came in later, but much of the old influence remained, and nothing was more suggestive than some of the artistic finds at Sparta which represented the goddess with lions clearly from a Minoan source. Delphi was connected with Crete, and large parts of the Greek epic were taken over, through a bilingual medium, from a much earlier cycle, along with two kinds of signs that could not belong to the age of Homer.

The PRESIDENT said the marvels of Crete were not altogether unfamiliar to the Society, as Sir Arthur Evans had already contributed a paper to *Archaeologia* on previous discoveries. Its civilization, in spite of wide ramifications, seemed to be *sui generis*, and all would recognize that its identification was due in great measure to Sir Arthur's own liberal expenditure of time and money on an undertaking of supreme importance to archaeology. The inadequate support afforded him was not entirely due to apathy on the part of the Government, but to public indifference, which was specially discreditable in view of the enthusiasm shown elsewhere in Europe. The objects shown on the screen would in themselves justify a national movement, and the neglect of such studies in England had already called forth more than one protest from the chair. The finding of finger-rings too small for any finger suggested that the graves were re-opened, as in other parts of the world, and the rings placed on the fleshless finger-bones; and he had previously remarked on the similarity of funeral customs at both ends of the Mediterranean. The brothers Siret found large urns used for interments in south-east Spain that were not capacious enough for two bodies, but served as a receptacle for the fleshless bones of two individuals. The Society highly appreciated the first-hand summary of recent finds in Crete, which Sir Arthur Evans was above all qualified to give.

Thanks were ordered to be returned for this communication, which will be printed in *Archaeologia*.

THURSDAY, 11th DECEMBER, 1913.

Sir CHARLES HERCULES READ, Knt., LL.D., President,
in the Chair.

The following gifts were announced, and thanks for the same ordered to be returned to the donors:

From V. B. Crowther-Beynon, Esq., F.S.A.:—The Rutland Magazine and County Historical Record. Vols. 1-5, 1904-12. 8vo. Oakham, 1904-12.

From the Author:—An introduction to English Church Architecture from the eleventh to the sixteenth century. By Francis Bond. 2 vols. 4to. Oxford, 1913.

From the Author:—A schedule of antiquities in the County of Surrey. By P. M. Johnston, F.S.A., assisted by Henry Nevill, F.S.A., and H. E. Malden. 8vo. Guildford, 1913.

From the Editor:—The extinct and dormant peerages of the northern counties of England. Edited by J. W. Clay, F.S.A. 8vo. London, 1913.

From the Author:—Pausilypon, the imperial villa near Naples. By R. T. Günther. 8vo. Oxford, 1913.

From the Author:—Tschudi, the harpsichord maker. By William Dale,
    F.S.A. 8vo. London, 1913.

From the Author:—Roman roads in Yorkshire. By Percival Ross. 8vo.
    n.p. 1913.

From W. H. Quarrell, Esq., F.S.A.:—A mezzotint engraved portrait of
    Richard Payne Knight, F.S.A.

From A. W. Gould, Esq.:—Photograph of an old oil-painting represent-
    ing One-Tree Hill, Greenwich Park.

William Vandeleur Crake, Esq., and Henry Vassall, Esq.,
were admitted Fellows.

Notice was given of a ballot for the election of Fellows to be
held on Thursday, January 15, 1914, and a list of the candidates
to be put to the ballot was read.

The Very Reverend J. ARMITAGE ROBINSON, D.D., F.S.A.,
Dean of Wells, read a paper on 'Effigies of Saxon Bishops
at Wells', which will be printed in *Archaeologia*.

In the choir aisles of the Cathedral Church of Wells there
is a series of recumbent effigies of Saxon bishops, which have
not received the attention they deserve. Solemn figures, boldly
sculptured, with a rich variety of dress and pose, they are the
equals in grace and dignity of the famous statues on the west
front. They are far better preserved, for they have not been
worn by the weather, and apart from some accidental breakages
they are in excellent condition. If they do not come from the
great sculptors who wrought the figures outside, they are the
work of their fathers before them, and they have something to
tell us of the development of English carving in the West. Not
less interesting than their art is the history of the successive
changes of name and of position which they have undergone in
the course of seven centuries.

The history of these effigies can only be briefly summarized
here. Two of them appear to be earlier than the other five. They
have very low mitres, resembling caps, whereas the others have
the triangular mitres common in the twelfth century; and other
details mark them off as more primitive. Possibly they were
made for the tombs of Bishops Dudoc († 1060) and Giso († 1088),
who were buried on the south and north sides of the high altar
in the Saxon church, and were carved to take the place of earlier
figures in the second half of the twelfth century. In the first
years of the next century six more figures were made to com-
memorate earlier Saxon bishops buried at Wells, and the whole
series was arranged on the sides of the presbytery of Bishop
Reginald's new church. When three new bays were built east-

ward a century later, the statues were rearranged behind the stallwork of the choir, so that they could be seen from the aisles only. In this position they remained from 1325 for more than five hundred years.

The effigies rested on stone casings which contained bones in small wooden boxes, and in each box was a leaden tablet giving the name of the bishop. Six of these tablets are still preserved, and it is interesting that the names correspond to the Wells local tradition of the episcopate more closely than to the scholarly tradition of William of Malmesbury and later authorities.

In 1848 the old stalls were destroyed, and stone stalls were substituted: as these were set back between the pillars, the effigies could no longer rest on the low wall between the choir and its aisles. Some of them were removed to the eastern part of the church, and three (apparently) to the undercroft beneath the Chapter-house. Two of the latter were brought back in 1870, but the third is no longer to be found. In the summer of the present year the installation of a heating apparatus called attention to the unsuitable and inconvenient position assigned to them in 1848, and gave the opportunity of putting them back as nearly as possible in the places which they had occupied for the five centuries before that date.

, Mr. ARTHUR GARDNER could not agree with the Dean that the two sculptures were earlier than the rest. To judge by the style, the drapery of the two with low mitres was more advanced, that of the others was clumsy, the effigies were flat, the folds had a rounded appearance and were all of the same breadth, and the heads were large and coarse. The two came nearer the statues on the west front, among which the earliest had large heads and shortish bodies, the folds of the drapery being of early type. The five would date from the time of Bishop Reginald, end of the twelfth or beginning of the thirteenth century; and in his opinion they were made when the new choir was built. There were at Salisbury Purbeck-marble effigies that had been brought from Old Sarum and were earlier than the church. Wells was then searching for early Bishops, and had a series carved, as was probably also the case at Hereford.

Mr. CRACE thought the foliated detail of the canopies was an item that had been overlooked, but certainly pointed to the thirteenth century. Similar foliage was visible where the crozier rested at the feet of one figure, and he thought that the earliest possible date for the drapery of another was late thirteenth century.

Mr. LETHABY considered the two with low mitres could not

be before 1230, the date being written all over them. The lead strips were perhaps not cast from bell-founder's letters, but from an old stock of moulds.

Mr. WALTERS thought there was no evidence that the inscriptions were bell-founder's work, nor that the forms were survivals, as Gothic lettering would not be earlier than the end of the thirteenth century.

Mr. EDWARD BELL was of opinion that the excellence of the drapery in one group suggested the best period of English sculpture, whereas the others were later and were apparently cut by an inferior hand in imitation of the earlier group.

Mr. HOPE laid special stress on the mitre. He had years before shown from episcopal seals that up to a certain date the mitre was worn with the horns at the sides, not at the front and back (*Proceedings*, xi, 284). The change dated from 1153, when Bishop Pudsey turned the horns to the front and back, but the old fashion lingered on till 1188, when all examples are arranged as on the Wells sculptures under discussion. In the doorway of the north porch at Wells was a sculpture with the same feature, hence the effigies could not be before Bishop Reginald's time. The latest of the group were those of Giso and Dudoc, which approximated to the sculptures on the west front and like them had croziers of wood. That point had been already noticed in *Archaeologia*, lix. 149. The five were of very rude work and were conspicuously bearded, another indication that they were earlier than the two others. He had already suggested[1] that the site of the Saxon church, which was re-hallowed in 1147, was to the south of the present church, in the vicars' cemetery; and the two churches for some time stood side by side. The earlier figures probably belonged to Reginald's building; and when the older church was pulled down, the two other effigies were probably carved to place over the transferred remains. The curious mitres were perhaps nothing but a piece of antiquarianism.

Rev. C. W. SHICKLE referred to the three bishops who migrated to Bath, where one of them (Reginald) did something to his credit in founding a hospital of which the speaker was Master.

The DEAN OF WELLS replied that he was glad of an opportunity of stating his opinion, which was formed before reading

[1] *Proc. Som. Arch. and Nat. Hist. Soc.*, lv, 55; *Archaeological Journal*, lxvii, 229.

ALABASTER TABLE OF THE PASSION OF CHRIST $(\frac{1}{3})$

the work by Messrs. Prior and Gardner. He could find no
parallels for the low mitres, and the argument from sheer art as
opposed to costume did not carry one far. He could not accept the later date proposed for the two effigies, but agreed that
the wooden staves were a sign of later date. The unprotected
feet had seemed to him evidence of early date; and the five had
very slight beards that hardly appeared in the photographs. He
had seen other instances of plain cushions under the head and
would not insist on that as an early feature. In spite of criticism he still believed that the N in WELLENSIS was an early form,
and was gratified to hear that the five might date from the
building of the new presbytery.

The PRESIDENT remarked that the present paper was not the
first contributed by the Dean, who was always welcome and had
already done much for Wells. The local monuments well employed his learned leisure, and the Society hoped to hear from
him again on one or other of the glories of Wells.

The Reverend W. O. B. ROGERS exhibited an alabaster table
of the Passion of Christ.

This table was discovered in 1834[1] at Plasn-pentre farm,
three miles from Valle Crucis Abbey, Denbighshire, of which it
was originally a grange. In or about that year the farm was
purchased by a member of the Rogers family, and this alabaster,
together with another representing St. Armel, was found under
the floor of a room in the gable. Both alabasters were removed
subsequently to High Lea House, near Plasn-pentre, where they
were put into niches in the hall. The alabaster exhibited is
shortly to be placed in Whitton Church, Hounslow, Middlesex,
of which the Rev. W. O. B. Rogers is vicar.

This alabaster, which is 2 ft. 11 in. high by 10 in. wide, represents our Lord seated upon the seamless coat and resting
against the Cross, remains of which can be seen behind the head.
The feet are bound with a rope, which passes upwards on the
right of the body and over the right shoulder. The arms are
broken off, but evidently were crossed on the knees and bound
at the wrists by the rope. A mark on the breast indicates that
the figure held in one hand a reed crossing the body from right
to left. The figure is naked except for a loin cloth and on the
head is the crown of thorns, in the torse of which real thorns
have been inserted. The figure is surrounded by the implements
of the Passion, and below are two shoulder-blades and two skulls,
one with a worm protruding from the orbit, while above the
right-hand shoulder-blade are the head and front feet of an

[1] *Arch. Cam.*, V, i, 215.

animal, possibly intended for a toad, issuing from its hole. · No traces of colour remain except possibly on the loin cloth, which is of a whiter colour than the rest of the alabaster.

The following extract from *Rites of Durham*[1] affords a striking parallel to the object exhibited :

Betwixt yᵉ tow neithermost pillers opposite to ỡ Laᐧ of Pieties Alter ther was an alter wᵗʰ a Roode repsenting yᵉ passion [of ỡ Saui̇ỡ] having his handes bounde, wᵗʰ a crowne of thorne on his head, being comonly called yᵉ bound roode.

Thanks were ordered to be returned for this communication and exhibition

---

THURSDAY, 18th DECEMBER, 1913.

WILLIAM MINET, Esq., M.A., Treasurer, in the Chair.

The following gifts were announced, and thanks for the same ordered to be returned to the donors :

From the Author, James Curle, Esq., F S A.:
  1. Roman and native remains in Caledonia. 8vo. London, 1913.
  2. The Romans in Scotland. 8vo   n p. n.d.
  3. Notes on some undescribed objects from the Roman fort at Newstead, Melrose 8vo. n.p. n.d.

From H E. Balch, Esq , F.S A :—Reproduction in colour of an ancient map of Mendip in Wells Museum.

Notice was again given of the ballot for the election of Fellows to be held on Thursday, January 15th, 1914, and the list of candidates to be put to the ballot was again read.

W. DALE, Esq., F.S.A , exhibited and read the following notes on a hoard of scrap bronze found near Andover ; an iron axe-head from Clausentum; a greenstone celt of foreign type found near Beaulieu; and worked flints from Dunbridge, Hants:

"The hoard of broken bronze implements I am showing was found in laying out a watercress bed by the side of the stream known as the Anton about a mile north-east of Andover Junction Railway Station. The spot where they were discovered is almost on the line of the Portway, the Roman road connecting Sorbiodunum with Calleva, and close to the point where the other road from Winchester to Cirencester crosses it. The peaty soil is

[1] *Surtees Society*, 107, p 41.

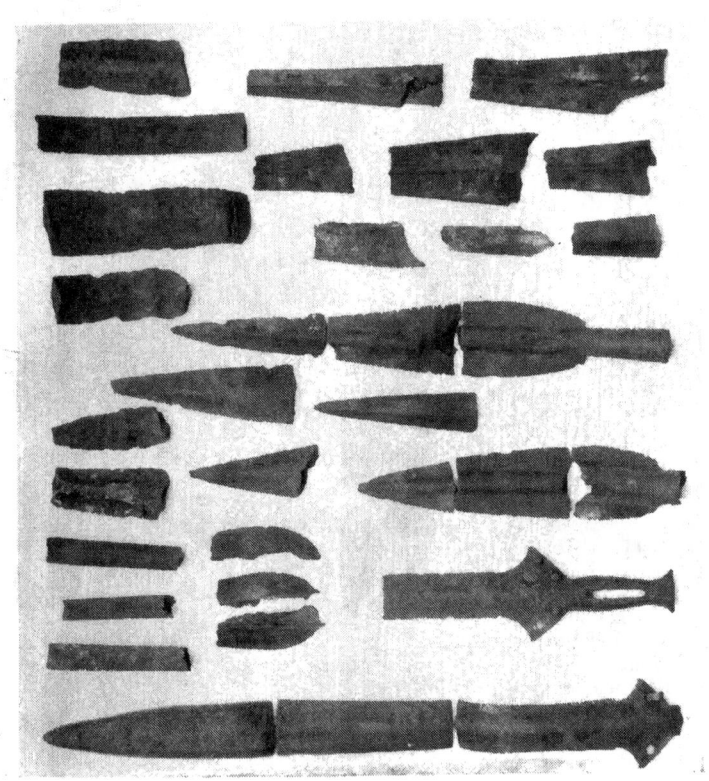

Fig. 1. HOARD OF SCRAP BRONZE FOUND NEAR ANDOVER ($\frac{1}{4}$)

here about 2 ft. thick and the hoard was found at the depth of a foot. It consists entirely of broken pieces and there are represented leaf-shaped swords, or perhaps, more properly speaking, rapiers, pieces of large winged spear-heads, some long ferrules, and portions of carefully made scabbards. The fragments lay all close together, and I am sure that I obtained all that were there. As, however, only a few of the broken portions match, it looks as if it were only part of a hoard.

The type of implements represented is very late, belonging to the latest period of the Age of Bronze in Britain. One of the rapiers was not more than an inch wide, and it will be noticed that in the two handles that have been preserved the characteristic notch at the bottom of the blade is scarcely perceptible. They are similar to the implements of the Blackmoor hoard which are figured in the *Victoria County History of Hampshire* in the chapter on Romano-British Hampshire by Dr. Haverfield. and the casual reader might conclude that the Blackmoor bronzes

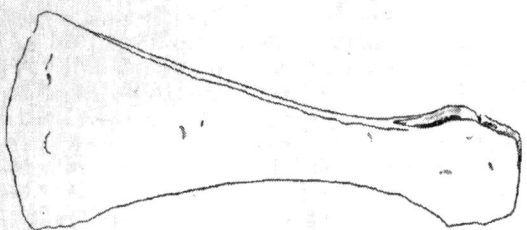

Fig. 2.   IRON AXE-HEAD FROM CLAUSENTUM ($\frac{1}{4}$).

were Roman, although it was probably not the writer's intention to convey that idea. No scabbards appear to have been found at Blackmoor.

The broken condition of the find is puzzling. The pieces were found in soft undisturbed peat, and the determined destruction of the implements dates from the age to which they belong. They appear to have been perfect weapons, and look too good to have been broken up as old metal for recasting.

The iron axe-head comes from the Roman station at Clausentum. It was found near the river in the same stratum of black earth which yields Roman pottery and coins. At the same time it is not necessarily a relic of the Roman period. Medieval objects are often found in this soft yielding earth, and it may be a battle-axe of the middle ages or even a domestic tool, although I incline to regard it as a military weapon. It is 12 in. long and weighs just 4 lb. I hope its exhibition in these rooms may lead to its age being fixed. From the same place I also show one of the small rings concerning which the gruesome theory was advanced a fortnight ago that they were for placing on the hand when the flesh had rotted off the bones.

The beautiful greenstone celt which is among my exhibits was found near Beaulieu, and is distinctly of a Breton or Continental type. At the last meeting of the British Association a paper was read by Mr O. G. S Crawford on 'Commerce between Britain and the Continent in the Neolithic and Bronze Ages'. His evidence concerning the former age was based on two greenstone celts in my own collection found in Hampshire not far from the sea. I was able to add to these the finding of a third, which is the one shown. The material from which it is made is pronounced by Professor Bonney to be diorite or hornblendic diabase, a rock which occurs in Brittany.

Several visits paid to the implement-bearing gravels of Dunbridge have resulted in obtaining some more implements which present the usual anomaly of some being much water-worn and others perfectly sharp It seems increasingly difficult to ascertain from the workmen the horizons where the implements occur. For instance, the wedge-shaped implement was said to have been found at the bottom, although its patination seems to show it came from quite the top of the gravel. Undoubtedly found on the surface-soil which caps the gravel are two roughly chipped implements which it has been our custom to call celts. The one of the colour of a gravel flint is somewhat of the Cissbury type. The other and larger of the two may be considered to approach an Aurignac type."

Mr. Reginald Smith considered the hoard of bronze important on several grounds. The metal was heavy for its bulk and would be apt to sink in peat, so that its position 1 ft. below the surface would indicate the maximum amount of peat-growth since the date of the deposit. That might be determined by the types contained in the hoard, and by the condition of the specimens. The sword with an imperfect handle (a breakage, not an unsuccessful casting) had evidently been broken into three pieces intentionally, and the long spear-heads had likewise been broken for convenience in carrying, the suggestion being that it was scrap-metal intended for recasting. A late date was indicated by one fragment of a spear-head that was merely a shell,[1] the hollow reaching the edge of the blades, and also by the rudimentary notches at the base of the second sword-blade.

[1] Canon Greenwell and Mr. Parker Brewis discussed this point in *Archaeologia*, lxi, pp 452, 465. Chapes and cylindrical ferrules are illustrated in the paper.

The notches were normal on swords both of bronze and iron in the Hallstatt period, and the wilful destruction of a sword that had apparently never been used might be accounted for by the introduction of iron, which was preferred for weapons. Whether Britain had a Hallstatt period or not, the deposit seemed to date from the fifth or sixth century B. C., though earlier oddments, such as the spear with solid blades, might easily be included. The sheath-like bronzes were frequently found in England, and were really the chapes of swords, the scabbard being of leather or wood. Both those and the cylindrical spear-ferrules were practically confined to Britain, a few being known from France.[1] The flint implements were of special interest, and included a chopper probably of the period of Le Moustier that should not have been at the base of the gravel, as typical St. Acheul forms (heavily stained with iron and somewhat rolled) were also exhibited from the pit. Such choppers were known from the gravels of north-east London and also from Cissbury mines. There was also a rolled white flake like the side-scrapers of Le Moustier, and a white unrolled pointed tool similar to several found by Mr. Worthington Smith deep in brick-earth near Caddington, and perhaps the ancestor of the Cissbury celt. Till the stratification could be finally determined, it was impossible to date the gravel, but recent finds in the New Forest suggested a St. Acheul date for the plateau gravel which was earlier than the Dunbridge river-deposits. The 'picks' from the surface were complete and typical, one with a chopping end and the other with a terminal plane: examples were known of both on one implement. At present the date was uncertain, but might soon be proved palaeolithic. The greenstone polished celt seemed to have been shaped by 'pecking'[2] before being polished, and the former process was characteristic of a group in Scandinavia called blunt-butted cylinder-celts (*prikhugning* or *butnakket Trindöx*). Implements of that material were best fashioned by grinding, not by flaking, and would be largely used in countries devoid of flint. The iron axe-head was not easy to date, but was unlike the Anglo-Saxon or Viking type, and might possibly be Roman, though a medieval date was not excluded.[3]

Mr. BUSHE-FOX said the axe-head was not the usual Roman form. The finger-ring was not of the original size, but had

---

[1] *Proceedings*, xxiii, 169; *L'Anthropologie*, xiv, 513; xi, 523.
[2] *Revue de l'École d'Anthropologie de Paris*, 1910, 22 (piquage).
[3] Subsequent comparison with those in the Silchester hoard of tools (*Archaeologia*, liv, 147) makes the latter date more probable.

been made for an adult and subsequently broken and the ends brought together.

HILARY JENKINSON, Esq., F.S.A., read the following paper on ' An Original Exchequer Account of 1304 with private tallies attached':

"I must begin this communication with an apology. I ought perhaps to excuse myself for harping continually upon the same subject—this of tallies,[1] but I hope to show that in the little file of manuscripts here illustrated I introduce to the Society an antiquity in a very full sense of the word.

Antiquities at the present time are being very generally raised to the honourable position of historical sources. All our discoveries now are collected into ordered series, each is assigned a relative place and receives an estimation relative to the extent to which it is able to link up itself and its contemporaries with predecessors or successors of the same order ; is valued, in fact, in so far as it helps to bring its class into an historical relation with historical interests of the present day. There remains, however, a charm in the true antiquity, the isolated example, the museum specimen, which makes a spectacular appeal, sums up and exhibits in itself a number of the curious, attractive, or striking characteristics which are found scattered over the whole class. The source or evidential quality is perhaps more common to manuscript, and the museum or spectacular one to material remains; but I would present the accompanying slight example as in its way a specimen, a curiosity in medieval administrative documents.

---

[1] I take this opportunity of mentioning some late tallies which I have not described before. I have been indebted to the kindness of the officials of both the London Museum and the Guildhall Museum while making an inspection of these specimens. The London Museum tallies consist of four of the date 1706 and two later ones ; perhaps the most interesting point about the four is the preservation along with them of three documents touching the assignment of the moneys involved, which were loans to the Treasury : it is perhaps well to emphasize the fact that all are Exchequer tallies (stocks) of the normal type. The Guildhall specimens, one of which is 3 ft. 8 in. in length and has a dent for a halfpenny, are all of the nineteenth century ; here again a special interest comes in, three of them relating to the repayment by the City of loans made to it by the Treasury for public works. I have been reminded that I never described in detail the large nineteenth-century tallies in the Public Record Office Museum and elsewhere in that Office. I took them to be sufficiently well known ; and, indeed, they (and other nineteenth-century tallies) have as a rule little of interest about them from the point of view of the history of the tally and its place in administration, except as illustrating the unwieldy length to which this instrument grew and the consequent difficulty experienced by those who tried (without medieval specimens before them) to interpret the passage in the *Dialogus*. Late tallies should always be readily traceable in other Records.

In that working out of the history of English medieval administration which those who realize its importance see slowly extending, it becomes necessary to distinguish certain influences which determined the evolution of records. We start—record-keeping started—with a heterogeneous mass of

EXCHEQUER ACCOUNT WITH PRIVATE TALLIES ATTACHED.

administrative documents preserved for official reference, of scraps of what may be called manuscript memory: among them we find scraps upon which are copied original documents which have been issued, scraps being memoranda of proceedings, and scraps which are themselves originals. The first of these two are generally separated off very early into very distinct classes by themselves—the Patent Rolls for instance, and the Plea Rolls. The third class remains the true miscellanea, the files of originals; throwing off, it is true, special files from time to time for all kinds of bulky divisions within itself, but

always keeping an ultimate residuum of pure miscellanea—
the Ancient Miscellanea of the King's Remembrancer of the
Exchequer, the Chancery files, the Ancient Indictments of the
King's Bench.

That is a rough summary of some of the theoretic facts which
one may draw from a general conspectus of classified examples
of records in these classes. It remains to display the present
curious specimen.

The pure miscellanea to which reference has been made may
come together (to continue the analysis a little further) from
three directions. They may be original documents officially
made and for some reason returned into official custody; or
they may be originals not made in the great offices, but made,
all the same, for their use; or they may be unofficial both in
compilation and in their primary aim, of official interest only by
accident and comparatively late in their career. Let us consider the provenance of the various parts of the present illustration, which comes from what was once the Ancient Miscellanea
of the Exchequer K.R.[1]

First we have, lying on the top of the file, a purely official
original—the writ or commission to John de Kirkeby, clerk,
ordering him to examine into the accounts of the Bishop of
Carlisle, farmer of the King's Castle and demesnes in that town:
this writ has been returned in virtue of its final clause—*remit-
tentis ibi tunc hoc breve*; *ibi* being, in view of the circumstances,
the Exchequer, then at York. Kirkeby is to examine the
accounts by view of the *visores* of the work done there and upon
their oath to certify the Treasurer and Barons whether the work
has been well and truly done.

Next we have, in the natural sequence, the accounts of the
work done; compiled privately or semi-privately, but intended
directly for that official information suggested in the writ to
which they form a return. They occupy the two membranes
seen below. The first of these is devoted to

Expense facte in Castro Karlioli circa bretachia et portas et alia
necessaria contra adventum Scotorum in marchiam a festo Nativitatis
sancti Iohannis Baptiste Anno regni regis Edwardi xxxj° prout patet infra
per visum Henrici Furbur Willelmi de la Sauserye usque festum Sancti
Michaelis proximo sequens.

The sum of this first membrane is £2 3s. 11d.

pro quibus affidatur caram [sic] Iohanne de Kirkeby clerico.

It will be noticed that the testimony of the two *visores* has
been placed on this membrane but cancelled because a reproduction of it on the second (most of which may be seen, reversed, in

---

[1] Its reference is now Exchequer Accounts, 482, 22.

the photograph) was considered sufficient, though in point of fact it related only to the one account upon the second membrane.

This second membrane is devoted to

> Operacio et emendacio diversarum domorum in Castro facte per Adam de Thorpp' Constabularium per visum Henrici le Furbur Willelmi de la Sauserie a festo Pentecoste a festo Pentecoste [*sic*] anno Regni Regis Edwardi xxx° usque festum sancti Michaelis proximo sequens.

The sum is given as £8 9s. 2½d.

> ut patet per talliam.

The testifying clause, which also refers to a (private) tally

> que attachiatur huic rotulo,

brings us to the last item—the two private tallies seen attached by thread to the head of the rolls. The inscriptions on these are as follows :

> De denariis receptis de Ada de Thorpp' ad operam Castri a festo Nativitatis sancti Iohannis Baptiste anno regis Edwardi xxxj° usque festum Sancti Michaelis proximo sequens,

the amount cut on this tally being £2 3s. 11d. ; and

> Contra Adam de Thorpp' Constabularium Castri Karlioli de expensis factis circa operam Castri a festo Pentecoste anno Regis Edwardi xxx°. usque festum Sancti Michaelis proximo sequens.

The amount cut on this second tally is £8 3s. 1½d.

It will be seen that these are purely private tallies between the parties concerned in the work dated by the time of the work— i.e. some time before the commission which incidentally resulted in their ultimate preservation at the Exchequer.

We have thus typical examples, filed together in a small space, of all the three main varieties of miscellanea to which I referred. The whole forms, I venture to say, an unusually neat and complete administrative curiosity.

Besides this point of interest, however, there are one or two small matters to be noticed with regard to the cutting and so forth of the tallies : they are mostly in the nature of confirmation of certain views which previously I have only been able to infer. The accounts themselves are interesting enough, but with an interest common to a long series of similar documents ; though I might perhaps mention the curious name of certain nails—fleywenges—three thousand of which, at a cost of 20d. per thousand, are mentioned in the second account along with the more ordinary 'spikinggys' and 'broddes'. Why the accounts for making two *bretachia* without the great gate and postern, and of erecting a springal, should be separate from those relating to repairs of the great gate, the tower, the Queen's chamber, the new chamber and the prison is not certain ; but they are clearly distinguished, and perhaps we may assume that this was to fit the two tallies which happened to have been made separately.

With regard to these tallies (both of them foils), we may notice in conclusion three points :

1. As might be expected in the case of the tallies of important officials used to Exchequer customs, the cutting conventions of that Office have been adopted in many points. The angles at both ends are the same ; the relative position of the larger and smaller amounts above and below the inscription is similar to what we see on the nineteenth-century Exchequer foil at Kensington ; and the thickness of the notches is according to Exchequer rule The writing begins in the proper place, though in each case it has spread over on to the following side ; upon which we find the date figuring quite correctly.

2 We have here examples of two of the kinds of wording which I noticed on private tallies in my first paper.[1] The first tally, that on the left, begins *de* and witnesses in favour of Adam de Thorp that he has paid out certain moneys entrusted to him, presumably, by the Bishop. The second witnesses, presumably on behalf of the Bishop against (*contra*) Adam de Thorp, that the latter has been entrusted with the amount which figures in the second account—in point of exact fact with a penny less. Both have the same effect so far as the Exchequer is concerned—that of acquitting the Bishop The *de* one, however, is the more direct as evidence for this purpose ; and it is possibly on this account that the *contra* one is accorded the extra note which we saw on the second membrane.

3. Finally, we have two new points, one on each tally. The tally on the right shows what we know to have existed in the nineteenth century but have not had medievally evidenced before either in written accounts or actual tallies, public or private ; that is the mark for a halfpenny, made presumably twice over (on stock and foil separately) with a jab of the point of the knife. This is seen faintly to the left of the thin (penny) cut at the left-hand end of the tally.

On the other tally, at about the middle of the half-exposed face, is what is quite new to me in any connexion—half a shilling cut, signifying sixpence.

Medieval private tallies are rare and rarely attached to accounts [2] I hope all the circumstances of the case will be held to justify the length of this note."

[1] *Archaeologia*, lxii, 367.
[2] There is, of course, nothing to prevent the preservation of private tallies in this way, and an examination of the printed List of Exchequer

The CHAIRMAN as Treasurer of the Society was interested in medieval as well as modern book-keeping, and thought the plan current in 1304 was ingenious as furnishing all in one a ledger account, cash account, and original voucher for payment. He remarked the absence of any auditor's certificate. It was possible to see in the document the germs of twentieth-century book-keeping.

H. CLIFFORD SMITH, Esq., M.A., F.S.A., exhibited the foot of an English Altar Cross of latten (fig. 1), on which he read the following note :

"The object rests on a sexfoil or six-lobed base 8½ in. in diameter, with a splayed edge ¾ in. deep turned out below in a narrow flange. From this rises a dome-like pedestal contracting at the top with an ogee curve, and surmounted by an openwork corona 1⅞ in. in diameter formed of twelve conjoined trefoils. The splayed edge of the base is engraved with a guilloche pattern; the upper surfaces of the lobes are engraved alternately in black letter (fig. 2) :

𝔍. 𝔥. 𝔰.   𝔥𝔈𝔏𝔓.

The dome of the pedestal is encircled with the words (fig. 3) :

𝔍. 𝔥. 𝔰.   𝔫𝔞𝔷𝔞𝔯𝔈𝔫𝔲𝔰   𝔯𝔈𝔵   𝔍𝔲𝔡𝔈𝔬𝔯ũ.

Into the corona has been fixed the brass stem of a candle-stick of later date.

The object was formerly in the Braikenridge Collection, which was formed early in the nineteenth century by George Weare Braikenridge and kept in a museum at his residence, Broomwell House, near Bristol. The collection was moved by his son Rev.

Accounts will supply a certain number of instances of the occurrence. I am indebted to Mr. R. J. Whitwell for calling my attention to some good examples, among them that which is the subject of the present paper. One such is interesting as occurring in the Class of Ministers' Accounts (M.A. 1122, 15). Another (Exch. Accounts, 261, 21) is remarkable for giving us no less than twenty-seven tallies, some of them stocks and some foils, according to the position of the accountant in question in the transaction which originally produced them. It is worth observing, also, that some of them, whose notches deal with amounts of metal, add a note explanatory of the amount in cash ; further, that an examination of private tallies in any quantity seems to point to the *contra* form of words being the most common ; i.e. the private tally witnesses chiefly against the person who has received, the Exchequer tally in favour of the person who has paid : a slight indication of the relative importance of receiver and payer in the two cases. Nearness of the person concerned to official life and, consequently, of the tally to the Exchequer convention may naturally be expected in most of the specimens found thus attached to Exchequer Accounts.

G. W. Braikenridge, to Clevedon, Somerset ; and after the death of his successor, W. Jerdone Braikenridge, the greater part was disposed of in 1908 in London by Messrs. Christie, Manson & Woods. The object in question was included in the sale of the remainder of the collection at Clevedon, and passed into the

Fig. 2.   INSCRIPTION AND ORNAMENT ON LOBES OF ALTAR CROSS FOOT.

hands of a Bristol dealer, from whom it was purchased recently by its present owner, Rev. F. Meyrick Jones.[1]

This interesting pre-Reformation altar ornament offers a striking comparison with two similar latten objects, both with sexfoil bases and dome pedestals, which have come to light in recent years. One, the foot of a portable cross from the parish church of Stoke Poges, Bucks., was shown before this Society on February 3rd, 1910.[2] The other, a complete cross with foot, was exhibited on the 27th of last month among the collection of latten objects from St. Sampson's Church, Guernsey.[3] It is to be observed that all trace of the gilding, which presumably once existed on this as on the Stoke Poges and Guernsey examples, has disappeared.

[1] It has since been acquired by the Victoria and Albert Museum.
[2] *Proceedings*, vol. xxiii, p. 49.
[3] See p. 4, *supra*.

Fig. 1.   FOOT OF AN ENGLISH ALTAR CROSS OF LATTEN ($\frac{1}{4}$)

As regards the date, there is good ground for supposing that all three pieces of latten-work are about the same period, and belong to the sixteenth rather than to the fifteenth century. In determining this question, ecclesiastical plate, the date of which is known by its marks or definite style, should serve as an almost certain guide, seeing that the latten-workers would presumably not be slow in following the models set by the goldsmiths.

The article on English medieval chalices and patens by Messrs. St. John Hope and Fallow in the forty-third volume of

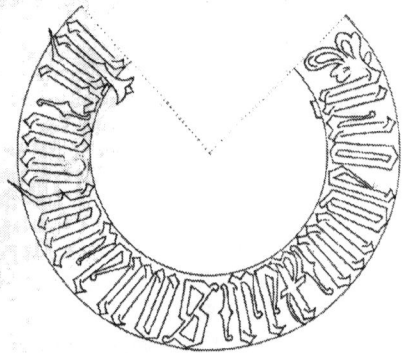

Fig. 3.   INSCRIPTION ON DOME OF ALTAR CROSS FOOT.

the *Archaeological Journal*[1] contains the standard classification of pre-Reformation chalices into eight types. Of these are two groups belonging to the Tudor period classed as type G and type H. In a supplementary classification of Tudor chalices in the sixty-first volume of the same Journal,[2] Mr. H. P. Mitchell, taking account of five additional examples which had come to light in the interval, was enabled to extend the known limits of type G to the period 1507–27, and to subdivide type H into two parts, *a* and *b*, of which the dated examples are included between the years 1525–7 and 1534 and 1536 respectively. The classification is based mainly on the form of the foot, 'the most salient feature of distinction,' and it is apparent that the type which the latten foot under consideration most closely resembles, exhibiting the sexfoil plinth and the domed pedestal surmounted by a corona or cresting, is the last medieval chalice-type, H*b*, of which the dated examples were plate-marked in 1534–5 and 1536–7. If it is objected that a date *circ.* 1535 is

[1] *Arch. Journ.*, vol. xliii, pp. 137 and 364.
[2] *Ibid.*, vol. lxi, p. 184.

too late to reconcile with the black-letter inscriptions on the latten foot, the answer is provided by the Highworth, Wilts., chalice of 1534-5 just mentioned, which bears inscriptions of the same character.[1]

The brass stem, already noted, which has been attached to this late Gothic foot is itself of Renaissance design, and belongs in all probability to the first half of the sixteenth century. And there is the possibility that the foot itself, having survived the general destruction of church ornaments under Edward VI, owed its preservation to the fact that the attachment to it of a stem enabled it to serve the practical purpose of a domestic candlestick."

Mr. Hope agreed as to the date of the 'candlestick', and observed that the inscription took an unusual form. The prayer for help was addressed to Jesus, not to our Lady. The feet of crosses first carried in Sunday processions had long been known from inventories, and by a curious coincidence three examples had lately been brought to the notice of the Society. The Wylye chalice with the mark of 1525 had a similar foot, crown, and black-letter inscription, and so furnished a date for the group of cross-bases.

E A Ebblewhite, Esq., F.S.A., exhibited the 'Bell' Salt, the 'Aris' Cup, and other plate belonging to the Worshipful Company of Tin Plate Workers, on which he communicated the following notes .

"The 'Bell' Salt. This salt-cellar was originally one of two 'Fair Silver Salts', made for Mrs Elizabeth Bell, widow of John Bell the Elder, clerk of the Parish Clerks' Company . one was given by her to the 'Parish Clerks' (which has since been lost), and the example shown was given to her son, John Bell the Younger, who succeeded his father in the clerkship. In 1679 he became also Clerk of the Tin Plate Workers' Company, who held their meetings in Parish Clerks' Hall; and shortly after his appointment he gave this salt-cellar to his new masters. The exhibit, which is of plain concave form, has on the upper part three projecting scroll-shaped brackets or arms for supporting a napkin, the salt being contained in a shallow circular depression on the upper surface. Beneath the circular spreading base is the following inscription in characters of the period 'The Gift of John Bell, Clarke to ye Company of Tinn Plate Workers'. Hall-mark—1671, London. Maker's mark—AD conjoined. Weight—14 oz 15 dwt.

[1] J E Nightingale, *The Church Plate of the County of Wilts* , p. 180

Fig. 1. THE 'BELL' SALT (½)

The 'Aris' Cup. Thomas Aris (1626-95), who was the first Master of this Company in 1670 and 1671-2, and Master of the Worshipful Company of Ironmongers in 1680-1, bequeathed money by his will dated 6th July, 1688, to enable the Master and Wardens of the Tin Plate Workers' Company 'To buy one silver bowl with my arms thereon to be engraven'. The cup here shown was accordingly bought in April 1695, and engraved on one side of the bowl with the arms of the Company (*A chevron between in chief two lamps, each with one burner, respecting each other, and in base a lamp with two burners*), in a cartouche surrounded by feather ornament, and—on the other side of the bowl—the full heraldic achievement of the donor (*On a chevron between three rams' heads erased as many roses. Crest: a man vested, holding a sword (?) in the sinister hand and supporting a spear (?) with the dexter hand*). The following inscription in characters of the period appears below the Aris arms: 'The Gift of Mr. Tho. Aris, first Master of the Tin Plate Workers' Company 1670'. Originally the cup had a contemporary pedestal, but it was replaced by the present one in 1771, when the following additional inscription was engraved on the bowl under the Company's arms: 'This Cup was repair'd and embellish'd with a new foot and pillar at the expence of Edward Walsby, Master, 1771'. Hall-mark on the bowl—London, 1694. Maker's mark—W.B. No marks on the pedestal."

M.

Mr. Hope said the salt was a popular form made in various materials: he had seen examples in silver and pewter, and himself possessed one in Lambeth delft. Very few people knew the use of them, and he had seen them exhibited upside down in museums.

The Director welcomed the exhibit as an indication of the treasures possessed by the minor City companies, but seldom inspected. He hoped that the present good example would be followed by other companies for the benefit of the Society.

Thanks were ordered to be returned for these communications and exhibitions.

THURSDAY, 15th JANUARY, 1914.

Sir CHARLES HERCULES READ, Knt., LL.D., President,
in the Chair.

The following gifts were announced, and thanks for the same
ordered to be returned to the donors:

From the Author:—The history of Wolverhampton Grammar School.
By G. P. Mander. 8vo. Wolverhampton, 1913.

From the Author:—Irish seal-matrices and seals. By E. C. R. Armstrong,
F.S.A. 8vo. Dublin, 1913.

From Rev. T. W. Oswald-Hicks:—The Register of English Monumental
Inscriptions. Vol. i. 8vo. London, 1912.

From Thomas Ashby, Esq., D.Litt., F.S.A.:—Catalogue of the British
Historical and Archaeological Section of the International Fine Arts
Exhibition at Rome, 1911. 4to. London, 1913.

From the Author:—Windsor Castle. An architectural history. By
W. H. St. John Hope, Litt.D., D.C.L. Two vols. and one portfolio
of plans. fol. London, 1913.

A special vote of thanks was passed to Mr. Hope for his gift
to the Library.

Votes of thanks were passed to the Editors of the *Athenæum*,
Notes and Queries, and the *Builder* for the gift of their publica-
tions during the past year.

L. A. LAWRENCE, Esq., F.S.A., exhibited a small gold head
of Apollo, some gold beads found at Volterra, a small gold arm-
let, and a specimen of gold ring-money.

This being an evening appointed for the election of Fellows,
no paper was read.

The ballot opened at 8.45 p.m. and closed at 9.30 p.m., when
the following were declared elected Fellows of the Society:

> Major Algernon Tudor Craig.
> William Blake Odgers, Esq., M.A., LL.D., K.C.
> Robert Bagster, Esq.
> William Alexander Cater, Esq.
> Rev. Henry Arnold Hudson, M.A.
> Captain Charles Walter Cottrell-Dormer.
> Charles George James Port, Esq.
> Cuthbert William Whitaker, Esq., M.A.
> Henry Oppenheimer, Esq.

THURSDAY, 22nd JANUARY, 1914.

The EARL OF CRAWFORD AND BALCARRES,
Vice-President, in the Chair.

The following gifts were announced, and thanks for the same ordered to be returned to the donors:

From the Author:—Decorative Ironwork from the xith to the xvinth century. By Charles ffoulkes, B. Litt. Oxon., F.S.A. 4to. London, 1913.

From Harold Sands, Esq., F.S.A.:

1. Slingsby and Slingsby Castle. By A. St. Clair Brooke. 8vo. London, 1902.
2. The Town of Denbigh and Denbigh Castle. By John Williams. 8vo. Denbigh, 1860.
3. The place-names of Nottinghamshire, their origin and development. By Heinrich Mutschmann. 8vo. Cambridge, 1913.
4. Warwick Castle and its Earls from Saxon times to the present day. By the Countess of Warwick. 2 vols. 8vo. London, 1903.

From the Right Hon. Viscount Dillon, D.C.L., F.S.A.:

1. Pageant of the birth, life and death of Richard Beauchamp, Earl of Warwick, K.G., 1389–1439. Edited by Viscount Dillon and W. H. St. John Hope. 4to. n.p n.d.
2. Degradation and reduction from knighthood. By Viscount Dillon. 8vo. London, 1913.

Cuthbert Wilfrid Whitaker, Esq., M.A., was admitted a Fellow.

G. McN. RUSHFORTH, Esq., M.A., F.S.A., read a paper on the Wheel of the Ten Ages of Life in Leominster Church:

"Several years ago when I first became acquainted with the wall-paintings in Kempley Church, Gloucestershire, I was struck, as every one who has visited the church must have been, by a design between the two windows in the north wall of the nave. It is a mere skeleton or framework in red paint, and consists of a central disc from which radiate ten spokes each ending in another disc or medallion (fig. 1). The wall on which it is painted, and, originally, the two windows, the interval between which it exactly fills, are of the early twelfth century; and the well-known paintings in the chancel cannot be very much later. But the nave walls were covered with pictures of various dates, and the surface has been so much altered by different layers of decoration and by varnishing, that it is not easy to find any immediate indication of the date of the design. Though the circles are accurately set out they seem to have been coarsely painted over at a later date.

Not long after I saw Leominster Church, and there on the north wall of the westernmost bay of the north aisle—that is to say in the Norman part of the building—was evidently the same design as at Kempley, but in better preservation (fig. 3). Not only were there patches of red paint within the medallions, suggesting figures or subjects of some kind, but the whole design was enclosed within an outer circumference or circle bearing traces of an inscription in Lombardic lettering, of which only two complete words, apparently the last, were obviously legible: *me decepit*. The design had a background of imitation masonry, each stone being ornamented with a scroll ending in a flower; and in the bottom left-hand corner was seated the figure of David playing on a harp. The style of these fragments suggests the latter half of the thirteenth century.

The remains of the inscription evidently offered the best chance of an identification, but for some time I met with no success. Recently I lighted by accident upon a series of iconographical papers by the late Mr. J. G. Waller, which appeared in the *Gentleman's Magazine* more than half a century ago; and in one of these, entitled 'The Wheel of Human Life',[1] he described a pictorial design in a well-known British Museum MS.—Arundel 83—consisting of ten circles or medallions illustrating the ten ages of life, radiating from a central circle containing the head of God, with a descriptive Latin verse inscribed round each. An inspection of the MS. (fol. 126 b) showed that the scheme of the design was exactly similar to that at Leominster, save that the inscriptions framed each picture instead of being placed on the outer circumference; but as the last two ended with the words *vita me decepit* the identification was certain (fig. 2).[2]

The Arundel Psalter belongs to the early years of the fourteenth century, and as we saw that the Leominster painting probably dates from the latter part of the thirteenth century, while that at Kempley may possibly be as old as the twelfth, the illumination cannot be the original, because it is, probably, the latest of the three examples of the design. But as it is the only one which is perfect it will be convenient to describe it first, and then compare the wall-paintings with it.

The central medallion contains the head of God with the cross nimbus—the centre of the ordered life of the universe. *Cuncta simul cerno : totum racione guberno.*

The ten ages begin at the bottom on the left hand, and move from left to right.

(1) A woman seated with a child on her knee before a fire over

---

[1] *Gent. Mag.*, xxxix (1853), 494.

[2] The illumination has been reproduced in another article on the same subject by Mr John Winter Jones in *Archaeologia*, xxxv (1853), p 167, pl v, and in Sir G. Warner's *Reproductions*, iii, pl. xxiv The latter also describes it in his *Illuminated MSS. in the British Museum*

To face page 48

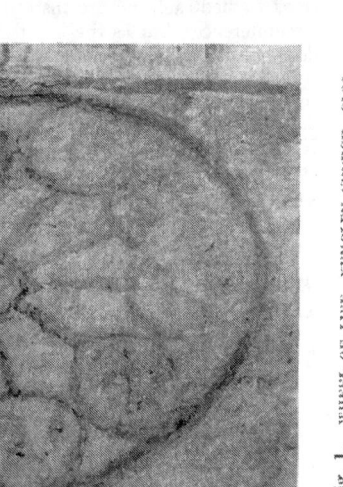

Fig. 1. WHEEL OF LIFE, KEMPLEY CHURCH, GLOS.

Fig. 2. WHEEL OF LIFE, ARUNDEL PSALTER, BRITISH MUSEUM

which a pot is boiling. The handle of a ladle protruding from
it shows that it contains something eatable, and not merely hot
water. The verse explains itself: *Mitis sum et humilis: lacte
vivo puro.*

The next two scenes, as the descriptive verses show, have been
transposed by mistake, proving, if nothing else did, that the artist
was copying and not inventing the design. The verses are
arranged in rhyming couplets, and, as the rhymes are correct as
they stand, it is the second and third pictures which have changed
places. We describe them in the correct order.

(2) A boy pointing to a pair of scales which he holds. *Num-
quam ero labilis: etatem mensuro.* Sir G. Warner describes this
as an apprentice, and Mr. Winter Jones as a man of business;
but this is the second stage—boyhood, from 7 to 14, and the
verse shows that the scales do not refer to occupation but to
character. It is the beginning of the age of reflection or self-
consciousness. The boy is aware that he is growing up, and
that he must realize and make the most of each stage of life if
he is not to make mistakes. The representation is not an obvious
one, but Sir G. Warner is, no doubt, right in describing the boy
as an apprentice. He was probably thinking of the Calendar
picture in Queen Mary's Psalter,[1] where September and the sign
of Libra are illustrated by the scene of a bargain between a buyer
and seller. Between them stands a youth holding the scales in
which the quantity of stuff is being weighed. He is, no doubt,
the merchant or shopman's assistant or apprentice, and we may
suppose that he appears at this stage in the Wheel of Life because
this is a common or typical occupation that the boy is set to
on reaching years of discretion. He has to weigh out the quantities of his master's goods, and at the same time, symbolically,
he begins to estimate the value and contents of life.

(3) A youth combing his hair before a round mirror which he
holds in his left hand. The age of puberty. He begins to take
interest in his personal appearance because this is the age of
courtship and love. The verse *Vita decens seculi speculo probatur* apparently means that he uses a mirror to assure himself
that he will make a presentable figure in the world.

(4) A young man on a white horse with a hawk on his wrist.
Non ymago speculi sed vita letatur. For the young man, real life
gives pleasure, and not the mere reflection of it.

(5) A king on his throne. *Rex sum rego seculum: mundus
meus totus.* The prime of life.

(6) A man in a long black robe lined with fur, the hood drawn
over his head, holding a staff. Not, I think, as Sir G. Warner

---

[1] British Museum, Royal MS. 2 B vii. In Sir G. Warner's edition
(London, 1912), pl. 140 and p. 25.

suggests, a monk, but the elderly man conscious of the approach of old age. *Sumo michi baculum morti fere notus.* His attitude and gesture perhaps suggest that he is looking back at the past instead of looking forward with hope to the future.

(7) A blind old man, with his right hand supported by a stick, and his left resting on the shoulder of a boy in front of him. The boy appears to be acting as a guide, but Mr. Winter Jones [1] suggested that it may illustrate the idea of some of the later examples of the Ages of Life, in which decrepitude is spoken of as the laughing-stock of children. The description is quite general. *Decrepitati deditus: mors erit michi esse.* Death is the only existence I can look forward to.

(8) An old man in bed attended by a doctor who holds up a vial, probably a urinal *Infirmitati deditus incipio deesse*

(9) A coffin on a bier, covered with a pall, between four tapers Behind stands a tonsured clerk in a surplice, reading the office of the dead. *Putavi q(uo)d viverem: vita me decepit.*

(10) A tomb in a churchyard with a cross on its cover. *Versus sum in cinerem · vita me decepit.*

The spandrel spaces in the four corners of the design are occupied by four figures representing the four chief ages of life. In the lower left-hand corner is *Infantia*, a boy in a long grey tunic seated on the ground, and pointing to a scroll on which his name is inscribed. I cannot accept Sir G..Warner's interpretation of this as a woman in labour. All the other figures are male The half-reclining attitude of the body, propped by one hand resting on the ground, is due merely to the conditions of the space to be filled. There is no trace of anguish in the features. Lastly, the infant Jesus on the Virgin's lap a few pages further on in the Psalter is represented in exactly the same way. Mr. Waller and Mr Winter Jones seem to have had no doubt that the figure was that of a boy. The remaining figures cause no difficulty. At the upper corner on this side is a king pointing to a scroll with *Iuventus*, the prime of life; opposite to him on the right is an old man—*Senectus*; and below is man in the last stage, reclining with his head supported by the left hand. His title—*Decrepitus*—appears from other instances to be, not an adjective, but a variety of *decrepitas*, formed on the analogy of *senectus*.

We are now in a position to appreciate the remains of the wall-painting at Leominster. The westernmost bay of the north aisle corresponds to the tower, and like the rest of this part of the church belongs to the first half of the twelfth century. A transverse arch springing from the north-east pier of the tower separates it from the rest of the aisle; it opens by another arch

[1] *Archaeologia*, xxxv, 174.

on the south into the tower; and a triplet window has been inserted in the west wall. The north wall, with which we are
concerned, is pierced by a door which led to the cloisters.
Above this comes a string-course, between which and the plain
unribbed cross vaulting is a contemporary round-headed window,
just like those in the nave clearstory. It is not set in the middle
of the wall, the larger space to the left being occupied by the
painting which we are about to consider. The smaller space to
the right of the window is covered with modern plaster, but as
the window itself was blocked before Sir Gilbert Scott's restoration of this part of the church about 1865, we may presume
that, when the window was opened and the painting discovered
on the left, the space on the right was also stripped, and nothing
discovered which was thought worth preserving. It can hardly
be doubted that, originally, it had been decorated at the
same date as the rest of the wall. Nor was this all. Prof.
Freeman, writing in 1853 in *Archaeologia Cambrensis* (2 S. IV,
19), says: 'The western bay [of the north aisle] was originally
separated by an arch from the rest of the aisle; at some later
period this arch was blocked with a solid wall. On the west
face of this wall remain considerable traces of mural paintings;
the date, subject, and merit of them I must leave to others better
versed in that branch of archaeology; but I may be allowed to
express a hope that somewhat better care than at present seems
to be the case may be taken both of them and generally of this
curious portion of the church, which is now blocked off as a
coalhole.' It was, no doubt, the St. Andrew's or St. Antony's
Chapel, to which there are various references;[1] and it looks as
if the whole chapel had been decorated in the style of the
picture which has survived. As a matter of fact, remains of the
same conventional ornament are to be seen, not only on the bare
stone-work of the string-course below it, but also on the piers
opposite. It would be hardly rash to suggest that the inserted
triplet window in the west wall belonged to this new treatment
of the chapel. Richard Symonds noted in 1645 'in the north
yle window of the old church, called St. Anthonyes Church, very
old' the arms of Croft.[2] By 'very old' I think he shows that
he recognized the difference between thirteenth-century and
(say) fifteenth-century glass. Perhaps we may conjecture that
the donors of the new decorations were the Crofts of Croft
Castle, only a few miles north-west of Leominster.

To come now to the painting itself, which we can follow in the
admirable reproduction by our Fellow Mr. C. J. Praetorius

[1] G. F. Townsend, *The Town and Borough of Leominster* (Leominster,
1862), p. 229 *note*.
[2] *Diary of the Marches of the Royal Army* (Camden Society, 1859), p. 267.

(fig. 3), it may be noticed that from the string-course to the crown of the vault is 10 ft. 5 in., the diameter of the wheel being 7 ft. 1 in., and that of the smaller circles 19¼ in. The decorative stoning is carefully finished off with a double line at the edge of the splay of the window. In addition to the seated figure of David on the left there seem to be traces of a figure or figures at the top of the wheel, surrounded by scroll work. The whole has been set out with no very great accuracy. No incised lines can be detected, but only the centre points from which the circles were struck. The only colours used, or at any rate surviving, are red, of more than one tone, and yellow. The backgrounds are white.

Let us now try to identify what is left of the subjects and the inscriptions, on the basis of the version in the Arundel Psalter, but with the possibility of variations from it. The two most obvious identifications are the seated king in the topmost circle, and the verse belonging to the ninth scene: *Putavi q(uo)d vivei em . vita me decepit* on the lower right-hand part of the circumference. These tell us two things: (1) that the subjects were arranged in the same order as in the Psalter, and (2) that each verse was placed, not round its picture, as in the Psalter, but on the adjacent part of the circumference. Hence arises a difficulty. If each verse took up about the same space as this one, there is room on the circumference for only eight at the most. The other two had to be provided for in another way, and this was done by inscribing them on a horizontal band which met the circle near the top (where the appropriate scenes were), and then followed its outer curve till it reached the corresponding point on the opposite side, where it became horizontal again. No trace of this seems to have survived on the right, but I think we shall see that it is necessary to assume what the principle of symmetry certainly suggests. Even with this provision for the extra verses, we shall find that the end of the tenth and last has to stray outside the circumference.

Beginning with the medallion in the centre, on the right side one may trace some of the long hair belonging to the head of God, and also part of the lower edge of the nimbus, which here did not, as in the Arundel Psalter, coincide with the circle or medallion in which the head is set. Here the head of God is a bust and its nimbus is considerably smaller than the circle which frames the picture. The inscription was placed outside the medallion, between the spokes ; but the end, on the right, is all that has survived :

[*Cuncta simul cerno, to*]*tum ratione guberno.*

The last syllable is placed above the line, suggesting that this

Fig. 3.   WHEEL OF LIFE, f

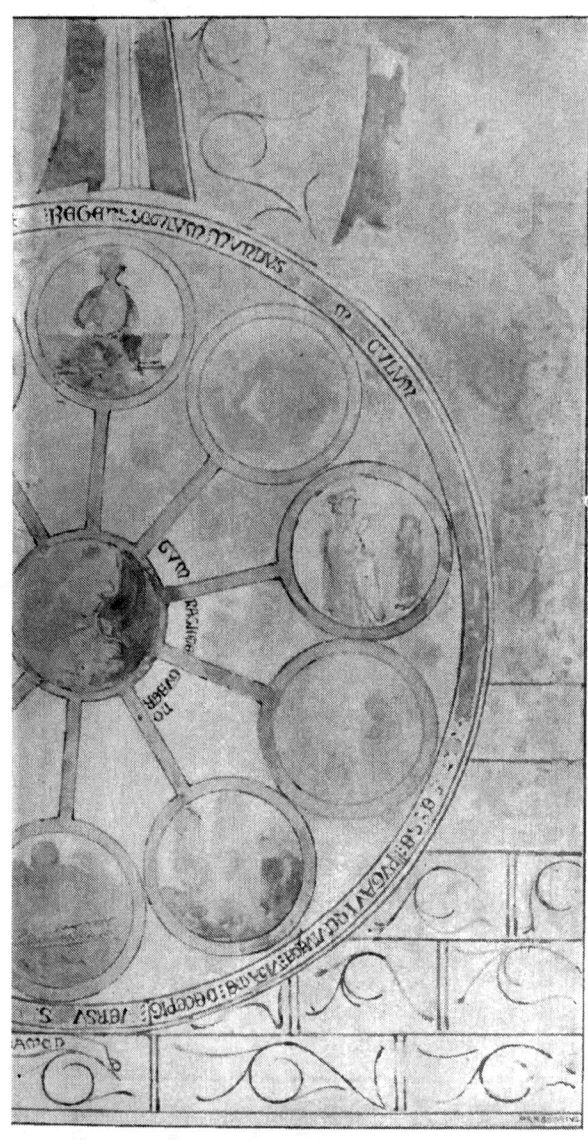

R CHURCH, HEREFORDSHIRE

compression was due to symmetry, and that the verse began in the corresponding space on the left side, where, however, all traces have vanished.

Next, taking the outer circles with the stages of life in order, the remains in 1 (Infancy) suggest a woman with her child in bed, and not the scene depicted in the Psalter, so that here we begin with a variation. On the circumference just beyond the circle are faint but certain traces of the end of the verse:

[*Mitis sum et humilis lacte v*]*ivo puro.*

(2) It is followed by the first letters of the verse of the next scene (Boyhood),

Num[*quam ero labilis etatem mensuro*],

but all traces of the scene itself and also of the next, (3) (Youth), have vanished. Most of the verse of the latter, however, survives in a fragmentary state. In the Arundel MS. this runs:

Vita decens seculi speculo probatur.

The first word is lost at Leominster, but the second is clearly *nitens*, a natural variant if we remember how *nitere* and *nitidus* are used in connexion with dress and personal appearance. The last word *probatur* is immediately followed by *re*[*x*], evidently the beginning of the fifth verse belonging to the king in the topmost circle. We must therefore look for the intermediate fourth verse in the outer inscription band, where it would be fairly close to its scene. Of the latter, (4) (Early Manhood), no traces are visible, but it can be seen that the inscription begins on the horizontal part of the band, to the left; and we at once become aware that it differs from the version in the MS. :

Non ymago speculi sed vita letatur.

The first word is *iam*; then, after a gap, comes a termination . . . *sus*, followed by *specie : vita me letatur.* I propose to restore this :

Iam non visus specie,

visus being the antithesis to *vita*, and part of the subject of *letatur.* 'No longer does mere appearance please me by its comeliness, but real life.' Mr. Praetorius has, however, pointed out to me that the final *e* of *specie* has a kind of tail attached to it, which looks like an abbreviation. In that case I would suggest *species, visús* becoming the genitive—'No longer does comeliness of appearance (or visage) please me'—which I think is an improvement. We now come to the circle at the top (5), with the king on his throne, one of the best-preserved subjects. The verse is immediately over it, and appears to read, with a slight variation from the Psalter :

Re[*x sum*] *regens seculum mundus* [*meus totus*].

Mr. Praetorius thought that the second word also began with
re, but I cannot make anything out of this; and as the traces
are very faint, I assume, provisionally, that the word was *sum*
Of scene 6, the first stage in the decline of life, nothing seems
to be left; but the remains of the word [*ba*]*culum* on the circumference close by show that its verse, of which one other letter
survives,

[*Sumo*] *m*[*ichi ba*]*culum* [*morti fere notus*],

was placed here, and not, as we should have expected on grounds
of symmetry, on the outer and partly horizontal band. The latter
must have contained the verse of the next scene (7), the only one
of which no letters have survived. There is certainly no room
for it on the circumference, as the remains of the following verse
show. Of the scene itself there are considerable traces which
suggest that the old man's left hand was not resting on the boy's
shoulder, but raised as if addressing or threatening him. Perhaps
the motive of age the laughing-stock of children, was here expressed more clearly than in the Psalter. Of the next scene (8)
little or nothing is left, and only the last letters of the verse:

[*Infirmitati deditus incipio de*]*esse*

In scene 9 there seems to be a standing figure on the left,
presumably a clerk, and there may be another next to him.
Most of the verse can be made out, and part is well preserved ·

Putavi q(*uo*)*d viverem : vita me decepit.*

viverem is not clear, and the way in which it is written may be the
fault of an illiterate artist . e. g. the final Ɛ may be an Ω turned the
wrong way. I cannot think of any alternative to *viverem*. There
are some fragments of the last scene (10), but we do not seem to
recognize in them the tomb of the Psalter. The hatching in front
may represent the ground, or may belong to a shrouded corpse
about to be interred. Behind there may have been three standing
figures, and I have sometimes thought that one at least is nimbed.
The first letters of the verse can be traced, and further on the
third word *cinerem*, after which the available space was brought
to an end by the beginning of the verse of the first scene, and
accordingly the last words were inscribed in smaller letters, and
in the reverse direction, on the decorative background outside
the circumference. It may be read thus :

Versus s[*um i*]*n cinerem* [*vi*]*ta me* [*d*]*e*[*cepit*].

Instead of the Four Ages of Life which accompany the wheel
in the Psalter, we have at Leominster, in the left-hand lower
corner, a seated figure of David playing on a harp The obvious
allusion would be to the 'three score years and ten' of Ps. xc, 10.
The harp appears to have eleven strings, if not more. Had

there been ten, we might have suggested a symbolical connexion between them and the ten ages of the wheel. Piero Valeriano [1] recognizes both the seven-stringed and ten-stringed lyre or harp as a symbol of human life and its ages; and passages in the Psalms (e. g. lvii, 9; xcii, 3; cxliv, 9) seem to have been interpreted in a similar manner. It is not impossible that the original of our design may have had a ten-stringed harp, the significance of which was not grasped by the Leominster copyist.

I have not been able to discover any literary source of the verses which accompany the scenes. Both of the metrical forms used, viz. the accentual rhymed couplets accompanying the stages of life, and the hexameter with its interior rhyme round the head of God, had their greatest vogue in the twelfth and thirteenth centuries.

In one case I have come across something of a parallel, and that is the verse round the central head of God. It differs from the others in metre, and in being a single line and not a couplet:

Cuncta simul cerno totum racione guberno.

I cannot help comparing with this the verse inscribed round the late thirteenth-century paten at Wyke in Hampshire:

Cuncta creo virtute rego pietate reformo. [2]

The central device is the Agnus Dei, but it is obvious how appropriate the words would be with the head of God or the Vernicle which so often appears as the central device on patens, though, apparently, there is no surviving instance of its use at such an early date. Sir William Hope places the paten about 1280,[3] so that it is more or less contemporary with the Leominster painting. I am inclined to suggest that its inscription, so unlike the ordinary legends on sacramental plate, was derived from some picture in which it was connected with a central head of God like those at Leominster and in the Arundel Psalter.

The Kempley wheel, which is on a smaller scale than that at Leominster, need not detain us, as it shows only the framework of the design in red. The surfaces of the alternate medallions are also reddish, which can hardly be due to the accident of survival. The lower left-hand spandrel space is filled by a piece of scroll-work, also in red, suggestive of a relatively early date. The circles of the design have been accurately set out, but the red paint has been coarsely applied, not always following the setting-out lines, and looks as if it were due to a later repainting.

It remains to say a few words about (1) the origin and analogies of this wheel design; (2) the representations of the ages of life.

---

[1] *Hieroglyphica* (Basel, 1567), p. 348.

[2] *Archaeological Journal*, xliii (1886), 154, pl. vii, 375.

[3] *Ibid.*, p. 375.

With regard to the medieval Wheel (*Rota*) designs we may distinguish:

(*a*) The design made up of concentric circles. This, no doubt, goes back to ancient times, especially in the form of the Time or Year Wheels (twelfth century), in which the centre is occupied by a symbolical figure of the Year, Time, Day and Night, or the head of God; while the surrounding zones show the four seasons, the winds, the months, the signs of the zodiac, etc.,[1] with which we sometimes find combined, as in the Byzantine Manual, the ages of life.[2] Another form of the concentric circle design, divided into segments by spokes, was used didactically to show the connexion between a number of different ideas or formulas. Among the schematic designs which are such a feature of the Arundel Psalter there is a Rota (so described) with the head of God in the centre, round which are set out, concentrically, the seven petitions of the Lord's prayer, the seven sacraments, the seven gifts of the spirit, the seven works of mercy, and so forth (fol. 129 b).

(*b*) Quite different is the representation of an actual spoked wheel in the act of being turned by a large human figure standing by or behind it, while smaller symbolical figures are attached to the spokes or the circumference. The commonest form of this is the Wheel of Fortune (e. g. in Rochester Cathedral), but it is also found in connexion with the Seven Deadly Sins, and with the ages of life.

(*c*) The design of the wheel of the Leominster type, with its radiating spokes ending in medallions, is distinct from these, but it does not stand alone. At Saint Denis[3] and at Chartres[4] are windows of the twelfth century in which just the same system of a central medallion, connected by radiating spokes with an outer circle of medallions, is used for the symbolism of the seven gifts of the Spirit. But the design was not confined to the representation of the seven spirits, for in a twelfth-century embroidery at Cologne it is used (as a pendant to one of the Time Wheels referred to above) for the twelve signs of the zodiac radiating from a central medallion containing figures of the sun and moon (fig. 4).[5] The space to be filled happens to be a square, but that does not destroy the circularity of the design, which is very like that of the Leominster wheel. Here we get much

---

[1] F. X. Kraus, *Geschichte der christlichen Kunst*, ii, 414 sqq

[2] Didron (Stokes), *Christian Iconography*, ii, 381. The words put into the mouth of the man in the last but one of the seven ages—' O Time, how thou hast deceived me!' recall *tita me decepit* of the Arundel and Leominster wheels, but this may be only a coincidence.

[3] Michel, *Histoire de l'art*, vol. 1, part ii, p 785, fig 419.

[4] Didron, *Annales archéologiques*, i, 217, *Christian Iconography* (Stokes), i, 486

[5] De Farcy, *La Broderie*, pl 48, 1, and p. 116.

To face page 56

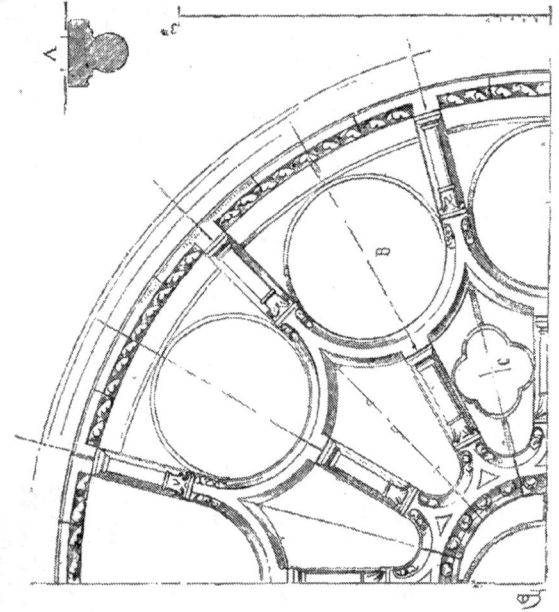

Fig. 5.   WEST WINDOW, NOTRE DAME, MANTES

(From Viollet-le-Duc)

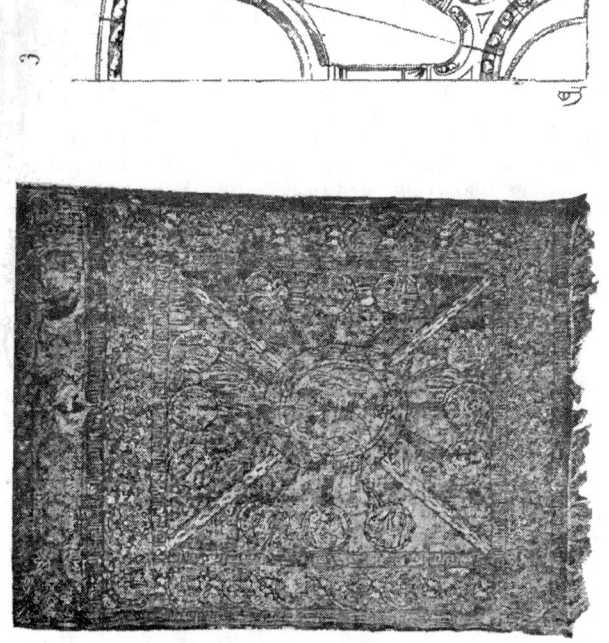

Fig. 4.   EMBROIDERY WITH WHEEL DESIGN AT COLOGNE

(From de Farcy, La Broderie, pl. 48)

nearer to our Wheel of Life, for the analogy between the seasons
and the ages of man is a commonplace. The design was, then,
evidently used for subjects which were practically secular; though
in our case, as often with the Time Wheels, the introduction of
the head of God in the centre imparts a religious element.

It is difficult not to think that this design has some connexion
with the earlier forms of the wheel window, which first appears
in the latter half of the twelfth century. That the architectural
form was applied to these circular designs is shown by the picture
of a Wheel of Fortune in the sketch-book of the thirteenth-
century architect, Wilars de Honecort,[1] where the figures of the
seven kings are set in an actual rose window. Nor does it stand
alone. In the *Hortus Deliciarum* of the twelfth-century abbess,
Herrad von Landsperg, we see Philosophy surrounded by the
Seven Liberal Arts set in a wheel window of contemporary
design.[2] We are brought nearer to our design by a window of
the type of that in St. James's, Bristol, where a central circle is
surrounded by an outer range of circles. But here we miss one
of the main features of our design, the connecting spokes which
suggest the radiating shafts or short columns connected by arches,
which are so important a feature of the earlier wheel windows.
Where, as in the great west window of Chartres (about 1225),
these shafts correspond with the centres of the outer series of
circles, we get the essential elements of our design, especially if
it be thought of, not in the terms of architectural draughts-
manship, but in actuality, with each of the radiating shafts or
spokes pointing, as it were, to its medallion picture in the glass.
Following this line of ideas, we are taken, I think, a step nearer
to the design of the Leominster wheel in the case of the early
wheel window in the west front of Notre-Dame at Mantes,
which Viollet-le-Duc[3] places in the last years of the twelfth
century (fig. 5). Here, owing to the exigencies of construction,
the spokes or shafts are brought into direct contact with the outer
medallions or circles, which are formed partly by the reversed
arch of the radiating arcade and partly by the iron framework
within it.

The subject of the representations of the Ages of Life has
been dealt with in various books and periodicals, among which
the first place must be given to Didron's treatise, *La Vie humaine*,
in the first volume of the *Annales archéologiques* (1844). About
the same time as Mr. Waller's paper in the *Gentleman's Magazine*, referred to above, *Archaeologia* (vol. xxxv (1853), p. 167)

---

[1] R. Willis, *Facsimile of the Sketch-Book of Wilars de Honecort* (London,
859), pl. xli.

[2] C. M. Engelhardt, *Herrad von Landsperg* (Stuttgart, 1818).

[3] *Dictionnaire raisonné de l'architecture française* (Paris, 1866), viii, 38.

contained an important article on the Ages of Life (including a beautiful reproduction of the Arundel Psalter wheel) by Mr. John Winter Jones. In 1859 Dr. Gustav Heider collected a great deal of valuable material in an article *Das Glücksrad* in the *Mittheilungen* of the Austro-Hungarian Central Commission.[1] A paper by Karl Weinhold, *Glücksrad und Lebensrad*, read before the Royal Academy of Berlin in 1892[2] also contains valuable suggestions; and a good deal of information may be gained from the works of Kraus, Bergner, Piper, Wackernagel, and others, and especially from the recent *Die Lebensalter* by Franz Boll (Teubner, Leipzig, 1913. Reprinted from the *Neue Jahrbücher für das klassische Altertum*, vol. xxxi).

The oldest literary evidence for the division of life into ten stages is an elegiac poem by Solon, preserved by Philo and Clement of Alexandria.[3] It depends, of course, on the number seven; there is no connexion between its descriptions and our pictures; and its only interest for us is that it is the oldest example of the Ten Age system. Mr. Winter Jones quotes a Hebrew poem of the twelfth century giving the same division; and as the influence of Jewish lore on the medieval writers and compilers is now recognized, it is not impossible that the system may have had a limited vogue in Western Europe about this time from some such source. While the Greek and Hebrew poems fairly divide the whole of life between their 'hebdomads', in the wheel of the Arundel MS. the last two stages are superfluous, for the man is already dead. This reveals the defect of the system, and explains why it was never very popular. The number of stages is too large, and as symmetry compels the identification of the middle point with the prime of life, it is not easy to differentiate five periods of its decline. As a great decorative design it consequently went out of fashion; and it is significant that in the Bodleian MS. Laud. 156, where a fifteenth-century scribe seems to have copied the schematic designs of Arundel 83, it is omitted. Nevertheless the Ten Ages had a certain popularity which we can trace in prints from the fifteenth century onwards in Germany, North Italy, France, and even England. Often the age is connected with the animal which was supposed to symbolize it, and generally (though not in the earliest examples) the figures are arranged on a sort of pyramid of steps, as in the seventeenth-century English picture illustrated in a recent volume of our *Proceedings*.[4]

With regard to this pyramid design Weinhold makes an

---

[1] iv (1859), 113.

[2] *Abhandlungen der k. Akademie der Wissenschaften zu Berlin*, 1892.

[3] Bergk, *Poetae Lyrici Graeci* (4th ed.), ii. 51.

[4] xxiv, 320.

interesting comparison between it and the half-wheel of the south transept at Amiens, where the idea of the Wheel of Fortune is combined with that of the Wheel of Life; the ascending figures being all young and happy, the descending ones old and miserable. There are eight on each side with the king at the top, but in the earlier rose window of the north transept at Saint-Étienne, Beauvais, which similarly illustrates both Fortune and Life, the ascending and descending figures number ten. This upper half of a wheel with its ascending and descending figures might easily suggest the pyramid of steps; but the idea is much older, as Weinhold shows by the passage in Aelian's *Varia Historia* (ii, 29), which says that the early Greek philosopher Pittacus set up in the temples at Mytilene ladders or steps to symbolize the ups and downs of human life.

As to the sources or influences which may be traced in these pictures a few suggestions can be made here. The first is the influence of astrology. Boll refers to the account in the *Tetrabiblos* of Claudius Ptolemaeus (second century A.D.) of the influence of the seven planets on the seven ages of life.[1] Taking into account the numerical difference of the systems, some of these can, I think, be traced in the Arundel Psalter pictures and verses. The first age is governed by the Moon, and the infant is described with its undeveloped mental powers and liquid nourishment, which recalls *Mitis sum et humilis: lacte vivo puro.* The second age belongs to Hermes and is marked by the beginnings of intelligence and knowledge, which agrees with our interpretation of the second scene. The third is dominated by Aphrodite, and is the age of puberty, therefore well illustrated by the third picture, in which, moreover, we may note that the looking-glass is one of the emblems of Venus. The fourth age, the prime of life, in this system is under the Sun, the king of the planets, when the man turns from amusements to the pursuit of honours and power, and our fifth figure illustrates this idea. The other pictures do not seem to have much connexion with the influences ascribed to the remaining planets, Mars, Jupiter, and Saturn.[2]

The second source is the Wheel of Fortune. Weinhold has shown how the Wheel of Fortune developed into the Wheel of Life.[3] Perhaps the earliest picture we have is in the *Hortus Deliciarum* of Herrad von Landsperg (twelfth century), where, as

---

[1] *Die Lebensalter,* p. 33.

[2] The passages come from the Fourth Book (περὶ χρόνων διαιρέσεως) of the *Tetrabiblos,* for which, until the appearance of a new edition in Teubner's *Bibliotheca,* reference must still be made to that printed at Basel in 1553 with the Latin version of Melanchthon (pp. 241–5).

[3] *Glücksrad und Lebensrad,* p. 21.

in Wilars de Honecort's design, the figures on the wheel are all kings. The topmost speaks some Latin verses, one of which contains the rare word *labilis*, which occurs in the Arundel Psalter:

Labilis ut ventus sic transit laeta iuventus.[1]

The changes of fortune were next illustrated by persons in various stations of life, but in all the Wheel of Fortune designs the king almost invariably maintains his position at the top of the wheel; and I think that the king at the summit of our wheel and of other Wheels of Life must be connected with this. Another common feature of the Wheels of Fortune and Life is the representation of a corpse in a coffin on a grave at the opposite extremity—the bottom of the wheel. It is noticeable that in our design the tomb occupies the same position.

Owing to the analogy between human life and the course of the year, another source which we might expect to have furnished suggestions is the pictorial system of the Calendars. The examples in Mr. James Fowler's well-known article on the Calendar pictures in *Archaeologia*, vol. xlv, provide one obvious instance—the man going out hawking, frequently on horseback, which occurs most commonly in April, but also for May and June, all months connected with the springtime of life and youth. Hence it formed an obvious treatment for the medallion in the Wheel of Life devoted to Early Manhood."

Mr. PRAETORIUS said the present deplorable state of the Leominster painting was due to the distemper covering. If that were removed, the white horse, for instance, might come to light in one of the upper medallions. Half the central medallion was clear, but the remainder should be cleaned. The painting was in the simplest style, only the light red earth and a second colour (probably madder root) being used, on a white ground. The second colour was a reddish brown, used for the scrolls; and the lower part was better executed than the top. The figure of David, and especially the hand, were vigorously painted, and his robe was originally brilliant crimson. Above the harp were detected red lines suggesting the left hand; and the lower sound-hole was well painted in purple and preserved. The roses were freely drawn, but the flowers had been painted a fugitive pink. The curious tomb in the lowest medallion had probably had a skeleton lying on it; and there were still five medallions to be cleaned of distemper.

REGINALD A. SMITH, Esq., F.S.A., read the following paper on four sculptures of the Viking period from Bibury, Gloucestershire, now in the British Museum:

---

[1] G. Heider, *Das Glücksrad*, p. 114.

"The greater part of southern England is practically devoid of Anglo-Saxon sculpture, and if the abundance of pre-Norman crosses in Cornwall is explained by the copious supply of raw material, it is difficult to see why Gloucestershire, for instance, should not have more relics of the period cut out of the local oolite. With the well-known exception at Gloucester, the later Anglo-Saxon period was not known to be represented in the county till several stone carvings came to light some years ago in the churchyard at Bibury, 4 miles north of Fairford, 6½ miles north-east of Cirencester, and 1 mile north of the Roman road known as Akeman Street.

It is to the Hon. and Rev. Canon F. G. Dutton, Vicar of Bibury, that the British Museum owes a selection from these early sculptures, which lay near the surface in the angle between the tower and south wall of the nave. Some fragments of Norman date are still stored in the church, but the four most interesting pieces were presented last year and form the subject of this communication.

The picturesque village is not easily accessible, and few visitors would have seen these relics even if space had been found for their exhibition locally; hence it was felt that objects of such rare interest would be more fittingly housed with the national collection, which should not be wholly sacrificed to the very proper desire to see such monuments preserved in the neighbourhood, if not on the spot, of their discovery. If logically carried out, such a policy would starve the national museums, and cancel the advantages they possess of a central situation and official prestige.

The four sculptures have their own peculiarities, and two are of special interest as being examples of Viking rather than native art, but it will be convenient to deal first with the two that are of a more familiar type.

The rectangular block here represented (fig. 1) is 32½ in. long, 14 in. wide, and 10 in. thick, the back and three of the four sides being plain. These may or may not be in their original condition, but the block seems to have been at one time intended for use as a horizontal slab, the arcading on the side being then in its normal position. It seems too short and thick for a grave-slab, but the raised border does not cross the upper face at one end, and if the enclosed pattern of two carrick-bends [1] in relief is complete it is not symmetrical, so that there may have been an extension at one end. The row of dots within the raised edge is remarkable, and is also wanting at one end, the return being visible at the other. One need not look far for

[1] The late Mr. Romilly Allen unfortunately called this the figure-of-eight knot, which is different and made with a single cord.

parallels, the carrick-bend being not at all uncommon, as for instance on two crosses in Cumberland—the standing cross of St. Bees (*V. C. H. Cumberland*, i, 262) and Waberthwaite cross (*ibid.*, facing p. 273).

The dots are hemispherical, not flat like those used to fill up small spaces on many Viking sculptures, but there may be some relation between them. If, however, this monument is a stone copy of a wooden coffin, the domed studs might well represent the nail-heads that would naturally follow the border. Still more unusual is the arcading on the side, for which I have failed to find a parallel in this country. The pattern requires no further description, though the absence should be noted of any

Fig. 1.   RECUMBENT STONE, BIBURY, GLOUCESTERSHIRE.

columns dividing the corresponding semicircles below. One is reminded of the hog-back gravestones, but the semicircles on them are turned the other way and occur in rows simulating the tiling of a roof.

Though referred to the Viking period, this sculpture has no feature characteristic of Scandinavian art, and in fact is altogether different in style from two of the three following. It is, however, not easy to find a name for the style, which is in striking contrast to the floral scroll-work of the Anglian series and the figure-subjects of the Irish crosses, so that Saxon or Anglo-Saxon seems the only alternative; but there is at present nothing to furnish a more exact date than the Viking period.

The next sculpture (fig. 2) is part of a slab 5 in. thick, $12\frac{1}{4}$ in. to $12\frac{3}{4}$ in. wide, and originally about 28 in. long, the present extreme length being 18 in. The front is covered with a regular interlaced pattern of a single broad band terminating in a pointed tail at the right-hand bottom corner.

The pattern, which may be easily completed, is simple
and indeed commonplace, but the tail warrants the conclusion
that the other end took the form of a head, and the pattern
must therefore rank as serpentine rather than pure interlacing.

Fig. 2.   SLAB WITH SNAKE-PATTERN, BIBURY, GLOUCESTERSHIRE.

A pattern practically identical but wrongly set out, apparently
with head and tail complete, occurs on one of the Maughold
stones in the Isle of Man ;[1] swan-like heads are also seen on the
lower block of Dolton font, Devon.[2]   The head and tail distinguish the pattern from most of the interlaced sculptures, and
point to Scandinavia, where the encircling band on a gravestone, generally carrying the runes, normally takes a serpentine

[1] P. M. C. Kermode, *Manx Crosses*, no. 51, detail on p. 34, fig. 22 (9).
[2] *Reliquary and Illustrated Archaeologist*, viii (1902), 247.

form. The broad plait on this Bibury stone much resembles
that on the red shaft at Cross Canonby (*V. C. H. Cumberland*,
i, 273), and in the same county is an example of serpentine
interlacing, on the cross already quoted at St. Bees. A still
better-known example is the Gosforth standing cross.

The remaining two stones belong to the same school or period,
and may to a large extent be discussed together. They are
quite unlike the majority of pre-Norman sculptures in Britain
or Ireland, and the opportunity presents itself of bringing together some at least of the same character found in this country,
and of reproducing a few parallels from Scandinavia, the head-
quarters of this peculiar art. Special attention has recently

Fig. 3.   DESIGNS ON TWO FACES OF SLAB, BIBURY, GLOUCESTERSHIRE.

been given to Scandinavian stone-work of the tenth and eleventh
centuries by Dr. Haakon Schetelig of Bergen, whose work has
been already referred to in connexion with the Winchester
bronze panel, and the Whitcombe stones described last session ;
and a more recent paper from his pen on the Scandinavian
affinities of Manx sculpture was contributed to the volume presented to Prof. Montelius of Stockholm, state-antiquary of
Sweden, on his seventieth birthday.

So far as it is purely geometrical, the smaller stone (fig. 3),
which measures 12¾ in. to 13¼ in. in width, 14½ in. in length,
and 2 in. in thickness, may be placed in the Ringerike group,
though one face is far more characteristic of that phase of
Scandinavian art than the other. The intersecting segments
have only a vague resemblance to the typical crossed bands seen
on the other face ; and the absence of the conventional foliage
(though this may have appeared on portions of the stone now
missing) strengthens the suspicion that the two faces are not
quite contemporary. Though parallels for the first design would

be hard to find, it must be remembered that work of Ringerike
style is rare in England, and if the intersecting segments cannot
be proved to be of that period, it would, on the other hand, be
rash to attribute them to any other.

The other face of this stone is easily recognized as belonging
to the Ringerike series, which has been isolated by Dr. Schetelig
and assigned, on unimpeachable evidence, to the first half of the
eleventh century. It may here be repeated that Ringerike, the
best-known centre for sculpture in this style, is in the Buskerud
district of Norway; but examples have been found elsewhere in
Scandinavia and in England of a fashion that interrupted the
traditional animal-ornament of the Teutons, and was apparently
the outcome of intercourse with the East. During the preceding
fifty years, perhaps longer, the prevailing style of decoration was
that best illustrated on the Danish Jellinge stone (about 980),
and about the time of our Norman Conquest the animal motive
again prevailed in Scandinavia but is poorly represented, as the
introduction of Christianity had meanwhile simplified monumental sculpture in Scandinavia, and reduced the amount of
funeral furniture.

A minute description of the ornament on the left face of
the third stone and on the fourth stone (fig. 4) would be a
difficult task, and is further unnecessary, as the completed rubbings here reproduced are considerably more intelligible than
the originals. The setting-out is faulty, and there is a free-
hand look about the work that cannot indeed compare with
contemporary Anglo-Saxon or Irish miniatures,[1] but has an
interest of its own from the archaeological point of view.
It now seems certain that the style was based on engraved
pendants and other imports from beyond the Caspian, which
are found from time to time with Cufic and other coins of
the eleventh century.[2] Parallels from Cumberland for the
Bibury stones have been already quoted, and it is instructive to
note that analogies are also found in the Isle of Man, both these
being districts strongly influenced by the Viking culture.

The pellets that occur in single or double rows within the
interlacing bands, and are also scattered over vacant spaces of
the design, have been recognized as a Scandinavian feature; and
by way of illustration may be cited the Norse cross at St. Bees
(V. C. H. Cumberland, i, 262), the stones at Desborough and
Moulton (V. C. H. Northants, ii, 193), and the panel in the

---

[1] A reminiscence of this style can perhaps be detected in the Psalter of
Ricemarch, an Irish illuminated manuscript of the late eleventh century.
See especially Bruun, Art of the Illuminated MSS. of the Middle Ages, pl. x,
p. 82.

[2] Schetelig, Kunst-Kultur, 1910, 38; Proceedings, xxiii, 400.

outer wall of Wroxeter Church, Shropshire. The Isle of Man furnishes several examples illustrated by Mr. Kermode.

Single rows of dots within plain narrow borders are frequent on Manx crosses, e. g. on Kirk Michael (no. 101) where the design of the upper limb of the cross recalls that of a bone disc from the City of London, in the national collection (*Proceedings*, 2nd ser., iii, 225; *V. C. H. London*, i, 163, fig. 6 on plate). The latter has, however, the dots in several rows, resembling a coat

Fig. 4.   DESIGN OF VIKING GRAVESTONE, BIBURY, GLOUCESTERSHIRE.

of mail, on a contorted male figure, the attitude of which is quite in keeping with the period (about 1,000), the crucified figure on the Jellinge stone (about 980) and the Kirby Stephen figure being probably of the same school. Dots in two, three, and four rows are also used on the interlaced animals of the Kirk Braddan cross (no. 108), which is assigned by Dr. Schetelig to about 990; and both on the Cunigunda and St. Cordula caskets.

The tapering bands that interlace at the crossing and are interrupted at other points by the leafy scrolls of the field are common to both these stones, but the larger stone has terminals at the base that may be regarded as the heads of monsters confronted. Animal motives are generally absent from this class of monuments, but the best-known example in England (the gravestone from St. Paul's Churchyard, in the Guildhall Museum) has a stag-like creature as its central feature, and somewhat similar heads are seen on the fragment from Somerford Keynes, Wilts. (fig. 5).

The claw-like projections filling the lower angles of the Bibury stone must on this view be regarded as crests or combs; there is a conspicuous tooth in both lower jaws (something like those of the animals flanking fig.9)closely allied to the pair on the right face of the Gloucester cross,[1] and a scroll or lappet passing in front of either eye and meeting below the chin.[2] There is, however, normally a spiral and lappet on either side of the base of these tapering bands, as on the Vang stone and

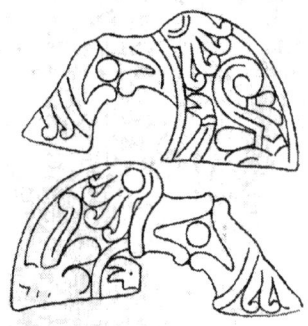

Fig. 5.   STONE CARVING, SOMERFORD KEYNES, WILTS.

Winchester panel (*Proceedings*, xxiii, 402 and 398), and it may be that the scrolls belong to the original design and the animal heads were an afterthought. The triple hooks on the back of the head appear in embryo on the London bone disc already mentioned, and are used with a sparing hand on the Winchester panel. The feet of the Teutonic decorative animal and the foliage adapted from Carlovingian art sometimes take this form, but the oriental bronze pendant from Vårby, Sweden, figured in *Proceedings*, xxiii, 400, furnishes a more plausible explanation, especially as it also exemplifies the joined S scrolls of the Bibury stone and something very like the union knot. The latter is a fusiform member with forked base, here springing from the axils of the scrolls and not placed as usual in the centre of the top as a kind of keystone, as on the Winchester panel and the bronze panel from the Thames at Hammersmith (*Proceedings*, xxiii, 400).

The termination of the scroll-work in two human heads is a feature of special interest and novelty. The same moustaches are worn by the soldiers seizing Christ on the cross of Muiredach at Monasterboice, Co. Louth,[3] and something similar but still

[1] *Trans. Bristol and Glouc. Arch. Soc.*, xiii, 122, pl. vi.
[2] Cf. design on tortoise-brooch, 8th century: Montelius, *Öfversigt öfver den nordiska Forntidens perioder* 30, fig. 39.
[3] Outline drawing of panel in R. Allen's *Early Christian Symbolism*, 201.

more grotesque is seen on three runic stones in Denmark, all of
the Ringerike style: the great Aarhus stone known as Aarhus II,
date about 1000 (fig. 6); the Sjœlle stone, west of Aarhus; and
the Skjern stone (fig. 7), west of Randers,[1] the head on which is
practically identical with that on the Lundagaard stone in
Scania.

There are enough examples in England to show that the
Ringerike style took root here, most of ours being stone monuments that were no doubt made on the spot and not imported

Fig. 6. MASK FROM GRAVESTONE,   Fig. 7. MASK FROM GRAVESTONE,
AARHUS, DENMARK.   SKJERN, DENMARK.

ready-made. There may be more specimens awaiting recognition
in the districts specially affected by the Vikings, but one would
hardly have expected such work in Gloucestershire, though Canon
Dutton informs me that Bibury has its Danish traditions. It can
hardly have been more than a passing phase in England, and it
may well be that the animal motive was not wholly abandoned.
There are several monuments that show a close connexion with
the Jellinge series, but must be regarded as debased examples,
produced perhaps in the half-century that separated the Jellinge
style from that named after Urnes in Norway. Dr. Schetelig
takes this view of several Manx stones,[2] the numbers in

---

[1] Both figured in P. G. Thorsen's *De Danske Runemindesmærker*, nos.
29, 48, 22; see also L. F. A. Wimmer, *De Danske Runemindesmærker*,
vol. i, pt. 2, pp. 126, 139; and vol. ii, p. 171. The Swedish stone is
vol. iii, p. 132.   [2] *Oscari Montelio*, 401.

Fig. 8. STONE CARVING, RAMSEY (MAUGHOLD), ISLE OF MAN.

Fig. 9. STONE CROSS, KIRK MICHAEL, ISLE OF MAN.

Mr. Kermode's book being 82 (Maughold), 89 and 90 (Michael), 96 (Ramsey), perhaps 104 (Michael) and 113 (Conchan), and the later school of Gaut (77, Ballaugh, and 110, Braddan). Two of the above list are reproduced here (figs. 8, 9), and others that seem to be late examples of the Jellinge style are also given in outline (figs. 10, 11, 12), as they have been discovered in counties

Fig. 10. CROSS-SHAFT, RAMSBURY, WILTS.   Fig. 11. CROSS-SHAFT, RAMSBURY, WILTS.

bordering on Gloucestershire and therefore presumably on the same artistic level.

The carvings represented by figs. 10 and 11 are two faces of the cross-shaft known as Ramsbury A,[1] and though contemporary portray the head of the lacertine animal from different points of view, a point of some importance in the study of this peculiar art. Fig. 10 is more true to type, but the interlacing shows in both cases a certain decadence; and the Ramsbury shaft, as well as that at West Camel, Som. (fig. 12),[2]

[1] *Wilts. Arch. Mag.*, xxvii, 64.
[2] Poole, *Old Crosses of Somerset*, 157.

may be provisionally assigned to the close of the Jellinge period, or the opening years of the eleventh century.

Perhaps the most typical example of the Jellinge style in England is the scabbard-chape found at York (*Proceedings*, xxii, 6). The carving found at Rowberrow, Som.,[1] seems to be a later specimen, and about the same date is the elaborate Gloucester stone,[2] especially the front and left side, where the animal is represented in top and side views. Examples of the Ringerike style are considerably rarer in England, and the following is a provisional list, those already mentioned being here repeated to make it as complete as possible:

Fig. 12. CROSS-SHAFT, WEST CAMEL,   Fig. 13. ENGRAVED BRONZE PLATE:
         SOMERSET.   BRITISH MUSEUM ($\frac{1}{1}$).

London, St. Paul's Churchyard, gravestone now in the Guildhall Museum, and two fragments of another in the British Museum, probably from the same spot; both figured in *V. C. H. London,* i, 168.

Bibury, Gloucs., two gravestones, figs. 3, 4.

Berks. (probably), engraved bronze plate in British Museum, with traces of gilding (fig. 13).

Winchester, Hants, bronze panel, figured in *Proceedings*, xxiii, 398.

London, Thames at Hammersmith, bronze model tombstone, figured in *Proceedings*, xxiii, 400.

London, bone comb in British Museum, figured in *V. C. H. London*, i, 164 (Roach Smith collection).

London, St. Martin's-le-Grand, bone cylinder in Guildhall Museum, figured in *V. C. H. London*, i, 169.

[1] Francis Bond, *Fonts and Font-covers*, 103.
[2] *Trans. Bristol and Glouc. Arch. Soc.*, xiii, 118; *Builder*, 1888, pp. 196 (plate), 218, 234, 253.

Dolton, Devon, upper block of font; Bond, *Fonts and Font
Covers*, 102, 103; *Reliquary and Illustrated Archaeo-
logist*, viii (1902), 251.
Somerford Keynes, Wilts., stone fragment, fig. 5, from *Wilts.
Arch. Mag*, xxvii, 65; details in *Reliquary and Illustrated
Archaeologist*, 1893, 49.

H. CLIFFORD SMITH, Esq., M.A., F.S.A., exhibited a profile
portrait of Christ, *temp.* James I, in oils on a circular oak panel.
Diameter 6¾ in. The background of the portrait is in gold. The
inscription in cursive hand in white on black is as follows:

This · present · fyguer · is The · symilitude · of · Our · Saviour · Christ
Jesu Imprinted · in · Emeralde · by · The · predecessors · of · the . Greet ·
Turke · and · sente · To · pope · Innocente The · viii · At · the · coste ·
of · the · Great · Turke · For · A · token · of · y⁸ · cause · Beinge · as · A ·
Rañsom · To Redeeme his · Brother · Maximilian The · Greate · which
was · taken Prisoner

Similar paintings with various garbled inscriptions stating the
portrait to be a copy of the emerald asserted to be preserved in
the Treasury of the Vatican are known, and there are references
to several such by Mr. Albert Way in the *Archaeological Journal*,
vol. xxix, p. 110. Engravings of the same character are more
commonly met with. The discovery of this further example is
worthy of record

Mr. G. F. HILL remarked that the profile bust of Christ was
derived from an Italian medal made in or soon after 1492, on
the reverse of which was an inscription claiming that the bust
was a reproduction of one on an emerald sent by Bajazet II to
Innocent VIII, in order that the Pope might retain Bajazet's
brother Djem in captivity. This legend was reproduced in all
essentials in the English inscription on the panel. The type of
bust, however, was not of Byzantine origin, but went back to
a Flemish original, and might be seen in the panel of the school
of the Van Eycks in the Berlin Gallery. The type was very
popular in the late fifteenth and sixteenth centuries, and was reproduced in innumerable forms (medals, reliefs, woodcuts, etc.).[1]

Thanks were ordered to be returned for these communications
and exhibition.

[1] See G. F. Hill, Medallic Portraits of Christ, in the *Reliquary and
Illustrated Archaeologist*, 1904, pp 173-93.

THURSDAY, 29th JANUARY, 1914.

Sir CHARLES HERCULES READ, Knt., LL.D., President,
in the Chair.

The following gifts were announced, and thanks for the same
ordered to be returned to the donors:

From Ralph Griffin, Esq., F.S.A.:
1. The Church and Fortress of Dover Castle. By Rev. John Puckle.
8vo. Oxford and London, 1864.
2. Le Psautier de Peterborough. Par J. van den Gheyn. fol.
Haarlem. n. d.
3. Vestiges of Antiquity, or, a series of etchings and engravings of the
ancient monastery of St. Augustine, etc., in Canterbury. By
T. Hastings. fol. London, 1813.

From W. de C. Prideaux, Esq.:—Sutcombe Church and its Builders. By
Edith K. Prideaux. 8vo. Exeter, 1913.

The following were admitted fellows:

William Alexander Cater, Esq.
Major Algernon Tudor Craig.
Henry Oppenheimer, Esq.

On the nomination of the President, the following were
appointed auditors of the Society's accounts for the past year:

Harold Sands, Esq.
Horace Wilmer, Esq.
Francis William Pixley, Esq.
Cecil Arthur Tennant, Esq.

The Reverend H. G. O. KENDALL, M.A., F.S.A., read the
following paper on 'Flint Implements from the surface near
Avebury: their classification and dates'.

"The district from which come the flint implements forming
the subject of this paper has Avebury for its centre. Within
its area are some unique prehistoric monuments, such as Silbury
Hill, the largest artificial mound in Europe; and Wansdyke,
running for miles along the shoulders of the hills. There are
also barrows, both long and round, the latter very numerous;
cromlechs, camps, enclosures, terraces, etc.

The implements have been turned up by the plough, and
picked up on the surface of the ground. On the red and yellow
clays, on the top of the highest downs, as well as on the Lower
Chalk plateau, many tools of 'eolithic' facies occur, with their
chipped surfaces stained green or yellow. With them, and of
equal or greater antiquity, are definitely flaked palaeoliths.
These older groups, belonging to a different age, require a paper
to themselves, and will not be treated of on the present occasion.

The best-known site for the later, unstained flints with white, blue, or black patination is Windmill Hill, one mile from Avebury. The top of the hill is surmounted by a camp. Within its boundaries are four round barrows, and many others are scattered about the sides and foot of the hill.

An immense number of chipped flints has been found on this site. Dr. Blackmore remarks that, in a collection formed many years ago, 'fabricators' were specially numerous (fig. 1). The writer has found several dozens of these instruments, varying from the very finest to quite coarse specimens. Arrow-heads of various types are numerous, and 'horseshoe' scrapers specially so. On each of two favourable days within the same week, fifty-five

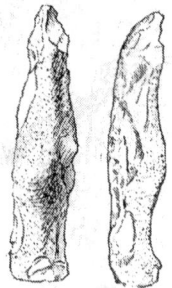

Fig. 1.   FABRICATOR, WINDMILL HILL (⅔).

Fig. 2.   LONG SCRAPER WITH PARALLEL FLAKING AND WHITE PATINA, WINDMILL HILL (⅔). IT RESEMBLES SPECIMENS OF THE CAVE DIVISION, PALAEO. AGE, FROM FRANCE.

good specimens were picked up, and the varieties are numerous and interesting.

Mr. Reginald Smith was the first to point out the extraordinary likeness between the Windmill Hill flints and those of the Aurignac stage of the Cave Division of the Palaeolithic Age. This extends not only to similarity of type but also of style, the long, narrow fluting being noticeable on many specimens.

Seven selected from this group form perfect replicas of those illustrated on p. 217 of Prof. Sollas's *Ancient Hunters*. There is the carinated scraper, of which several exactly similar specimens have come to hand; the knob-headed scraper, both with large and with small scraping end; the narrow form of tool which links the keeled scraper with the beaked *burin* or graver; the beaked graver itself; and a broad plane with a high back.

A considerable number of long scrapers on blades occur (fig. 2). Most of them have the oldest patina, a thick white. The flak-

ing on the outer face is clean, tending to parallelism. The proportion of long scrapers in the later
periods is perhaps rather less. In any
case, those of later date do not so often
show the cave style of flaking. It must
be remembered, however, that the shorter
horseshoe scrapers (fig. 3) are much more
numerous than the long form in all the
periods, including the earliest. Attention
should be drawn, in passing, to the tool
figured as fig. 4. It lies between a long
scraper and a fabricator. The round end
is rubbed smooth. Rubbed ends, edges,
etc., are frequently found on scrapers,
flakes, etc., in this district. Sometimes
very fine edges have been rubbed.

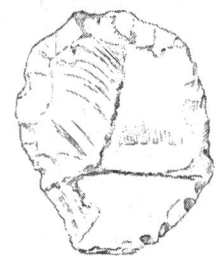

Fig. 3. 'HORSESHOE'
SCRAPER, WHITE PATINA,
COMPARATIVELY COARSE
CHIPPING, WINDMILL HILL
($\frac{2}{3}$).

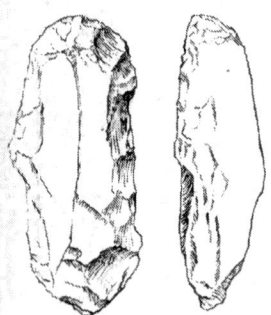

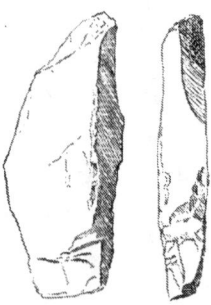

Fig. 4. IMPLEMENT FROM WINDMILL   Fig. 5. GRAVER-LIKE TOOL, SLICED
HILL ($\frac{2}{3}$).   AFTER THE MANNER OF THE FRENCH
                                        BURIN, WINDMILL HILL ($\frac{2}{3}$).

Small planes for holding in the fingers are frequently found.
The planing end varies from broad to narrow. Some specimens,
again, are steep-ended and others acute-edged.

Several dozens of graver-like tools have been picked up by the
writer (fig. 5). Generally, though not always, they seem to
belong to the oldest group. In some cases they have been sliced
down one edge, after the traditional manner of French Cave *burins*.
They are of several forms: triangular, long and narrow, and beak-
shaped, and are seldom as clean and regular in their flaking as
French specimens.[1] This may be due to the badness, and possibly

---

[1] A graver found by the writer at Wangford, Suffolk, should be mentioned. It is a perfect likeness of some gravers of the Madeleine period
and is of a dark brown colour.

also the abundance of the flint in North Wiltshire, whereas in South France the material would be more carefully used. The flint of this neighbourhood is not only of poor quality, but, as a rule, the blocks are small. The general run of the chipped flints, therefore, is also small at Windmill Hill. An attempt seems to have been made to form graving-tools of the basal ends of three or four scrapers, which are retouched along the edges, after the manner of some Cave scrapers.

There are some remarkable likenesses between chipped flints from Windmill Hill and specimens from France of the Solutré period. A blade with a curved edge and a blue-white patina is

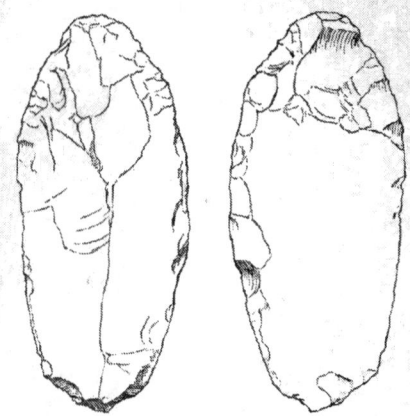

Fig. 6. 'LAUREL-LEAF' IMPLEMENT. WINDMILL HILL ($\frac{2}{3}$).

a replica, almost chip for chip, of one from Laugerie Haute. Another variety, which is shorter and has a truncated base, is similarly duplicated by a specimen from the Grotte de Rocheberthier, le Placard. Some implements of laurel-leaf type (fig. 6) resemble the French specimens, and, like them, many are broken. It is noticeable that out of a series of some two dozen broken pieces from Windmill Hill, only two are points, and the remainder are bases. This fact, coupled with the nature of their edges, suggests that some were purposely made as they are now found and were used as cutting tools, the middle fracture serving as a rest for the forefinger. Others, however, are no doubt fragments of once complete laurel-leaf implements. A large number of small flakes closely resemble Le Moustier 'points' in outline. Some have untouched edges, whilst others have been retouched, on one face only, and made into well-shaped knives (fig. 7). There are also some larger knives with coarser retouches, i.e. edge-chipping.

So far, the flints from Windmill Hill alone have been considered. But there are other sites in the neighbourhood which are of great interest. These may be divided into four classes:

1. The tops of the highest downs and of a few of the lower hills are covered with patches and pockets of red and yellow clay, together with a thin flint drift. The chipped flints on these sites (other than the much older stained specimens) are either sharp and of unchanged black or grey flint, or else have their ridges slightly dulled and are of a colour which may be described,

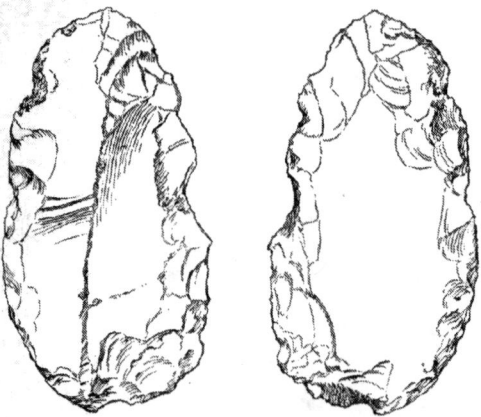

Fig. 7. KNIFE WITH COARSE RETOUCHES. WINDMILL HILL ($\frac{4}{5}$).

generally, as dark blue. Very occasionally a white specimen is found. The characteristic types from these horizons include 'cores' or, as some prefer to call them, 'cones' and 'prisms', tending to regularity of shape, and bearing long, narrow facets with a tendency to parallelism. There are many horseshoe scrapers, a small proportion of fine thumb-scrapers; and a few arrow-heads, barbed, as well as leaf-shaped, etc. The only specimens of pygmy implements (in the technical sense of the term) which have come to hand in ten years were found on one of these sites, viz. Hackpen Hill. The field in question is the best site for cones and prisms, and for fine, narrow flakes. The pygmies are all sharp and of unchanged flint.

2. Below the foregoing positions come the chalk hill-sites, such as the face of the escarpments and the highest part of Windmill Hill. These are frequently covered with about 6 in.

of black soil. The majority of the chipped flints show white or blue-white patinas.

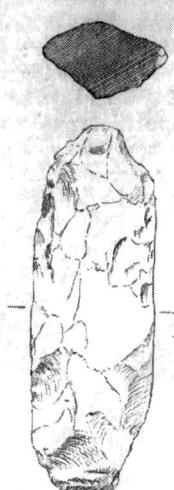

Fig. 8. CELT-LIKE TOOL, WITH ENDS RUBBED AND SMOOTH-ED AS WELL AS THE SIDES, WINDMILL HILL (⅔).

Some of the characteristic implements and tools have been already mentioned. There are also arrowheads, which on Windmill Hill occur in a great variety of types. 'Lumps', or small blocks chipped all over, sometimes show the familiar triangular section and have three chopping edges. They shade off into rude hand-celts and the 'tea-cosy' type of cutting tool. The identity of these and other tools from Windmill Hill, and similar sites in North Wilts, with types from Cissbury and Grime's Graves is manifest. Dozens of pieces of broken-up polished celts have been found (fig. 8). There is also a considerable number of small ovate implements (fig. 9).

3. On the footslopes of the downs there is sometimes to be seen a pale, tawny soil, or wash, as it may be termed.

A few white chipped flints are picked up on these sites, but a large proportion have a patina that may be termed light blue. To this group belongs an implement of River-drift type, picked up by Mr. Cunnington, jun., in Clatford Bottom, north of the Bath road (fig. 10). A large proportion of implements from the surface, described by collectors as of palaeolithic type, only resemble River-drift palaeoliths in outline and general shape, not in style of workmanship. The specimen under consideration is, however, remarkably like a River-drift implement in both those respects. The light-blue flints frequently exhibit a quantity of dark orange blotches of iron stain, that are manifestly ancient, for they have, in some instances, been partially removed by re-chipping in a later prehistoric (at latest Romano-British) period.

The light-blue tools are sometimes much striated. The striations and small white lines bear a close resemblance to those abundant on palaeoliths from Knowle Farm Pit and Hackpen Hill. Striations are formed, also, on the tools with a thick white patina. The white marks on the group under consideration sometimes cross the iron stains. A certain proportion of narrow lines of iron stain may be modern.

The flakes are almost always thick, clumsy, and irregular. Comparatively shapeless lumps abound, and there are a few finer implements.

4. The valley bottoms that form the fourth group of sites lie at heights of more than 400 ft. or 500 ft. above O. D., though they are more than 300 ft. or 400 ft. below the highest downs.

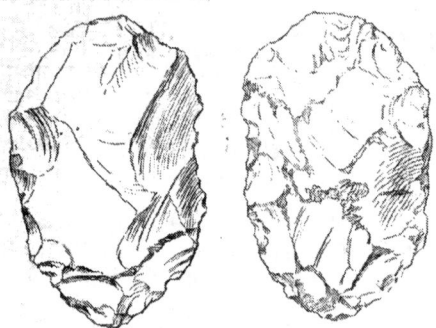

Fig. 9. SMALL OVATE IMPLEMENT, WHITE PATINA. WINDMILL HILL ($\frac{2}{3}$).

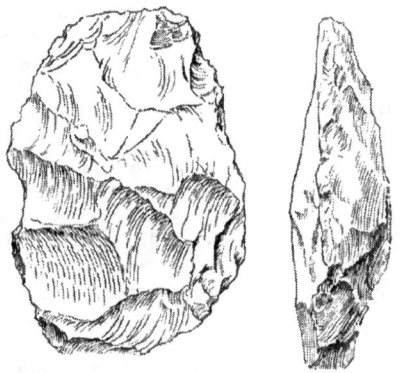

Fig. 10. IMPLEMENT FROM CLATFORD BOTTOM ($\frac{2}{3}$).

The top of Hackpen Hill is 875 ft. above O. D., and Milk Hill is but little short of 1,000 ft.

The valleys frequently contain a dark red clayey deposit, with a large number of naturally fractured flints having a blue patina and but slight traces of wear. A section, at the foot of Monkton Down, revealed a large sarsen entirely enclosed by the clayey deposit in a bowl-shaped hollow of the chalk. It was too big to have been water-borne.

The chipped flints of the valley bottoms bear a strong resemblance in colour to those of the high hill-tops. There is this difference, however, that whilst a highly lustrous and much striated specimen may occasionally be found on the upper level, they are numerous below. Lustre and striation, as in other instances, seem to go together, and also to occur most commonly in low positions.

The classification and dating of the chipped flints are most difficult, but the attempt may be made by one well acquainted with the ground. It is not pretended that every flint can be put into its proper place, but that the evidence shows the existence of four or five periods. Patina is of considerable value in making comparisons within a given district, but is not claimed as an absolute criterion of age.

There are various puzzling anomalies to be discussed, e. g. some tools may be decayed and white, and others, of the same period, unchanged; or a majority may be white on both faces, whilst a few are white on one face and black on the other.

The fact is, that while the majority of flints belonging to a given period may have had a normal history, the circumstances of a smaller number may have been abnormal; e g. most flints of one period of the Bronze Age may have been exposed under conditions which induced decay, and now have a blue-white patina. A beautifully chipped knife, on the other hand, had been placed, with a Bronze Age burial at Winterbourne Monkton, under a large sarsen, and was covered, in addition, by a foot or more of black soil. It was, therefore, well protected, and is sharp and unchanged to this day [1] It is these flints with abnormal histories that make the task of classification so difficult.

Tools with multiple patination facilitate the comparative dating of the chipped flints of a neighbourhood. There are specimens from the surface in the writer's collection from Herts., Suffolk, etc., with the following history. At some ancient period a block of flint has been chosen, chipped into shape and eventually lost, or left by its owner on the ground. During a period of time, perhaps a long one, the flint lay on or near the surface of the ground, subject to conditions which caused the decay of its faces. The exterior of the stone was affected to an appreciable depth, and the facets turned to a blue-white colour Eventually, the flint was picked up by a man of a later period, and was by him rechipped for his own purposes. The rechipping removed part, but not all, of the older blue-white facets, the line of demarcation between these and the newer chippings being perfectly distinct. Again the tool was abandoned, and once more it underwent decay. Either the conditions inducing decay were on this occasion not so strong, or the time during which the stone lay exposed was shorter. At any rate, the exterior of

[1] The specimen is in the Devizes Museum.

the flint was affected but slightly, and the black flint, showing
through the thin film of decay, gives a blue colour to these
facets, quite distinct from the blue-white of the original chipping.
Once more was the tool found and re-chipped, and once more it
lay on the ground, or just under the soil, when done with ; and
though, at the least, some two thousand years have passed by
since its final abandonment, no change has taken place on its
surface, save that the latter is now smooth and lustrous ; whereas,
when freshly chipped, it was dull and rough.   The stone shows,
ultimately, three different patinations : the blue-white facets
(partially removed by the blue) ; the blue (which have been
broken into and to some extent replaced by the black) ; and,
lastly, the black, which have remained untouched to this day.
Here is irrefragable evidence of at least three periods, apparently
of considerable length, in one district.   Whilst it is admitted
that some specimens are puzzling and difficult to place, yet a pro-
longed study of one district makes it evident that a large number
of specimens with a normal history can be assigned to one or other
of the periods represented on the tool with multiple patination.

The examination of a considerable number of the latter, and
comparisons with great quantities of tools having a single patina,
result in the determination of at least five periods among the
surface implements of North Wilts., as follows, the sequence
dates being given by numbers :

110. Chipped flints with a thick white patina, the re-chippings
of a later period showing blue-white.

120. The blue-white ; re-chippings light blue.

130. The light blue ; re-chippings (quite distinct) showing
dark blue.

140. The dark blue ; with black re-chippings.

150. The black or grey ; unchanged in colour, but lustrous.

To periods nos. 110 and 120 belong the majority of the Windmill Hill flints.   Those of period 130 are found on the foot-hill
sites ; 140 and 150 on the tops of the downs.   Perhaps the valley
flints belong to these two last periods.

Thick white patina and comparatively coarse chipping are
found associated.   The work on the blue-whites is usually finer.
Truncated prisms of regular shape are rare in those periods,
whilst 'lumps' are numerous.   None of the former has, as yet,
been found in period 130 at all.   Cones (figs. 11, 12) are less
numerous and less regular in outline (often retaining a portion
of the crust of the flint) in 110 and 120 than in 140 and 150.
There is a certain proportion of long, narrow flakes in 110 and
120.   They are rare or absent in 130.   Regular, truncated
prisms and cones are numerous in 140 and 150.   'Pygmies',
which have been found only in period 150 in North Wilts., and

then in small quantity, have also been found by the writer, in association with prisms and cones, at Dozmare Pool and Booby Bay, Cornwall, and at Wangford in Suffolk. The cones and prisms occur in Hertfordshire, in the Lea Valley, and on various sites abroad.

It is evident that the re-chipped polished celts with white patination are among the oldest of the surface flints of the

Fig. 11.   UNALTERED CONE OF BLACK FLINT, WITH NARROW, PARALLEL FLAKING.   ELCOT, MARLBOROUGH ($\frac{2}{3}$).

Fig. 12.   CONE WITH BROAD, FLAT FLAKING.   PERIOD 110.   THE OUTLINE IS USUALLY LESS REGULAR THAN IN PERIODS 140 AND 150.   WINDMILL HILL ($\frac{2}{3}$).

neighbourhood. Re-chippings make it absolutely certain that the white patina is the oldest. Not only is the polished surface of the broken celts white, but the facets formed on them by re-chipping are white also.

If, therefore, any of the surface flints of this neighbourhood are to be assigned to one of the periods of the Cave division of the Palaeolithic Age, these polished celts must certainly be included.

A sequence of five periods among the surface flints round Avebury has thus been made out, as the result of ten years' study. Can an actual date be given to any of these periods?

a. Certain very finely chipped tools from the black soil on the tops of the round barrows have a dark blue patina, and bear other resemblances to the flints of periods 140 and 150 from the high hill-tops.

b. Two late Celtic pits, of beehive shape, were discovered at the foot of Winterbourne Monkton Down, in the making of

a reservoir, during 1913, and another on Wadon Hill.[1] Flint
flakes, scrapers, and cones were dug out of these pits, and out
of one of them fragments of pottery. Some of these were fitted
together again, and formed two cooking pots. In the same pit
was a small earthenware crucible for melting bronze, of which
metal traces were seen. 'A considerable number of similar
small crucibles were found in the Glastonbury Lake Village, and
are fully described and illustrated in *The Glastonbury Lake
Village*, vol. i, pp. 300–9, where a list is given of crucibles
found elsewhere. Most of these are of the Late Celtic period,
to which also no doubt the Monkton Pits belonged. General
Pitt-Rivers found a single example in each of the Romano-
British villages of Rotherley and Woodcuts.'[2]

The flint tools are sharp, the patina dark blue and sometimes
grey. It is evident that they were made by the occupants or
users of the pits. Other chipped flints, dug out near by, immediately above the chalk and beneath some six inches of blackish
humus, are also sharp. The blue colour of their facets is less dark
than on those from the pits.

c. Beneath a pale tawny wash, varying from one to two feet
in depth, flint flakes, etc., similar to the last-named, have been
taken out by the writer *in situ*, together with pottery which has
been pronounced to be as late as the Roman period.

d. There has been a recent find of a quantity of flint flakes,
scrapers, cones, prisms, and some finer implements near the Marlborough Sewage Works, at Elcot, in the same field where the
Marlborough bucket was found. Pottery and bronze relics were
dug out, according to Mr. Joshua Brooke, of Marlborough, at
about the same depth as the flints, the bronze articles being of
undoubted Late Celtic character. The stratum in which the
articles were found lies beneath 1 ft. or more of humus, and immediately overlies gravelly clay from which it is quite distinct. It
is traceable by a line of small natural flints, which occur with
the chipped specimens. Mr. Brooke possesses a large triangular
arrow-head and a 'fish-throttle' from this site. The chipped
flints are identical with those from Hackpen Hill and, like them,
are of two periods. The older specimens have a dark blue patina.
The clearly defined re-chippings of the later period are unchanged
black or grey. The tools of the older period agree in condition
and style with the specimens from the Late Celtic pits.

The evidence, given under *a, b, c,* and *d* goes to show that all
the chipped flints thereunder described having the older of the

---

[1] Stukeley calls it Weedon Hill.
[2] Rev. E. H. Goddard, *Wilts. Arch. and Nat. Hist. Mag.*, vol. xxxviii,
June, 1913. Mrs. Cunnington also considers that all the indications point
to a Late Celtic age for these pits.

two patinas (usually dark blue) belong to the Late Celtic Period. This being so, the later, unchanged specimens must be Romano-British. The Late Celtic flints would be on or very near to the surface when Roman and Briton settled down together in the neighbourhood. The Romano-Britons frequently re-chipped and re-used the earlier tools, and it is evident that there would be considerable mingling by the time that the site was deserted.

If Late Celtic specimens be taken as a basis, the question arises whether any of the earlier groups can also be dated.

The elaborately barbed and delicately chipped arrow-head (fig. 13), has the blue-white patina belonging to period 120. Arrow-heads of this type have been found in the closest association with burials of the Bronze Age, and not, so far as is

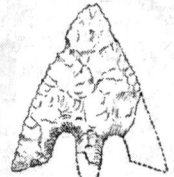

Fig. 13.   ARROW-HEAD.   WINDMILL HILL ($\frac{3}{4}$).

known, with interments in Long Barrows. This points to the finely made tools of this character being of the Bronze Age. The light blue group, of sequence-date 130, being later than these, yet earlier than the Late Celtic specimens, must therefore be ascribed to a later period of the Bronze Age.

There still remains the industry numbered 110 to be dealt with. It contains the oldest specimens, with a thick white patina. The probability that white polished celts belong to this period has been already mentioned. It is tempting to round off these efforts at dating flint implements from the surface, by assigning these earliest specimens to the Neolithic Age. But in deference to the persistent investigations which Mr. Reginald Smith has instituted and is making, and the remarkable resemblances to French Cave types, the writer refrains from definitely dating period 110 until further light is thrown on the subject.

Flints from one or other of the groups described in this paper must eventually be assigned to the Neolithic Age. But it must be remembered that five is the least number of periods that the evidence seems to warrant, and it is possible that among the older specimens subdivisions may yet have to be made.

N.B.—It is suggested that the stereotyping of the following nomenclature would conduce to clearness and prevent confusion : Pre-Crag, Palaeolithic, Neolithic, Bronze, and Iron *Ages*.

Plateau (hitherto known as 'Eolithic'), River Drift, and Cave *Divisions* of the Palaeolithic Age. Sub-divisions of these *Divisions* (e. g. Chelles, Solutré, etc.) should be spoken of as *Periods*.

Any sub-division of the other *Ages* should be into *Periods*, as e. g. Iron Age, La Tène Period I, La Tène Period II, etc. This system has been adhered to in the foregoing paper."

Mr. REGINALD SMITH remarked that the tendency in Scandinavia was to reduce the length of the Stone Age, but it was surprising to find a flint industry in the Late Celtic period. In spite of the occasional chipping of flint in Merovingian times, it seemed to him that proof was wanted of the true association of patinated flints and British pottery, in view of the abundance of flint chips in the soil of the district. He instanced the discovery of flint scrapers and other forms in the material of round barrows, the earth having been scooped up from outside the circumference, and older surfaces being possibly reached in the process. Thus the Saxon barrow at Taplow contained flint flakes at the top and later remains in descending order, exactly the reverse of their original position in the soil. It was difficult to imagine blue patina produced in the comparatively short space of two thousand years; and the frequency of patinated flints in and round the barrows might be explained by the disturbance of the soil in the Bronze Age. Discoveries of various kind were bound to occur where the land is bared to a certain depth over a large area, as in the ironstone region. Prehistoric classifications were based not so much on resemblances but on groups of resemblances, and several forms from Windmill Hill seemed to him to correspond closely with Cave period flints in France from one particular horizon. The latter were accurately and finally dated, and it was allowable to assign the British specimens to the same period if there was no good evidence to the contrary. Palaeolithic Cave man inhabited caves in the limestone region, but cannot be proved to have avoided south-east England, where no caves existed. Unless the whole area between the Dordogne caves and Wales were deserted, Cave man must have left his flints on or near the surface, and it was the business of archaeology to sort the surface finds by comparison with dated series. For instance, blade-scrapers were the normal type in the Cave period, yet collectors habitually assigned surface examples to the Neolithic period, without inquiring whether Neolithic man ever made that pattern. Patina again was very deceptive and was largely a matter of accident. It seemed an established fact that white patina required a very long period of exposure, but once a flint was white further progress in patination could only be measured by its

depth, revealed only by breaking the flint.   Blue or unchanged
flints might be as old as the white, patination having been
arrested or prevented by situation or some other accident;
and it should be remembered that the earliest Cave flints were
normally unchanged, whether found in the cave of Le Moustier
or in brick-earth as at High Lodge, Mildenhall; whereas many
Solutré and Aurignac specimens were pure white. A much safer
indication of date, when controlled by a number of coincidences,
was form, which lay at the root of the dominant French classification, and with proper safeguards was a useful criterion. There
were difficulties in the way of regarding all or even the majority
of white flints as palaeolithic, but when large groups of that
colour were found exhibiting the same style and the same forms,
it was prudent to consider such a date possible.   There were
white arrow-heads and white polished celts re-chipped at a later
date, both considered typical of the later Stone Age.   There
were also polished specimens, with a porcellanous creamy patina,
that showed white where re-chipped, and a great antiquity might
be claimed for the polishing.   It was possible that warmth, such
as the embers of a funeral pyre, accelerated the process of patination, and exposure on the surface to the sun seemed to bring
about the same result.   The discovery of hand-axes, of which
one was exhibited, on the surface but with a bluish patina not
far advanced, proved that later palaeolithic finds might occur
on the surface also, as they undoubtedly did in numbers; and the
Windmill Hill series contained several that in his opinion were
undoubtedly of the Cave period.   Mr. Kendall's work in Wilts.
had been most successful, and raised many points that could only
be settled by continued search in that and other districts. Circum-
scribing the area compensated to some extent for the inevitable
uncertainty of surface association.

Mr. DALL congratulated the author on a painstaking piece of
work, but felt that much should be put to the suspense account.
In 1882 he had visited Mr. John Brown at Avebury, who first
discovered the site on Windmill Hill and had a good collection,
but its fate was unknown.   It included a long pick, the like of
which Sir John Evans had never seen.   For himself the most
striking feature of the series on exhibition was the white patina,
but there were several finely chipped pieces, especially among
those with blue patina   He thought the variety of conditions
rendered conclusions from the various patinas very dubious.   It
was often found that chipped celts had been re-sharpened: having
broken in use, they were again adapted for hafting.   Butt ends
were usually found, and he thought that the other parts had been
taken away for re-chipping and so were not found on the same

site. Some of the polished celts found in Hampshire had a thick
white patina, and if those were to be assigned to an earlier date
on that account, what was to become of the Neolithic period?

Mr. KENDALL replied that the local flint was not only small
but of poor quality, hence the small dimensions of the Windmill
Hill series. The average size was shown by the exhibits. The
dark blue patina was found on the top of barrows and in Late
Celtic pits at Elcot, all the specimens being quite sharp and, in
his opinion, contemporary with the other relics. The Elcot section
showed the flints in a thin stone layer under 1 ft. of soil, overlying stiff clay, and apparently river-drift below. Those found
on the summit of barrows had a dark-blue patina. The dark
blues were rarely found on Windmill Hill, and the white flints
were older. Polished celts were often re-chipped to form entirely
different tools, and he showed the two best specimens in his
collection. It seemed clear that they were older than many
surface flints of the district and had been wantonly broken up.
If any group of the surface finds was to be classed as Cave period,
the same would apply to the polished celts.

The PRESIDENT said Mr. Kendall had given a clear demonstra-
tion of his views with regard to the flints found in his district,
and would hardly object to being regarded as an enthusiast.
Collectors like him and Dr. Sturge did much for the study of
early man that museum officials found beyond their powers.
Local research extending over several years could alone establish
the types and their sequence, by a study of the conditions under
which each group was deposited. The work was for the moment
unremunerative, but would be appreciated in the future by the
scientific world. The science of pre-history was only sixty or
seventy years old, and it had taken a long time to establish the
human origin of any flint specimens. In the present case the
only evidence of date and origin lay in the objects themselves.
Often additional evidence was afforded by the geological aspect,
by the associated fauna, by stratification and isolation in caves
that eliminated the possibility of error. But surface finds could
only be classified on broad lines, as England was a small island
that had been thickly and continuously inhabited, so that human
relics of all dates might be found in association on the surface.
The task of re-sorting the accumulation was an arduous one, but
the exhibits showed certain distinct groups that probably fitted
into a sequence. It had long been disputed whether certain celts
received their polish before or after they were chipped, and the
question of precedence remained. The chemical change, which
seemed to be the cause of patination, often went very deep, and

he had seen specimens of flint altered all through, no black core showing in a section; but what caused that extraordinary change it was impossible to say. It was certainly not age alone, as most specimens of Le Moustier date, at the very beginning of the palaeolithic Cave period, showed no change, whether found in French caves or on certain British sites. Some admittedly neo-lithic flints were on the other hand altered to a measurable depth by some unknown agent. Therefore patina was a fallacious test of age, and he had long urged that form was in itself no better criterion. The graving-tool or French *burin* was a curious form difficult to produce, with a strong point for marking bone; and its appearance in Wiltshire was certainly a fact of importance. The whole subject was one of peculiar interest, though perhaps the few who treated it seriously were apt to take for granted in others a close acquaintance with technicalities and classifications that were by no means common property. There was much to be done in England, and Mr. Kendall's close investigation of a definite area was a useful contribution to the more scientific side of archaeology.

Thanks were ordered to be returned for this communication.

THURSDAY, 5th FEBRUARY, 1914.

SIR CHARLES HERCULES READ, Kt., LL.D. President, in the Chair.

The following gifts were announced, and thanks for the same ordered to be returned to the donors:

From the Author:—Markham memorials. By Sir Clements Markham. 2 vols. 4to. London, 1913.

From Harold Sands, Esq., F.S.A.:
1. Castles of England and Wales. By Herbert A. Evans. 8vo. London.
2. Old and new London. By Walter Thornbury and Edward Walford. 6 vols. 8vo. London. n.d.
3. Extracts from the documentary history of the Tower of London. By Harold Sands, F.S.A. 2 parts. 8vo. London, 1912–13.

From the Author:—The hundred of Stanborough or Dippeforda in the time of Testa de Nevil, A.D. 1243. By Rev. O. J. Reichel, F.S.A. 8vo. n.p. 1913.

From the Author, Horace Sandars, Esq., F.S.A.:
1. The weapons of the Iberians. With supplement containing text of the passages from classical historians. 4to. Oxford, 1913.

2. False Iberian weapons and other forged antiquities from Spain. 8vo. Oxford, 1913.

3. Notes on the Puente Quebrada on the Guadalimar river, near Linares, province of Jaén (Spain). 4to. Madrid, 1913.

The following were admitted fellows:
Robert Bagster, Esq.
Captain Charles Walter Cottrell-Dormer.

W. H. ST. JOHN HOPE, Esq., Litt.D., D.C.L., read the first part of a paper on the Funeral, Monument and Chantry Chapel of King Henry V at Westminster, in which he dealt with the funeral. Of this there were at least three contemporary accounts: a French one of Engerraud de Monstrelet, a version in Latin by Thomas of Walsingham, and what is probably an official account in English (now in the Heralds' College). There was also a later version in English in Edmund Hall's Chronicle. These all agreed in the main as to the king's death in 1422 in the Bois de Vincennes, and the removal of his body after embalming to Paris, and thence to Rouen, where it lay some time. Thence it was conveyed with great pomp and solemnity, to Abbeville, and so to Calais, where it was brought oversea to England. The body was landed at Dover just two months after the king's death, and after resting at divers places on the way, at each of which a splendid herse was set up, was finally brought to London, and so to Westminster, where it was buried in the abbey church of St. Peter. So magnificent a funeral had not been seen in England for 200 years. There were certain discrepancies in the accounts as to the number of horses that drew the charet with the king's body and effigy of boiled leather, and as to the armorial devices on the trappers. Mr. Hope showed how these differences might be reconciled, and quoted from the accounts of the sacrist of the Abbey evidence that there were finally four horses with new trappers with the king's badges, all of which became with other things the perquisite of the Abbey because the horses drew the charet up the nave of the church. Mr. Hope also discussed an interesting variation between the badges on the trappers and those now visible upon the King's Chantry Chapel. These consisted of the Bohun swan and the king's antelope chained to beacons on one side and to oak trees on the other. But it was clear from the trappers and other contemporary evidence that the king actually bore the antelope in two aspects: first, as engaged in 'busie laboure', drawing in a horse-mill; and, secondly, as taking 'victorious reste', reposing on a stage, with gold branches over him. On the chapel the horse-mill had been blundered by the carver into a beacon, no example of which, as a badge of King Henry V, seemed to occur elsewhere.

Mr. Tipping remarked on the association of the swan badge with a mill, beacon, or tree. He was the owner of an old house (Mathern Palace, near Chepstow) that had belonged to the bishops of Llandaff and been rebuilt by Bishop Zouche in the reign of Henry V, as recorded on a stone in Monmouth museum. On pulling down an old doorway, he had found stones bearing on one face traces of the swan and tree, and over the latter was a bird. He was unable to explain the significance of that addition, but thought the design was the badge of Henry V.

The President was disappointed to notice that the paper had not given rise to a discussion, especially as questions of heraldry had arisen. He did not think the discrepancy as to the number of horses was important or remarkable, as reports, even of eye-witnesses, seldom tallied exactly at any period. The author would no doubt agree that a blunder on the part of the mason was hardly a satisfactory explanation of the irregularities noticed on the frieze of the chapel, but nothing better occurred to himself at the moment. The Society would look forward to the sequel of the paper and convey its thanks to Mr. Hope for an interesting account of an historic pageant.

T. M. Legge, Esq., M.D., exhibited a collection of fragments of English fifteenth-century stained glass, most of which had been acquired in Norfolk and was of the Norwich school.

Mr. Hope noticed the arms of the City of Rochester on one of the pieces of glass, which, as the author subsequently explained, did not belong to the series from East Anglia. The arms were not invented till the days of Elizabeth, and their use might prove a clue to the origin of the fragment.

The President remarked on the Trappist attitude of the meeting and on the rare appearance of stained glass as exhibits. Few things were so portable or more easily shown to advantage. It was also curious that nothing had been written on the subject in the severe archaeological spirit since Charles Winston's admirable work on Glass-painting appeared in 1847 (second edition, 1867). East Anglia was known to have had an art of its own and to have been practically isolated, so that one would have expected such work to be confided to a local school of glass-workers, and to exhibit striking peculiarities, in view of the exotic character of the population. There was an admirable treatise on the various methods of decay in glass to be found in *Archaeologia*, vol. xlvi, from the pen of the late James Fowler, which might throw some light on the specimens kindly brought by Dr. Legge.

Thanks were ordered to be returned for this communication and exhibition.

THURSDAY, 12th FEBRUARY, 1914.

The EARL OF CRAWFORD AND BALCARRES,
Vice-President, in the Chair.

The following gifts were announced, and thanks for the same ordered to be returned to the donors:

From the Author:—Loddenden and the Usbornes of Loddenden. The story of a Kentish homestead. By H. S. Cowper, F.S.A. 4to. Ashford, 1914.

From E. A. B. Barnard, Esq., F.S.A.: Churchwardens' accounts of the parish of Badsey, with Aldington, Worcestershire, from 1525 to 1571. 8vo. Hampstead, 1913.

The following were admitted fellows:
Charles George James Port, Esq.
Rev. Henry Arnold Hudson, M.A.

W. H. ST. JOHN HOPE, Esq., Litt.D., D.C.L., read the second part of his paper on the Funeral, Monument and Chantry Chapel of King Henry V at Westminster, in which he dealt with the monument and chapel. The site of the king's burial-place had been fixed by the king himself in 1415 to be 'among the tombs of the kings in the place where the relics of the saints are kept'. This was behind the Trinity altar to the east of St. Edward's shrine, and here a platform of Caen stone, supplied by John Arderne, was built out into the ambulatory in September, 1422, for the king's grave and tomb.

The platform was afterwards cased with marble, and a tomb of the same material set up on it, carrying an effigy of the king made of oak, with a plating and ornaments of silver-gilt. The tomb was protected by a closure of iron and wood made by Roger Johnson, smith, in 1431. The wonderful bridge-like chapel that formed a canopy to the king's tomb was begun in 1439, of stone obtained the previous year, and its setting up was marked by an entry, in the Sacrist's account for 1440-1, of the plucking down and sale of Johnson's ironwork, and of the taking down of the wooden closure of the Trinity altar *pro novo edificio ibidem erigendo*. The chapel was built partly of Purbeck marble, and partly of a hard limestone, but mostly of firestone, and consisted of a vaulted basement spanning the king's tomb and the ambulatory, and a chapel above reached by twin stair-turrets. The tomb was again protected by an iron grate, but this was not sufficient to hinder the theft of all the ornamental parts of

the king's effigy before 1467. On account of this a further
protection was added, it is said by King Henry VII, in the form
of the existing iron screen and gates at the west end of the
chapel; but burglars again broke in in 1545–6, and robbed the
effigy of the rest of its silver-gilt plating. Mr. Hope described
at length the statues that adorned the turrets, including those of
King Sebert and King Henry III, St. John as the pilgrim, and
King Edward the Confessor, St. Katharine and King Edmund,
with two figures of cardinals, who, the Provost of King's thought,
might be St. Ambrose and St. Bonaventura. Mr. Hope also
described the arrangements of the chapel, with the remarkable
series of cupboards around the altar, and the great displays of
imagery over the altar with large figures of the Holy Trinity
(lost), the Blessed Virgin and the Angel of the Annunciation,
St. Edmund and St. Edward, St. George and St. Denis. The
numerous figures on the outside of the chapel were associated on
each side with a coronation scene. Mr. Hope suggested that
these depicted the acclamation with the simultaneous donning
of their hoods (before coronets had come into fashion) by the
lords present, and the enthronement and homage of the peers.
The king was also represented riding across country, in England,
perhaps, and in France, with allegorical figures over him of
ladies holding books with accounts of his great deeds and works.
The master mason of the chapel was John of Thirsk, who
was appointed master mason of the Abbey in 1421, and
died in 1452. Above the chapel were now fixed a tilting helm,
a shield formerly bearing the king's arms in painted gesso,
and a saddle once covered with blue velvet. These interesting
objects, which were exhibited by kind leave of the Dean of
Westminster, Bishop Ryle, probably formed part of the funeral
trappings which became the perquisite of the abbot and convent,
through their being brought into the abbey church on the day
of King Henry's burial. Lastly, Mr. Hope referred to the considerable traces of the limewash with which the whole of the
marble and firestone portions of the tomb and chapel, including
all the imagery, had originally been covered. Where this
remained, the surfaces were still intact; where it had gone, the
surfaces were crumbling to powder, and there could be no question that common sense called for the bold policy of a speedy
renewal of the protective distemper, if so grand a monument was
to be handed on to posterity in its present condition.

Mr. LETHABY stated that in the triforium at Westminster
was a set of wrought-iron door-standards with spoke bars that
had probably formed part of the closure at the east end of the
door into Henry V's Chapel.

Major FARQUHARSON thought it remarkable to see on the table a piece of armour that had been carried in one of the most memorable funerals in our history. Though it had some curious features, the helmet was quite authentic, and he regarded it as an unfinished tilting helm adapted for the funeral. The front part was very thick, to withstand a lance-thrust, but the back was thin and left unfinished, as being of less importance. It would have carried mantling and had evidently been gilt in front. It was quite a practical piece of armour but had not been worn by the king at Agincourt, where he is recorded to have worn a *bel bascinet à bavière*. The term casque was incorrect in the present case. The hole at the top was roughly made for a crest of light wood.

Mr. STEPHENSON recalled the tradition that the two slabs of which rubbings were exhibited marked the graves of John and Margaret, children of William de Valence. Some of the letters and the stem of a cross were still visible on one, and the mosaic slab had similar lettering. Restorations of both were given in Mr. Lethaby's *Westminster Abbey and the King's Craftsmen*, p. 318.

Mr. J. G. WOOD inquired as to the recurrence of the antelope, swan, and beacon. Years ago tiles had been found in the priory church at Monmouth bearing a swan, a badge which was thought to have come to Henry V through his mother, Mary de Bohun.

Mr. C. L. KINGSFORD said that a chronicle of 1431 mentioned under Nov. 7 that the tomb was set up at the cost of Queen Katherine and the workmen's names were English. It also detailed the arrangements made in the City of London, and proved that the procession did not pass from London Bridge along Lombard Street, but by way of Gracechurch Street and Cornhill. The identification of one of the stone figures on the screen in the chapel must be incorrect, as Thomas Langley was never called Cardinal in England.

Mr. HOPE replied that, a week before, he had given a full account of the king's badges and pointed out that the beacon was not one of them but merely a blunder for the horse-mill which was drawn by the antelope. He had quoted the account mentioned of the City's part in the funeral and had seen the original manuscript. The costumes worn were black, not white. With regard to the cardinals represented, he had quoted the Provost of King's, and was prepared to stand by that opinion.

The CHAIRMAN referred to the paper as one that would be memorable in the history of the Society, and expressed the thanks of the meeting to Mr. Hope, and the Dean and Chapter who had generously lent the exhibits.

Thanks were ordered to be returned for this communication, which will be printed in *Archaeologia*.

THURSDAY, 19th FEBRUARY, 1914.

Sir CHARLES HERCULES READ, Knt., LL.D., President, in the Chair.

The following gifts were announced, and thanks for the same ordered to be returned to the donors :

From Philip Norman, Esq., LL.D., V.-P.S.A.:—A volume of tracts relating to the Society of Antiquaries of London, written by John Bruce, T. J. Pettigrew, Sir Fortunatus Dwarris, etc. 1852.

From the Compiler, Robert Bateman, Esq.:—The Manchester Whitworth Institute. Catalogue of a loan collection of works by William Blake, February to March, 1914. Sm. 4to. London, 1914.

Notice was given of a ballot for the election of Fellows to be held on Thursday, March 5th, 1914, and a list of the candidates to be put to the ballot was read.

J. P. BUSHE-FOX, Esq., read the report on the excavations at Wroxeter in 1913, which will be printed in *Reports*.

During the excavations carried on in 1913 an area of about 1½ acres was explored and two buildings were uncovered. One proved to be a temple, and the other a large dwelling-house. The latter had a frontage of 115 ft., and extended back from the street line for 200 ft., although its limit in this direction has not yet been ascertained. As this building was not completely excavated it was not dealt with in this report.

The temple, which measured 98 ft. by 56 ft., consisted of a podium supporting a cella or shrine which stood at the back of an enclosed space with a paved courtyard and a three-sided ambulatory in front. The entrance was from the main street under a portico of six columns. That the building must have been a fine one was shown by the number of carved architectural fragments found. Portions of several life-sized statues were also discovered, as well as the carved head of a horse and a small female head in stone. There were also some small fragments of a bronze statue. Although parts of two altars came to light, no inscription was met with, so it was not possible to say to whom the temple was dedicated. This type of temple was commonly found on Roman sites, and several similar examples were shown from the Continent and North Africa. The building appeared to have been erected about the middle of the second century, and to have fallen into disuse about the end of the third century.

A great number of small finds were discovered. They consisted of many brooches, pins, ornaments, etc. Among the most noteworthy were a finely cut amethyst paste gem engraved with a figure of Venus, a small cameo of a Medusa head, and a well carved clasp-knife handle, in the form of a crouching tiger. A large amount of beautifully decorated Samian ware was found, a considerable portion of it dating from the first century. The potters' stamps recorded amounted to about 200, and represented most of the large continental factories of the period. The coins were in excess of those found in 1912, and numbered 476. They ranged from the Republican period to the end of the fourth century. Two coins of the Emperor Theodosius I were discovered, thus adding another decade to the life of the town. Four silver coins of the Emperor Carausius were worthy of note : one of these was of the Adventus type, with the RSR mintmark, and was extremely rare. Several articles were met with showing that working in metal and bone was practised on the site.

Sir ARTHUR EVANS said the paper showed the high civilization attained during the Roman occupation of Britain ; and such a settlement on the Limes proved that the Romans had Wales well in hand. He claimed the rare coin of Carausius for Britain : the Rouen fabric was quite different and barbarous, and the letters RSR might stand for Richborough, but perhaps did not indicate the place of mintage at all, and the coin might have been struck at London or Colchester.

Professor HAVERFIELD congratulated the Society on having such a fine site as Wroxeter to explore, and Mr. Bushe-Fox on a most successful season. The last report was an excellent piece of work, far above the average, and the second year's work had been most ably described to the meeting. The construction of the temple, though simple enough when represented in a diagram, was not easy to detect on the spot, and its elucidation was somewhat of a feat. The other temple-plans shown on the screen were of two types : one classical, as at Pompeii and Wroxeter, the other Celtic and N. Gaulish, as at Caerwent.

The Wroxeter building was non-Celtic and of Mediterranean origin. If the last letter of the inscription SETMAPEM stood for *manu*, the rest was not, as Sir John Rhŷs argued, Celtic: he himself preferred to read L in place of T. A Celtic legend would be an interesting discovery and such had come to light in Gaul, but the few inscriptions on tiles, etc., in Britain were in Latin. To prove the use of the Celtic language in such towns as Wroxeter, words as well as personal names were required.

Professor GOWLAND joined in congratulating Mr. Bushe-Fox and the Society on the work done at Wroxeter. Metallurgical specimens were few, and it was surprising that lead was so scarce, as the site was near a mining district and no less than five pigs of lead bearing Hadrian's name had been found in the neighbourhood. There were specimens of lead ore exhibited that had been obtained from surface workings, and curiously enough a large nail of that metal. One of the bronze specimens was a complete casting, showing that the Romans used four or five times the amount of metal that would be used at the present day; the excess served to press down the molten metal well into the mould. The upper part of another casting showed the channel through which the metal was poured, and also casts of the air-holes made to allow the air to escape from the mould. Further, the crucible had been used as at the present day; it was thrust into the fire, and not protected from the fire below. In earlier times the crucible was nearly buried in the hearth, and the fire piled over it. There were pieces of slag that had been produced in the melting of bronze, and an important specimen formed part of the hearth of a cupellation furnace, for extracting silver from lead. The use of such furnaces had been conclusively proved at Silchester. The Romans also used bone ash in the construction of the hearth, and its use had continued to the present time. Mr. Bushe-Fox had excavated on another site, on the south coast, extensive remains of the same industry, and one lump weighing 30 lb. contained £20 worth of silver.

Mr. WALTERS had examined some of the pottery on the spot during a few days' visit in September, but had no comments to make on the series exhibited. Among those who had assisted at Wroxeter was his colleague at the British Museum, Mr. Pryce, who had devoted his attention to bottle-necks.

Mr. STEPHENSON thought the progress made at Wroxeter reflected great credit on Mr. Bushe-Fox and the Society generally. There was a large house to be opened up next season, and it was to be hoped that farther north along the main street they would come upon the public buildings. The continuation of the work would need all the funds that the Treasurer and individual Fellows could provide.

Mr. REGINALD SMITH thought the large leaden nail might be a survival of the old notion of currency perpetuated in the name *drachma*—a handful of rods more or less in the form of nails, as the unit of value. If that were so, the nail would be a votive offering of money in a primitive and traditional form. There were Roman bronzes in the form of nails with incised ornament, that could not have been used in the ordinary way. Though there were earlier buildings on the temple site, there was nothing later, nor did the small finds seem to date beyond the middle of the third century. Was the site respected after the destruction of the temple, or was there another reason for the absence of later remains?

Mr. GARRAWAY RICE remarked that lead nails or pegs were used for fixing the roof-slates of buildings exposed to fumes, like gasworks; and he thought their use might have been necessitated at Wroxeter by the presence of noxious fumes due to some industry.

Dr. WRIGHT noted the sea-horse as a motive from the eastern Mediterranean; and drew attention to the accurate rendering of certain anatomical details on the stone carving exhibited.

The PRESIDENT thought that an additional reason for carrying on excavations of ancient sites was that a training ground was thereby provided for young antiquaries. The British Museum assistant who had specialized in bottle-necks would no doubt proceed to treat the bottle as a whole and do useful work in that direction. The Society would be interested to know that the first Franks Student in the University of London had also spent some time at Wroxeter. He seemed to remember seeing at Leyden a large series of pipeclay figures, invariably of Venus, but had never come across a perfect example in Britain, though many fragments had been found in London. Another interesting relic was the deer-horn pick, which was usually found in much more ancient surroundings, as at Avebury, Grime's Graves, and Cissbury. The Roman example from Wroxeter was one more object-lesson in archaeological caution. In connexion with the Roman control of Wales he cited the milestone inscribed 8 miles from Canovium (near Conway) in the British Museum, which was alone sufficient evidence of peace and order. He approved the idea that the leaden nail was votive, such offerings being often useless copies of weapons or implements. The Society would appreciate the work done at Wroxeter, and the meeting had enjoyed listening to a business-like report, admirably illustrated.

PHILIP NEWMAN, Esq., F.S.A., exhibited an illuminated Letters Patent of Henry VIII to John Lambart of Calton, co. York., on which W. Paley Baildon, Esq., F.S.A., read the following note:

"The original document exhibited by Mr. Newman is of some interest. It is a grant, dated March 4, 31 Henry VIII, 1539-40, under the great seal, to John Lambart of Calton in Craven, Yorkshire, gentleman, of certain rents and lands at Malham, Ayrton, Scothorp and Hellifield, all in the neighbourhood of Skipton and Settle, which had formed part of the possessions of Bolton Priory, as fully as Richard Mone, late Prior, or his predecessors, held and enjoyed the same, to be held of the king in chief by the service of a twentieth part of a knight's fee and a rent of 14s. 5d. yearly for all service. The consideration money was £129 11s. 8d.

So far it is all commonplace enough; but the document itself is very unusual from the fact that it is illuminated and has on it the arms of the grantee. The top line, containing the words 'Henricus Octavus Dei gracie Anglie et Francie Rex Fidei', is placed on a border ornamented with sprays of roses. The initial letters H, O, and R are painted with gold strap-work on a blue ground, the O and the R also containing painted roses. The letter A is painted yellow on a square blue panel. The capital H of Henricus contains a picture of the king, holding the orb and sceptre; he is clothed in a pink gown, and a blue robe powdered with a conventional flower in yellow. He is seated on a throne, which has a canopy with a green frame, hung with cloth of gold with a red arabesque pattern. In the centre of the top line is a shield with the arms of France and England quarterly under a crown. The dexter supporter is a sitting lion crowned proper, holding a blue banner with a gold rose (?) on it. The sinister supporter is a silver rampant dragon, holding a blue banner with a gold fleur-de-lis. There is a gold fleur-de-lis over the word 'Francie'. The design of the lettering and ornamentation is common enough in patents, but is usually in pen-work only; I have never seen one similarly illuminated.

On the dexter margin of the vellum is painted a large shield bearing the arms of Lambert, viz. gules, a chevron between three lambs passant silver, a chief checky gold and azure. The silver here (and elsewhere) has turned black, and on this shield appears to have been painted black at a later date. Underneath is a scroll bearing the word NOTHOSOLITHOS. So far as I am able to

translate this word it means 'imitation stone', but what significance that may have as a motto I cannot say.

On the sinister margin is drawn in pen and ink, not coloured,
a monster having the head, arms and body of a woman, and the
four legs and body of a cloven-footed animal; in her hands she
holds a scroll with the word NOTHOSOLITHOS. Underneath
is a silver six-foil with a red centre. The monster is the crest of
the Lamberts, which is described in the Visitation of Yorkshire,
1584–5, as a female centaur proper, crined or, holding a flower
argent, leaved and stalked vert. There is some uncertainty what
this beast really was, for Harley MS. 1487 (fo. 354 b) shows a
conventional sphinx, with four limbs only, and Harley MS. 1394
(fo. 200) shows the head, arms, and body of a woman joined to
the hind-quarters of a hoofed animal with a dog's tail. It is
possible that the crest was intended for Lamia, the Greek fabulous
monster, said to live on human flesh, and that the heralds were
not quite clear how this interesting creature should be drawn.

All this fancy-work must have been inserted at the instance of
John Lambert, the grantee, about whom a good deal is known,
and little to his credit. He was a lawyer (not of Lincoln's Inn),
vice-chancellor of the Duchy of Lancaster, and had been steward
to Bolton Priory. The last fact probably accounts for his getting
a considerable slice of the Priory lands, as he was in a position to
make early application. He was, beyond reasonable doubt, the
forger of a considerable series of charters to bolster up a spurious
pedigree showing his descent from Count Lambert of Louvain,
who died in 1004. Some of these were denounced as forgeries by
Whitaker in the first edition of his *History of Craven* (1805), and
were subsequently made the text of one of Dr. J. H. Round's
most slashing articles in *The Ancestor*, vol. iii. The document
here shown is, I feel no doubt, a part of the scheme devised and
carried out by Lambert for the spurious glorification of his
family.

The six-foil is evidently in allusion to a quartering, of very
doubtful authenticity, allowed to the Yorkshire Lamberts at the
Visitation of 1584–5, which has been adopted as their arms by
several families of Lambert claiming descent from the Yorkshire
house, and through it, of course, from Count Lambert. The
Visitation gives the coat as gules, an annulet or, between three
chaplets argent. The charges are variously described as nar-
cissuses, roses, chaplets, cinq-foils, and six-foils. Here the object
is very clearly drawn as a six-foil."

Lord BOLTON, F.S.A., exhibited and presented a deed, with the
seal of the Abbot of Furness attached, between the Abbot and
Convent of Sawley and the Abbot and Convent of Furness

regarding the tithes of the manor of Wynterbourne within the parish of Gargrave.

Thanks were ordered to be returned for these communications and exhibitions.

Thursday, 26th February, 1914.

Sir CHARLES HERCULES READ, Knt., LL.D., President, in the Chair.

The following gifts were announced, and thanks for the same ordered to be returned to the donors:

From the Author:—The Avowries of Cheshire (Reprinted from the English Historical Review, January 1914). By R. Stewart-Brown, F.S.A. 8vo. London, 1914.

From the Librarian of the London Library:—Catalogue of the London Library, St. James's Square, London. By C. T. H. Wright and C. J. Purnell. 2 vols. 4to. London, 1913–14.

From the Royal Anthropological Institute:—Description of the test specimen of the rostro-carinate industry found beneath the Norwich Crag. By Sir Ray Lankester, K.C.B., F.R.S. 8vo. London, 1914.

William Blake Odgers, Esq., K.C., LL.D., was admitted a Fellow.

Notice was again given of the ballot for the election of Fellows to be held on Thursday, March 5, 1914, and the list of the candidates to be put to the ballot was read.

W. H. St. John Hope, Esq., Litt.D., D.C.L., read the Report on the Excavation of the Cathedral Church of Old Sarum in 1913.

"I have the honour of submitting to the Society of Antiquaries, on behalf of my colleagues, Lt.-Col. Hawley and Mr. D. H. Montgomerie, and myself, a report on the excavations at Old Sarum during the year 1913.

The chief part of our operations during the preceding year was confined to tracing the outline of the cathedral church and to such provision as could be foreseen for the complete clearance of the cathedral site.

One fact that had been ascertained was that on the north side of the church there was a deep deposit of broken-up building rubbish. The disposal of this rubbish presented a difficulty, since the only places to which it could be transported still

awaited excavation. It luckily happened that at some not
very remote period a large excavation for chalk had been made
on the north side of the hill of Old Sarum, the filling up of
which would restore its broken outline. There being no ob-
jections to this, a wooden bridge was thrown across the ditch,
with a shoot at its inner end, by which any excavated material
might be transferred from a full wagon on the top to an empty
one on the bridge, and this in turn could be run across and
emptied into the chalk pit.

These preliminaries having been settled, on 28th April the
bridge was begun. Some trial trenches were also cut across the
eastern part of the church. By 2nd May we were able to begin
laying down the tramway from the shoot towards the church.
A fortnight later, during the laying of a second line of
rails, a quite unexpected discovery was made, in the form of a
deposit of ridge tiles. More of these were found the following
day, and it was then seen that they had been laid side by side
in four rows, each of eight tiles. With them were also a
number of ordinary roofing tiles. The deposit had been sys-
tematically laid at a quite early date, apparently for some
drainage purpose, and the ends of the rows were closed by pairs
of L-shaped stones, disposed bridge-wise, with a supporting
block under. The tiles are covered outside with a fine green
glaze, and cannot well be later in date than the middle of the
twelfth century. Many fragments of ridge tiles of similar form
were found when we excavated the castle.

Beyond the discovery of many pieces of worked and moulded
stonework, nothing worth recording occurred during the laying
of the tramway lines, which in due time reached the church and
enabled us to begin the clearing of its site.

Before describing the remains of the church it will be advisable
to recall a few facts belonging to its history.

The transfer of the bishopric of Sherborne to Old Sarum, in
accordance with the edict of the Council of London of 1075, which
directed the transfer of episcopal sees from villages to more popu-
lous places, involves not only the suggestion but the probability
that there already existed at Old Sarum a church into which the
bishop's-stool could be transferred. Bishop Hermann, in whose
days the transfer was made, is said to have begun a church of
new work, but to have died of old age before the time of its
dedication. His successor Osmund, who was consecrated in
1078, finished the building, which Simeon of Durham says was
hallowed with the help of Walkelin bishop of Winchester and
John bishop of Bath on Monday, 5th April, 1092.

Five days after the church had been consecrated, it was struck
by lightning and seriously damaged. William of Malmesbury,

writing of the events in the fifth year of King William Rufus, says that the violence of the lightning utterly threw down the roof of the tower of the church and shook down much of the walling.

Many traces of this catastrophe have come to light during the recent excavations in the shape of scorched and reddened stones and pieces of moulded work, used up as rubble in the later walling of the church.

William of Malmesbury also states that bishop Roger, who held the see from 1103 to 1139, 'made new the church of Salisbury and adorned it with ornaments, so that it is inferior to none in England but surpasses many; and he himself not untruly can say to God, "Lord, I have loved the glory of thy house".'[1]

In or about the year 1227, for reasons that were fully set forth in our 1909 Report, the ecclesiastical establishment and most of the civil population removed from Old Sarum to the new church and city in the plain below. The old church was thereupon disused, and partly destroyed against the possibility of a return to it. In any case the building seems to have become derelict, and to have passed into the king's hands.

In 1327 licence was granted for the dean and chapter to enclose with a battled wall the close of their church. This was followed, by letters patent of 1st March 1330–1, by the gift of the king, to the bishop and to the dean and chapter of Salisbury, of all the stones of the old cathedral church of Old Sarum, and of the houses within the king's castle there which the bishop and canons of that church formerly occupied, for the repair of their church and for the enclosure of the precinct of the same.

The church and all the buildings annexed to it were accordingly razed to the ground, and the site of them became practically a waste place.

The excavations of 1912 showed that the church thus destroyed had consisted of an aisled and square-ended presbytery with eastern chapels, north and south transepts, with a south porch, and of a nave and aisles with an added section at the west end. We also found that a building with a groined subvault adjoined the north end of the transept, in connexion probably with a cloister north of the presbytery. The broad outline of the church had been noted during a dry summer so far back as 1835, and was partly confirmed by excavations in the following year.

Now it has long been obvious to those who are acquainted with the laying out of eleventh-century churches that the plan of the cathedral church of Old Sarum, as marked by these excavations, and more fully by those of 1912, could not possibly

[1] *Gesta Regum Anglorum* (Rolls Series, 90), ii, 484.

CURTAIN

GA

WEST GATE

10 0 20 40

10 0

be that of the church of bishop Osmund. We had also noticed that the eastern parts of the church and its western addition were built with yellow mortar, while the nave was as clearly built with white mortar. An early opportunity was accordingly taken of cutting a trench down the middle line in the hope of finding traces of an earlier building. This trench, which was begun about the middle of the later presbytery, had not been carried far before a cross wall was met with, nearly 7 ft. thick, and apparently curved instead of straight. It was accordingly traced north and south, and, though mutilated for later works at both ends, proved to be the main apse of bishop Osmund's church, and to be built with the white mortar. Further, it had against it on its western side a foundation of rubble masonry 8 ft. long and from 4 ft. to 4½ ft. wide, which formed the base either of the altar hallowed by the three bishops in 1092, or (what is more probable) of the bishop's throne.

It was not possible at the time to proceed further with our investigations, but as soon as the area of the transepts had been cleared, it did not take long to find and trace out the other apses of Osmund's church and to recover its complete plan, as well as to establish its relation to the later work.

The first church was 173 ft. long from east to west, and 113½ ft. across the transepts. It consisted of an apsidal presbytery, with narrow north and south aisles, square-ended outside but probably apsidal within, north and south transepts, each with an eastern apse, a tower over the crossing, and a nave and aisles.

Of these the nave and aisles only had remained to the end. The rest had all been pulled down to make way for later works, and nothing was left save their foundations. These are fortunately of good flint rubble with white mortar, and of massive character, and are everywhere carried down to the solid chalk. What exactly stood upon them is of course guesswork, but from analogy with contemporary examples of the same type of church it is possible to reconstruct the building with some degree of certainty.

It is also clear from what remains of it that bishop Osmund's church at Old Sarum may be added to an interesting class built under Norman influence during the second half of the eleventh century, of which several contemporary examples exist in this country.

At some unrecorded date early in the twelfth century the canons of Salisbury began to lay out to the north-east of their church a four-sided cloister. It cannot be called square, since its sides are all unequal, and it may not be described as rectangular, since none of its angles is a right angle. The south side measures 137 ft., the north 133½ ft., the east 125½ ft., and the west 113¼ ft. The cloister therefore was approximately about as large as that at Christchurch, Canterbury, and had covered alleys on all four sides. Such an adjunct to a purely secular church did not serve the same purpose as a monastic cloister, the alleys of which were more or less living places, but usually contained the burying ground, and the alleys were to enable processions to go about this under cover. The cloister or Palm churchyard at Wells was so laid out by bishop Joscelin about 1240, and that attached to St Paul's was long known as 'pardon churchyard'. The Old Sarum cloister is perhaps the earliest example of its kind in this country.

At the same time as the laying-out of the cloister there was built against its west side a two-storied structure of remarkable character (fig. 2). What remains of it is a subvault or crypt, measuring internally 60 ft. from east to west and 26 ft. from north to south. It is four bays long, and divided into two alleys by three large round pillars 5 ft. in diameter, with corresponding semicircular responds about the walls. Upon these, as may be proved by the mortar casts of the springing stones, rested a ribbed vault, now unhappily destroyed The whole of the interior of the crypt is also greatly ruined, and both walls and pillars have been stripped of nearly all their original ashlar facing, which had a chamfered plinth at the floor level. The crypt was lighted by eight windows with stepped sills, one in each bay, on the east, north, and west, but the south wall had not any windows through being built up against the old church. It has, however, in both the third and fourth bays the remains of a round-headed almery, while the first bay contained the entrance. In the second bay on this side was a well in the floor, 6 ft in diameter. It seems to have had two courses of masonry round the top, below which the shaft is sunk through the solid chalk; no attempt has yet been made to clear it. The south-east compartment of the crypt is almost filled by the block of a staircase into it. The steps had treads 14 in. wide, and there were six up to the doorway, which was fitted with a drawbar. The doorway itself and all the work above are unfortunately hopelessly ruined. The walls of the crypt are built throughout of flint rubble with the white mortar, but vary in thickness, that of the east and west walls being 10 ft., of the north wall 12 ft., and of the south wall 8 ft. Both north and south walls had also two broad pilaster buttresses, in line with the first and third pillars

In order to form this crypt a deep excavation was made outside the north transept of bishop Osmund's church, with a vertical face against which the south wall was built. This wall is not quite parallel with the transept, nor does it touch it, but it is so

Fig. 2.   THE CRYPT, LOOKING EAST

near that a chase must have been cut in the church wall to enable
the western buttress to be carried up. The west wall of the
crypt, as the plan shows, is in line with the west side of Osmund's
transept and probably butted up against it.

For what purpose the crypt was built is uncertain, nor is it clear
for what it was at first used. A subvault of such massive construction could not have been built for itself, and it is practically
certain that another large room stood upon it. This was most
likely the chapter-house, but there is nothing to show how and
where it was entered. It could, however, without difficulty have
had a way into it from the transept in the westernmost bay.

The laying out of the cloister evidently suggested, if it was
not part of a scheme in connexion with, the enlargement of the
church by a new presbytery, which was followed by a rebuilding
of the transepts, also on a larger scale. This work, from the
architectural details, seems not to have begun much before the
second quarter of the twelfth century, and represents 'the church
of Salisbury' which, according to William of Malmesbury, was
'new made' by that great builder, bishop Roger, who held the
see from 1103 to 1139.

The new work is characterized throughout by the use of a
mortar of a bright yellow colour, instead of the white mortar
of the older work. It was probably begun on the north side by
building a wall southwards in line with the east wall of the crypt,
and then returning it eastwards for two-thirds of the length of
the cloister against a vertical face cut for it in the chalk. Care
was taken at the same time to set out the new presbytery in line
with the older church. There was probably a pause to enable
the services to be transferred from the old church to the new
building when finished, and then Osmund's work was demolished
as far as the nave and the rebuilding continued westward.

Owing to the wholesale destruction of the church in the fourteenth century hardly any of the twelfth-century building
remains above the floor level, and in the presbytery not a fragment is left of pillar or respond. It is nevertheless possible to
recover many of its details, and, what is more extraordinary,
most of the pattern and colouring of the floor! To the considerable difference between the levels on the two sides of the
presbytery is due the fortunate circumstance that the lower parts
of the walls forming the south-west corner of the cloister were,
early in the destruction, buried in rubbish. The rubble cores
here have at the base several courses of excellent ashlar masonry,
showing the chamfered lowest member, with two battering courses
above, of the plinth, and the bases of two of the transept pilaster
buttresses. The two bottom steps are also left of a wide ascending flight from the cloister into the church.

The new presbytery was of four bays, with piers set upon a low wall raised above the floor in the same way as in the cathedral church of the Salisbury of to-day. The arcades opened into aisles, which were carried a bay eastwards and joined by an ambulatory behind the presbytery end. The presbytery not improbably had an arcade of three narrower arches towards the ambulatory, with its eastern windows above. Beyond the ambulatory, which was a step higher than the aisles, was a row of chapels.

The west end of the presbytery abutted upon a tower over the crossing, carried by compound piers arranged with their longer axes east and west. Of these only the core of the northwest pier remains, to a height of about 3 ft.; the others have entirely perished. They can, however, all be laid down on plan. The north transept had for its end the north wall of the chapterhouse, or whatever the building was over the crypt, but its east and west sides were planned without any reference to the chapterhouse buttresses. The sides of the transepts were pierced with three arches opening into eastern and western aisles of the same width, $12\frac{1}{2}$ ft., as those of the presbytery. To carry these arcades, the lower piers, and the arches extending from them, wide and continuous concrete foundations of great strength were laid, which cut through, and in some places obscure, the similar foundations of bishop Osmund's church. In the north transept the piers that stood upon these foundations can only be traced by their mortar beds, which are also marked out in an interesting way by the lines incised in the concrete by the master-mason. In the south transept the lowest courses of the pier blocks remain in place, and are $6\frac{1}{2}$ ft. square. In both transepts the arches must have been unequal.

Both transepts have other unusual features beside western as well as eastern aisles. The north transept, for instance, had in the middle bay of its eastern aisle a flight of seven steps coming up from a landing, on to which there opened a wide doorway, approached by two more steps, from the cloister (fig. 3). In the north end of the same aisle was another flight of steps leading down into the earlier crypt, which probably was now used as the vestry and treasury. There seems, therefore, to have been no convenient place in this aisle for the two altars that otherwise could have been in it, and they may accordingly have stood in the transept against the piers.

The south transept probably had its two altars in the eastern aisle. This has also at the south end a thickening of the wall internally, which suggests an entrance there into the lobby or passage at the foot of a vice. The south end of the transept proper has a broad bench across it, interrupted in the middle by

Fig. 4. PURBECK MARBLE COFFIN, FOUND IN THE CANONS' CEMETERY

Fig. 5. GRAVES, WITH HEAD AND FOOT STONES, ON SOUTH SIDE OF NAVE

two steps. There was also a third step at the higher level forming the sill of a wide doorway from without. The existence of this is confirmed by the foundation walls of the porch that covered it. This porch has a projection of 20 ft., and was about 13 ft. wide within, with a stone bench along each side. Some of its stone floor remains in place, and the step of the outer arch, much worn, also exists in parts.

The transepts are plainly defined by the rubble cores of the walls, which remain all round to a height of about 3 ft., but all the ashlar facing has been stripped off save a few odd stones. There is an irregularity in the west wall of the south transept which is not easy to account for.

From these general remarks on the plan of the newer work of the church we may pass to the consideration of its details and arrangements.

Mention has already been made of the recovery of the pattern and colouring of the floor; to which may be added the evidence for the position of sundry steps and consequent changes of level. The whole of the new work, except in one or two places, was paved throughout with squared blocks of stone, either of the white Chilmark or the delicate green from Hurdcote. These blocks were faced on one side only, leaving the other quite rough; in order, therefore, to obtain a level surface, the blocks were laid in a very thick bed of mortar. When the church was dismantled these blocks were taken up, leaving the mortar beds exposed, with here and there embedded chips of the displaced stones. By diligent brushing of the dust and rubbish out of the hollows we have been able to recover from these beds the disposition of the blocks, and Lt.-Col. Hawley noticed one damp day the alternating colours of the stone chips. Mr. Montgomerie and I have accordingly been able to measure and lay down on paper the patterns, with the colouring, of a large extent of the floor, and so to recover what may at present be looked upon as a unique feature of a twelfth-century English church.

It has been pointed out that the ambulatory behind the high altar had to the east of it a row of chapels. The two at each end, in continuation of the aisles, had a step at the entrance, and two more steps up to the altar. How this was arranged it is impossible now to say, and it is also uncertain whether the chapels were not apsidal within though square-ended without.

The space between the end chapels presents several problems. There was certainly a step up to it from the ambulatory, and the middle part contained a chapel, but after that difficulties begin. The chapel was only 14 ft. 9 in. wide and at least 30 ft. long, and was crossed by a step at 20 ft. from the entrance, and by another 3 ft. farther east. Upon this platform stood the altar.

From the fragments scattered about, it seems to have been covered by a slab of black marble or touch. How the chapel ended is a question. The mass of rough foundation behind the altar is so irregular that it may just as likely have helped to support an apse as a square end. The altar platform was paved with rows of stone blocks, alternately white and green, and some of the mortar beds remained in part in front and to the north of the altar. The chapel floor also retained the mortar bed of a curious pavement of interlacing circles, but not of the same material as the altar platform, the stones composing it having been flat and not rough underneath. Between this middle chapel and those north and south of it there is on each side an intervening space nearly 15 ft. broad which has to be accounted for. This interval has on either hand fragmentary masses of rubble walling. Next the outer chapels, these clearly belonged to walls 6 ft. thick, in line with the side walls of the presbytery. The fragments next the middle chapel were certainly 5½ ft. thick, so that the interval between the walls was about 3 ft. The only feasible suggestion as to the use of these narrow areas is that they either formed passages to vices at their eastern ends, or themselves contained ascending flights of steps to the upper works.

The southern end of the ambulatory is blocked by a mass of rubble masonry about 8 ft. square built athwart it. This is clearly of medieval date, but as it has been stripped of any facing stones it is difficult to imagine its purpose. It may have been a tomb, but in any case it must have effectually barred the procession way.

There is the further possibility that this obtrusive fragment may belong to works done to retain the chapel for a certain chantry in the old cathedral church which the dean and canons obtained licence in 1331 to rebuild in any other place 'within the castle'. A chapel of the Blessed Mary 'where the bishop's seat was wont to be' is mentioned in the Liberate Roll of 1246, and Leland says that in his day the only token of the cathedral church 'is but a chapelle of Our Lady yet standing and mainteynid'.

Both the ambulatory and the presbytery aisles, as well as the eastern chapels, had groined vaults.

The presbytery is still enclosed to the height of some inches by the rubble cores of its walls, which were 6 ft. thick, but there are no definite traces of the arcades. In the first bay, to the south of the altar-place, there are the remains of a stone-lined grave within the wall, and there is the foot of a similar grave in the second bay. Now it is recorded of dean William de Wanda that on the feast of the Trinity in the year 1226 he caused to be removed 'from the castle of Sarum to the new fabric the bodies

Fig. 6.   COFFIN-LIDS IN THE CANONS' CEMETERY

Fig. 7.   COFFIN AND COFFIN-LID IN THE CANONS' CEMETERY

of three bishops, namely, the body of the blessed Osmund, the body of bishop Roger, and the body of bishop Jocelin[1]. For two of these bishops, Roger and Jocelin, there still exist monumental effigies brought down from Old Sarum, and it is very probable that they originally occupied the recesses in the presbytery wall. Bishop Osmund was no doubt first buried in a place of honour in his own church, but when its eastern parts were demolished, he was most likely taken up and translated to the north side of the altar in the new presbytery, where there are some indications of another tomb. His memorial at Salisbury is a marble tomb of peculiar fashion, with three oval openings in each side, which seems to date from William de Wanda's translation. The presbytery was raised as to its western half a step above the aisles, and there must have been other steps eastwards up to the altar platform, but owing to their nearness to the present ground level all traces of them have long been destroyed by the plough.

During the excavation of this end it was found that at a depth of 6 in. below the foundation level there was an expanse of plaster flooring. Part of it was destroyed, but a little more than half its width is preserved. Careful examination showed that the plaster surface is scored with groups of parallel lines and with at least one curved line, and it seems fairly certain that, like the chapter-house floor at Wells, this had been laid for use as a setting-out board for the master-mason while the presbytery was in building. It would be interesting to know if any other such example has been noticed.

In the middle of the presbytery there is a stone socket in the floor. Its position is so far east of the quire that any desk here could not have been used by the chanters or rulers; the socket most likely therefore marks the place of the desk in the presbytery, at which, according to bishop Osmund's *Customs*, the Gospel was read on weekdays. In later times the desk, which was usually surmounted by an eagle, stood at the north end of the altar.

The main level of the presbytery extended westwards to a platform filling the fourth bay. This platform seems to have had at each end the openings known as the upper entrances into the quire, and on the west was a step, that called the *gradus chori*. The quire proper extended under the crossing, with the stalls arranged on either side against the tower piers and dwarf walls within the arches, and abutted westwards against the *pulpitum*. This filled up the narrow space west of the tower and was a more or less solid construction of masonry, 14 ft. deep, with a passage between quire and nave through the middle. On one side or the other there would be a staircase to the loft on top, from which the Epistle and Gospel were read from a brass eagle desk on Sundays and festivals. Enough was left of the base of the *pulpitum* to enable it to be laid down on plan.

The eastern aisles of the transepts were a step lower than those of the presbytery, and had a continuous stretch of flooring, upon which any altars or altar platforms must have been built. The aisle floor extended outwards to the western face of the arcade, and then another step lowered the level to that of the main area of the transept and of its western aisle.

It has already been pointed out that the nave and aisles of bishop Osmund's church remained in use throughout.

The arch at the east end was blocked by the *pulpitum* of the new work. This had in front of it a platform raised two steps above the floor of the nave and aisles, with another step from it into the passage through to the quire. Upon the platform apparently stood two altars, one on either side of the quire door. The wall blocking the arch at the east end of the south aisle also probably had an altar against it. The corresponding wall on the north, on the other hand, must have had a doorway through it, for the passage of the Sunday and other processions, which after visiting and censing all the other altars in the church, passed down the aisle of the nave to the font, and then turning up the nave made the accustomed station before the Rood above the *pulpitum*. The usual order for these processions was to start from the north door of the presbytery and turn eastwards so as to visit the altars beyond the presbytery ; then turning westwards to traverse the transept and go down the *south* aisle of the nave. But the order here must have been reversed : first, because access to the south aisle was barred by the wall blocking its arch, and secondly, because the cloister lay on the north instead of the south. From the platform for the nave altars there were no more steps westwards, but the floor sloped gently down to the west end. There is one other feature to be noted in connexion with the nave, and that is the existence of a doorway in the middle bay of the south aisle. As this was built with the yellow mortar it was evidently an insertion.

The addition to the front of bishop Osmund's nave is built of flint rubble with the yellow mortar and was originally faced with ashlar. It is noteworthy for the massiveness of its foundations. What the foundations exactly carried is uncertain, but it was evidently meant to be something heavy.

The whole front is about 75 ft. broad, and its depth 30½ ft. to the nave wall. Internally there are two cross walls 5 ft. thick dividing the area into three. The southern of these walls ranges with the nave arcade, but the northern is just 2 ft. out of line. The west wall was 8 ft. thick at the base, and the end walls about 5 ft. At the angles are projections for stair turrets.

Fig. 8. COFFIN-LID WITH INSCRIPTION TO GODWIN, PRECENTOR OF SALISBURY

Fig. 9. ARCHITECTURAL FRAGMENTS

The questions now arise, whether the foundations carried towers, and if so, were there two, after the Norman manner, or only one in the English fashion?

Any two towers must have been quite oblong in plan, with side walls thinner than their ends. The middle division, on the other hand, could have been surmounted by a tower practically square in plan, with proper supports eastwards, northwards and southwards. It could also have had arches opening into the end divisions and so have reproduced the original arrangement of the cathedral churches of Winchester, Hereford, and Ely, and the abbey church of St. Edmundsbury. Further than this we cannot go, since nothing remains to us above the foundations, and there is nothing to *prove* that anything was ever built upon them.

Before leaving the church it may be recorded that various trenches were cut across the nave in the hope of finding traces of an earlier building. Nothing, however, was found to confirm this, but one of the trenches passed through a depression containing very black rubbish, which yielded a little pre-Roman British pottery and part of a bronze brooch of the same date.

The church as altered by bishop Roger must have had an internal length, including the added western member, of 316 ft, and across the transepts of 138 ft. It shares its peculiar feature of western as well as eastern aisles to the transepts with a few churches of quite the first rank, including Winchester, Ely, Westminster, Beverley, Lincoln, and York. The church is also noteworthy for being one of the first to have an aisled and square-ended presbytery with eastern chapels: Hereford and Romsey being among the few other contemporary instances of a plan that was adopted later at Byland and Abbey Dore, Lichfield, St. Albans, Exeter, Wells, and elsewhere.

The last section of last year's work was one of the most interesting.

It had been noted in 1912 that from the south-east angle of the transept there was a wall, 2 ft. thick, extending eastwards for some distance and apparently enclosing a burial-ground. Parts of several coffins and gravestones were disclosed while the church walls were being traced, and a fine coffin of unpolished Purbeck marble, which contained the skeleton of a priest with a pewter chalice, was removed and transferred to the cathedral church of Salisbury (fig. 4).

On 7th October we began cutting trenches across the area, and were quickly rewarded by coming upon a coped tomb with a long Latin inscription, and another beside it with a massive but plain cover of Purbeck marble. The work was continued with increasing energy on the two following days and resulted in the finding of more than a dozen other tombs and coffins.

It will be noticed that the quadrangular foundation discovered in 1912, supposed to have been the base of a churchyard cross, stands at what was perhaps the corner of the enclosure of the graveyard, but nothing could be found of an eastern boundary.

The description of the tombs is as follows (figs. 5-7):

Of no. I only the greenstone bearers are left. No. II has an oolite slab with middle rib and roll-moulded edges, and a foot-stone, partly broken, bearing a cross potent. No. III is a plain slab of Purbeck marble much weathered. No. IV is an oolite slab with double chamfered sides, and a middle rib which bears a small cross formy. The slab tapers with a slight curve, and is of very graceful design.

Of no. V only the lower part remains, made up of oolite slabs, with a rough upper surface. No. VI has been partly destroyed and shows only some of its oolite bearers. No. VII is a flat oolite slab, cracked across, having on its rough surface six shallow square depressions which seem intended as sockets for pillars carrying an upper stone. On the flat top of no. VIII is carved a wheel cross on a stem starting from a stepped base; at the foot is a plain stone with segmental head.

Close to and south of the above is a greenstone coffin, no. IX, with shaped interior. Part only of its covering slab remains, also of greenstone, without ornament. West of this pair is a rather remarkable tomb, no. X, cut from a single block of greenstone, without taper; the side edges are chamfered and the ends form a broad slope. South-west of this are a pair of which the northern-most is reduced to its greenstone bearers; the other, no. XII, re-sembles closely no. II, even to the design of its cross which is cut upon the headstone.

Further to the west stands a single tomb, no. XIII, in good preservation, with a coped greenstone slab, and head- and foot-stones of oolite. The former has a circular head carrying a cross formy on its outer face; it seems to have been intended for a smaller tomb and in a reversed position, for the present outer side has a recess below with curved head.

Near the angle between the south transept and the wall of the church our excavations revealed a remarkable group of inter-ments, numbering seven in all; four of these, nos. XIV to XVII, stand nearly side by side. The first (no. XIV) is a plain slab of greenstone with chamfered edges; at a few inches distance on the south is another and similar one (no. XV), save that it bears a long rhyming inscription along the sides, another inscription on the head, and an incised cross at the foot. The longer inscription appears to read:

Fig. 10. ARCHITECTURAL REMAINS OF VAULTING, ETC.

Fig. 11. EARLY CROCKETED GABLE MOULDINGS, FOUND OUTSIDE THE
SOUTH TRANSEPT

(South side)

+ECCE TVIS ALWARD ERVAS RAMNESBERIARVM
+QVI FVERAS QVOD DEBVERAS FLOS FOMES EARVM.

(North side)

+SEXTA DIES IANI MVNDO TVRBIVAT INANI
QVA MVNDVM MVNDA MVNDAT BAPTISMATIS VNDA.

The inscription on the head is

PVLIIMATANTAĐES
SIT+VERA QES,

and should perhaps read *ultima tanta dies sit tibi vera quies*.

Of Alward of Ramsbury nothing seems to be known, but he may be the Ailward who witnesses a charter of bishop Roger of a date about 1108.

Beyond the above tomb is another (no. XVI), having a very large and well-cut stone of hard oolite, in extraordinarily good condition, seeing that its upper surface was but a few inches below the modern soil level. Both sides and ends have broad sloping faces, but the stone is quite plain and uninscribed. The weight of the block has forced down its bearers, but without dislodging them, and the whole tomb has a tilt to the west. Tomb XVII, which lies a few feet south of the last, is the most interesting, in that its upper surface is covered with six lines of a rhyming inscription in Latin hexameters (fig. 8). Unhappily, the material chosen by the carver was a soft oolite, and the slab has cracked and crumbled with the failure of its supports and the weight of the soil and rubbish above it. It has therefore not been possible to do more than to photograph the stone carefully and to take rubbings of the best-preserved portions. So far as it can be read the inscription seems to be as follows:

(South slope)

ProDITus A PVERO GODWINus [   ] VITA
MANDATIS STVDVIT DIVINIS MenTE PerITA
PreSBITer ANSELMO SACRATVS CANTVRIENSI
CANTOR In ECCLesiA MICVIT SERESBERIENSI.

(North slope)

ME QVI CVLTOREM STABI[li] viRTVTE B[onor]VM
eT CORRECTOREM LIBERVM FECIT VICIORum
[   ] FACIAT SVPer ASTRA LEVARI
CETIBVS YMNIRIS ELE [   ]ARI.

Tomb XVIII, a greenstone coffin with shaped interior, is placed against the south wall of the church, and a little beyond it are the rough foundations of another (no. XIX). No. XX, farther west, was the fine coffin of Purbeck marble described in last year's Report.

Besides this interesting and almost unique collection of memorials of dignitaries and canons of Old Sarum, none of which can well be later than the first quarter of the thirteenth century, mention must again be made of several others that were found in 1912 when following the south side of the nave. These have all been laid down on our plan, and were mostly plain and uninscribed coffin lids of oolite or greenstone, slightly rounded or ridged down the middle. Just outside the third bay of the aisle two were found side by side. Each stone has in low relief a cross paty on a shaft starting from a stepped base, and had other stones bearing crosses set up at each end. Both head-stones remain : one has a plain wheel cross on each side; the other has on both sides a cross paty with square ends, plain on the back but more ornate on the front, and the outer vertical edge is covered with a row of lozenges containing crosses. The footstone of the southern stone is badly damaged, but its fellow is more perfect; both had wheel crosses on both sides in low re-lief. This remarkable group of stones, which are all wrought in the soft greenstone, dates from the eleventh century, and probably forms the memorial of some unknown citizen and his wife. A small tomb, probably that of a child, was disclosed in the excavation bank facing the north wall of the nave.

In addition to the discoveries south and east of the church, something more must be said about the cloister north of it. Its dimensions have already been noted; also the fact that it had covered alleys on all four sides. These alleys were 12 ft. wide on three sides, but the south alley was 13 ft. wide. The wall towards the garth that carried the pentise roof could be traced all round and was 2 ft. thick, but only more or less of its foundation remained, and there was nothing to suggest what had stood upon it. From the large number of fragments found, the pentise seems to have been roofed with tiles. The rain water from the roofs and garth had been carried off by a stone drain roofed originally with planks covered with mortar. Part of this was traced, running out under the north-east angle. That end of the south alley which extended eastwards beyond the church had been filled at some time by a dwelling-house. This had at least two rooms on the ground level of the alley, each with a hearth of tiles laid on edge, and there was a third room filling up the corner of the cloister with a doorway in its north wall. This room had also a garderobe pit on the south, which seems to have been in the line of a flight of steps that once led from the cloister up to the cemetery. The garderobe was 5 ft. 3 in. long, 4 ft. broad, and 14 ft. deep,

Fig. 12. ARCH-STONES OF A LARGE NORMAN DOORWAY

and yielded a good many blocks of ashlar. At the bottom were the remains of two glass flagons with thick necks and wide lip-rims, but no pottery.

There has not yet been any opportunity of clearing, or examining for graves, the area of the cloister garth.

Outside of and attached to the north-west angle of the cloister are some remains of another building, but the further investigation of this and others of which indications have been found farther west will form part of the work of the present year.

The clearing of the cloister alleys brought to light some interesting illustrations of the way in which the buildings were destroyed. Large cavities had been cut in the masonry and props of wood inserted as the work proceeded. Then these had been set on fire, and, as they burnt through, the walling above subsided into the hollows in fractured masses or was overthrown in bulk. By the steps up into the transept may be seen two such masses. One on the north of the doorway has dropped about 3 ft., and has in it part of the chase for the drawbar of the door. Another fragment at the junction of the transept and presbytery retains its ashlar facing, and the floor of a locker or recess of some kind. Towards the east end of the presbytery lie two overthrown lengths of wall core, from behind which were recovered quite a number of carved and moulded stones as well as ashlar blocks.

During the five and a half months of last year's operations and those of the preceding year a very considerable number of architectural remains was accumulated (figs. 9, 10). From many of these it is possible to form an idea not only of the general richness of the twelfth-century work, but to go far towards reconstructing some of the parts on paper. This, however, has yet to be done. Of carved heads of varying degrees of grotesqueness there is quite a collection, including two of large size belonging to a series round some important doorway (fig. 12). One of these has a sixfold tongue protruding from the mouth, and the other a mermaid hanging on to the teeth. The curious thing is that these two heads, and it is to be presumed the rest that completed the half-circle, were carved upside down. Outside the end of the south transept there were found in 1912 a considerable number of stones that had belonged to a row of small gables, part perhaps of the decoration of the south doorway or of the porch that covered it. These gables are peculiar in exhibiting what are probably the earliest examples of true crockets (fig. 11). They seem also to have enclosed some such ornaments as the large rosette which was found with them. Several gables were surmounted by pairs of creatures, one having two lions gnawing a

round object. carved with considerable spirit (fig. 13); another
had two birds, and a third a plain cylindrical finial. Proof that
parts of the new presbytery were vaulted is afforded by a number
of lengths of ribs, and of a key with a damaged boss in form of
a floriated cross in a beaded circle. Quite a number of small
blocks are carved with rosettes and other devices in relief, and
many others of the series may be seen built into the close wall
in Salisbury; they probably formed components of ornamental
diapers   There are also one or two examples of the springing
blocks of pairs of arches with zigzag patterns which, combined
with such diapers, would furnish a design almost identical with
that of the contemporary triforium at Rochester. Many other
details, such as carved and simple capitals, pieces of string-
courses, and arch mouldings of various patterns, still await drawing out and classifying, for which we hope to find time during
the forthcoming season.

Among the minor objects discovered may be mentioned a
number of fragments of plain and patterned floor tiles, which
were found for the most part scattered in or about the eastern
part of the church and in the south alley of the cloister   The
stone flooring already described can be traced over so much of
the church that it is difficult to see where these tiles could have
been laid, but possibly on the destroyed platform of the high
altar.

A more remarkable discovery is that of quite a considerable
quantity of pieces of verde-antico and red porphyry of various
sizes. These materials are so rare in this country, Westminster
and Canterbury (both at Christchurch and St. Augustin's Abbey)
being the only other known places of their occurrence, that it
would be very important to say how they could have been used
here. They were, however, so scattered about that this is impossible   There was, moreover, no shrine or important tomb
here that we are aware of, yet these precious materials were
used in a church that was destroyed before the Canterbury and
Westminster works were begun [1]

One other singular discovery deserves notice, this time within
the church. During the clearance of the north end of the
ambulatory the remains of several human skeletons were found,
lying on the floor level in such a way as to suggest that they
had been thrown out of stone coffins when the church was destroyed. With one of these skeletons was deposited a wonder-
fully perfect set of leg-irons, consisting of two closing rings
which were still riveted and connected by two long and one
round link. The unfortunate man whose bones these were had
evidently therefore been buried in his fetters. He must have
been a person of note, or he would not have received burial at

 To face page 116

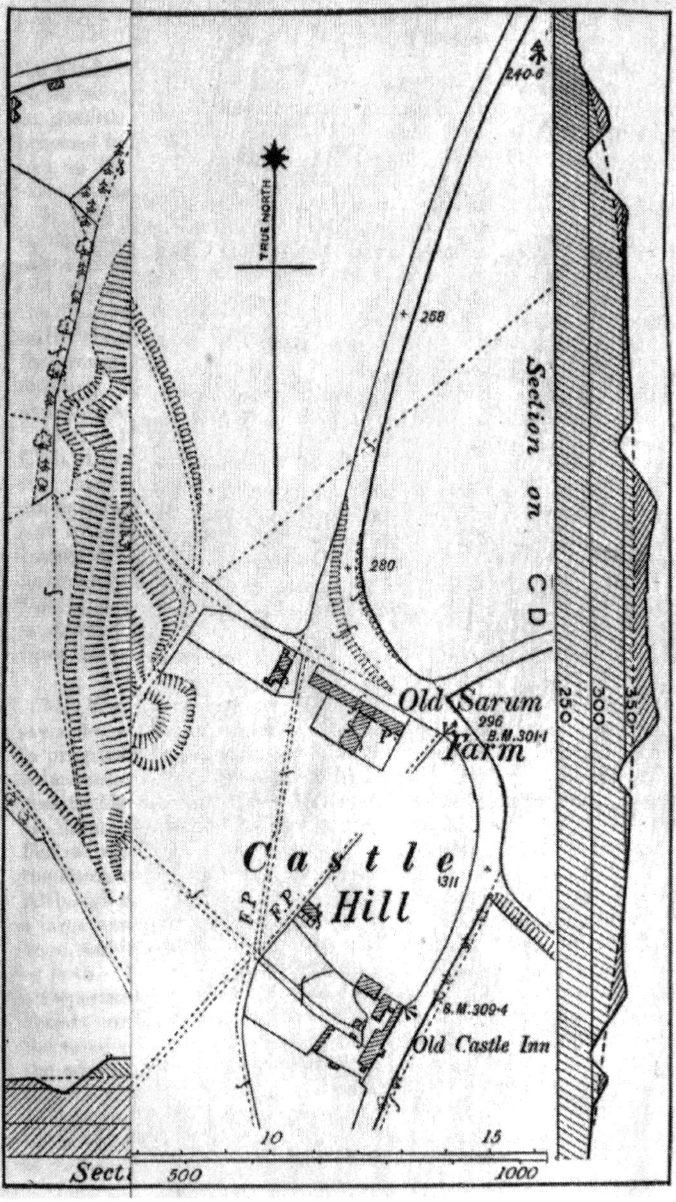

the hands of the canons in an honourable part of their church. So far no one has been able to suggest his name, but it ought to be possible to find what notable person could have been imprisoned in the castle between the building of the new presbytery in the middle of the twelfth century and its destruction early in the thirteenth

It only remains to add that the supervision of the work day by day was undertaken, as in previous years, with his usual care and patience by Lt.-Col. Hawley. I myself also visited Old Sarum at frequent intervals and was able to take part in the discovery and planning of many of the interesting features in the church. Mr. Montgomerie joined us towards the end of the season and stayed on for many weeks taking photographs, finishing the plan, and supervising the protective works necessary against the winter.

During the season visits were paid us by the Hampshire Field Club, the Bournemouth Science Club, a joint gathering of the Cambrian Archaeological Association and the Wiltshire Archaeological Society, the Surrey Archaeological Society, and by a large party of members of the Royal Archaeological Institute. A projected visit of the Society of Antiquaries unfortunately fell through, but many of the Fellows came over from time to time, and the interest shown by visitors in general is attested by the £112 received as gate-money, and the £16 from the sale of our reports."

Mr WILMER took the opportunity presented by the report to say a few words on the financial aspect of the two excavations in progress under the auspices of the Society. A study of the balance-sheet would reveal the extent of the Society's indebtedness to Mr. Tapp, who filled the office of Treasurer last year. He himself ventured to ask for the collaboration of certain Fellows who last year helped to collect funds for the work, as the Research Fund was small and many calls were made upon it. Although 80 per cent. was allocated to the excavations, there was a large sum still to be found. Voluntary efforts had to be relied upon, and individual appeals made on behalf of either excavation or both. There would be drawbacks to a State subsidy, but till a Department and Minister of Fine Arts were established, the Society must pay its own way. There was no question as to the value of the work, and many problems would be solved by the advance of critical science. He would make the appeal for funds a personal one, and did not feel called upon to apologize for begging on behalf of such a cause The great interest shown in the paper was a tribute to the Council's wisdom and enterprise as well as to the ability of those in charge on the spot.

Mr. PEERS congratulated the Society on witnessing the disinterment of another English cathedral, which added one more to the interesting series of late eleventh-century plans immediately succeeding the Conquest. There was no question that the Conquest did smother native architecture, but it also brought over a notable endowment of architectural skill. Up to the middle of the twelfth century England led the way in architecture, but after that date the lead was taken by the French. In 1901 he had laid before the Society the details of Romsey Abbey, where an apse was found within the lines of the twelfth-century central tower, belonging to an earlier building. The enlargement of the pre-Conquest church was probably begun after 1085, when the abbey obtained an accession of wealth; and did not range with the French plan adopted in other places in England, showing that the Saxon plan survived the Conquest. Sarum was an interesting example of the imported plan, with a short presbytery of one bay, while Westminster had a two-bay presbytery, and Christchurch (Hants) three bays. St. Albans, with four bays, was inspired by St. Stephen's at Caen, and the French plan was becoming universal at the time when Sarum was built, at the end of the eleventh century. Early in the twelfth century the Sarum church was enlarged in a characteristically English way, with a square east end; the main span was widened, so that the tower piers were not on the line of the old arcades but outside them, and it was evidently intended to rebuild the nave on this larger scale. This was never done, and walls were therefore built between the transepts and the aisles of the nave, to mask the change of line between the old nave arcades and the newer tower piers. The west end of the nave was also lengthened, but as in this case the span of the added work corresponded with that of the nave, it was clear that this lengthening was either earlier than the eastern extension of the church, or was made after the idea of rebuilding the nave was abandoned.

Rev. E. E. DORLING was able to supplement what had been said about Godwin the precentor, who had previously been chancellor of Salisbury. His name appeared with that of other witnesses about 1108. It was generally believed at Salisbury that the tomb of Jocelyn had a restored head. The late Mr. Arthur Malden was engaged at the time of his lamented death in a search for further information about Aylward, but there seemed to be nothing in his papers about either him or Godwin.

The PRESIDENT spoke of the work at Old Sarum as one of the Society's heaviest responsibilities, and had omitted to mention, when Mr. Bushe-Fox's report on Wroxeter was presented, that the Research Fund was much indebted to Birmingham University for showing interest in that site to the extent of £500. The Society was only too pleased to recognize this valuable co-operation, and Lord Barnard, as owner of the site, would not overlook Birmingham's claims to a share in the proceeds of the excavations. The proposed visit of a party to Old Sarum had unfortunately fallen through, and nothing but a personal acquaintance with the site could bring home the points discussed by Mr. Hope. The reappearance of a ground-plan that had been buried 600 years was in itself an imposing event, and there were details enough for the most exacting architect. The Society fully appreciated the achievements of those in charge of the work at Old Sarum : Mr. Hope's knowledge and lucidity were everywhere recognized ; and Colonel Hawley, who was unfortunately unable to be present, as well as Mr. Montgomerie, deserved the Society's warmest thanks. The new bridge had been mentioned in passing, but he might add that its construction cost £77, one of those incidental expenses for which there was little to show but which nevertheless encroached on the funds available. He did not share the belief that a Minister of Fine Arts would save the situation, and thought that before entering on such a scheme it would be well to inquire how the Department worked in France, from those serving under the minister in question.

Thanks were ordered to be returned for this communication.

Thursday, 5th March, 1914.

Sir CHARLES HERCULES READ, Knt., LL.D., President, in the Chair.

The following gifts were announced, and thanks for the same ordered to be returned to the donors :

From L. B. Phillips, Esq., F.S.A.:—Traité de l'horlogerie mécanique et pratique. Par Thiout l'ainé. 2 tomes. 4to. Paris, 1741.

From Señor José Ramon Mélida, Hon. F.S.A.:—Excavaciones de Numancia. Memoria presentada al Ministerio de Instrucción Pública y Bellas Artes por la Comisión Ejecutiva. fol. Madrid, 1912.

From C. R. Peers, Esq., Secretary :—Report of the Inspector of Ancient Monuments for the year ending 31st March, 1913. 4to. London. n.d.

E. NEIL BAYNES, Esq., F.S.A., exhibited the matrix of the seal of the extinct borough of Newborough, Anglesey, dissolved in 1814, and a brass to Marcelie Lloyd, 1609, from the disused church of Llanwenllwyfo, Anglesey.[1]

L. A. LAWRENCE, Esq., F.S.A., exhibited a collection of posy rings.

TALFOURD ELY, Esq., D.Litt., F.S.A., exhibited an oil portrait on copper supposed to represent Richard Cromwell.

This being an evening appointed for the election of Fellows no papers were read.

The ballot opened at 8.45 p.m. and closed at 9.30 p.m., when the following were declared duly elected Fellows of the Society :

Charles Harry St. John Hornby, Esq., B.A.
Rev. Philip Thomas Byard Clayton, M.A.
Henry William Lewer, Esq.
Robert Copp Fowler, Esq., B.A.
William de Courcy Prideaux, Esq.
Jonathan Edward Hodgkin, Esq.
Arthur William Gould, Esq.
Colonel Sir Clement Molyneux Royds, C.B.
Arthur Thomas Bolton, Esq.

THURSDAY, 12th MARCH, 1914.

Sir CHARLES HERCULES READ, Knt., LL.D., President,
in the Chair.

The following gifts were announced and thanks for the same ordered to be returned to the donors :

From John Gibson, Esq.:—Guide to the Priory Church of St. Andrew, Hexham. By C. C. Hodges. 8vo. Hexham, 1913.

From Harold Sands, Esq., F.S.A.:—Barking Abbey in the middle ages. By Walter A. Locks. 8vo. London, 1913.

From Mill Stephenson, Esq., B.A., F.S.A.:—Two thousand years of gild life. By Rev. J. M. Lambert. 8vo. Hull, 1891.

[1] See *Arch. Camb.* III, v, 170.

Fig. 1. STAUNTON HAROLD CHAPEL: EXTERIOR FROM NORTH-WEST

The following were admitted Fellows :
Henry William Lewer, Esq.
William de Courcy Prideaux, Esq.
Robert Copp Fowler, Esq., B.A.

Earl FERRERS, F.S.A., on behalf of the Rev. ROLAND BOROUGH, read the following paper on the private chapel of the Earl Ferrers at Staunton Harold :

"In the year 1653, no doubt owing to the overthrow of the Prayer Book services in the parish church, Sir Robert Shirley built a large and spacious church close to his own mansion at Staunton Harold. When it was completed the Lord Protector demanded a large sum of money from him on the ground that if he could afford to build a church he could afford to provide him with a regiment of soldiers. On his refusal he was imprisoned in the Tower and died suddenly soon afterwards.

The casual observer on first catching sight of the building would be inclined to mistake it for a church of the fourteenth or fifteenth century (fig. 1). It consists of a chancel, a nave with north and south aisles, and a west tower containing a ring of eight bells. The nave has a clearstory and is separated from the aisles by arcades of three bays. The nave roof is almost flat : the other roofs are very low-pitched, and all the walls have embattled parapets. The tower, the west door of which forms the only entrance to the church, is a massive structure of three stages, with pairs of buttresses at the angles. The uppermost stage has two two-light windows in each face and large crocketed angle-pinnacles with vanes.

The chancel is low in proportion to the nave, and is separated from it by a low pointed arch having a blank wall-space above ; its details and those of the nave arcades have a close general resemblance to medieval work. There is, however, a complete departure from the English medieval type in the roofs, and also in the woodwork, which is of the kind usual in the early part of the seventeenth century.

Round the outside of the chancel runs an inscription, as follows :

SIR ROBERT SHIRLEY BARONET : FOVNDER OF THIS CHVRCH : ANNO DOMINI 1653 ON WHOSE SOVL : GOD HATH MERCY.

It looks as though his successor wished to cling to old phrases so far as possible, but fighting shy of the precatory 'have' substituted the assumption 'hath'. Over the entrance (fig. 2), which is at the west end as already mentioned, is this beautiful and touching inscription:

In the yeare : 1653.
when all things sacred were throughout yᵉ nation
either demollisht or profaned
Sʳ Robert Shirley Barronet
Founded this Church
whose singular praise it is
to have done the best things in yᵉ worst times
And
hoped them in the most callamitous
The Righteous shall be had in everlasting remembrance.

On entering the church (fig. 3), the first thing that catches the eye is the fine wrought-iron chancel-screen and gates, surmounted by the Shirley Arms. There is a broad gangway between the pews, which are of fine workmanship, of the square type with doors, but not unduly high. Every seat faces east. There are also smaller gangways in the aisles. The oak panelling is carried up the pillars as high as the capitals, and to a corresponding height along the walls.

The walls were originally plastered and distempered, but the plaster, becoming cracked, was unfortunately removed altogether only a short time ago. The stonework beneath is rough and unfinished.

The roofs are boarded and almost flat, and are painted in a most uncommon way with a representation of the Creation. Clouds are the predominating feature, while the sun and moon are in evidence in the nave ; and just before the entrance to the chancel, within a 'glory', is the Sacred Name of God רהֹרָה. This is a noteworthy example of the very superficial knowledge of Hebrew in those days. *Vau* (ו) is so clumsily written as to be more like *rēsh* (ר), while the first letter ought to be *yōd* (י) and not *vau* at all. Moreover, the insertion of the pointing of the *k'ri* (what is read) *Adonai*, would have been thought out of place by anybody who knew that the word Jehovah was formed accidentally from the vowels of Adonai (the Lord) being combined with the *K'thiv* (what was written), namely the tetragrammaton J H V H.

On the chancel ceiling, just over the altar, is the word Θεός surrounded by a circle of winged heads represented alternately as singing 'Halleluiah' and 'Sanctus, Sanctus, Sanctus'. The chancel is on the same level as the nave, with no step either up or down, and is quite empty, without stalls of any kind. There is an ascent of three steps to the presbytery.

Until quite recently these steps were fitted with movable kneeling-benches with flat tops, permanently hung with house-ling-cloths of dark blue or purple cloth, *en suite* with all the hangings and upholstery in the church.

The Decalogue is now written on one small table to the north of the altar, the Creed and Lord's Prayer being contained on

Fig. 2. STAUNTON HAROLD CHAPEL: WEST FRONT

another to the south. This, however, was done within living memory, the original Tables of the Commandments being over the chancel arch and so large as to be easily read from the west gallery.

The presbytery is paved with squares of black and white marble, and the nave with good flagstones.

The altar itself is just an inch short of 3 ft. high, and the original pall and tasselled cushions are still in use. The colour is, or was, a dark red-purple, with heavy gold fringe, and the altar-pall is pulled out at the lower corners, giving the altar the appearance of being longer than it really is. Altar coverings of this kind are sometimes to be seen in thirteenth-century miniatures, and although their place was taken latterly by the flat straight-hanging frontal familiar to us now, this large loose-fitting type survived in places. There is an interesting eighteenth-century example in a well-known French devotional book.

The design in the midst of the front consists of rays surrounding a crown of thorns, within which is the sacred monogram surmounted by a cross, while the three nails and a.heart are beneath. The heart appears also on the almsdish.

A pulpit-hanging with the same design on a smaller scale was found in the house a few years ago, but has not so far been restored to.use.

The linen altar-cloth is fringed all round and reaches to the ground in front, and beside the corporas there is a long narrow strip of very old and fine linen. This seems to be a survival of the early medieval type of corporas, which had four folds to the length and three to the breadth. The two eastern folds were turned up behind the chalice and used to cover it. Afterwards, the easternmost fold was severed from the rest and formed a separate strip such as this.

The altar-pall and cushions are removed out of service-time, while the ornaments appear only at the Communion. These consist of two very fine gilt candlesticks, a large and handsome alms-basin, two flagons, two chalices with covers, two standing patens with covers, and two knives (but these are modern) (fig. 4). In accordance with the medieval custom, these are all set out upon the altar by way of decoration, even when all are not required for use. The covers to the chalices and patens are surmounted by crosses. The flagons have 'Holiness to the Lord' on their lids, while the body is engraved with the crown of thorns surrounding the words 'The Blood of the New and Æternal Testament'. Each chalice has engraved upon its side a figure of the Good Shepherd carrying a lamb upon His shoulders, while one has also the inscription 'My blood is drink indeed', and on its cover 'My flesh is meat indeed'. On the paten-covers are the

words 'My Love is crucified', and on the patens themselves
'This is the true Bread that came down from heaven'. The
plate is dated 1640 and 1654, and has been dealt with more
fully in Trollope's *Church Plate of Leicestershire*.[1]

The custom has only lately been discontinued of placing two
handsomely bound books or *textus*, for the Epistle and Gospel
respectively, on the altar north and south, leaning against the
east wall between the alms-basin and candlesticks. These were
in addition to the two service-books, and it is a very striking
survival of an early custom. There were other cases of survival at Winchester Cathedral, Christ Church, Oxford, and
Peterborough, but probably all trace has now disappeared except from old pictures. There are also rubrics for the same in
eighteenth-century French missals.

The original books are in the library at Staunton Harold,
and have crucifixes engraved on both back and front. The
books that replaced them are now in the church chest, and a
painting in the library shows that at one time they were placed
outside the candlesticks at the extreme ends. The Bidding
Prayer has never been discontinued.

Marks on the stone-work prove that the pulpit had a sounding-board at one time, and its removal is a disaster, as the position of the pulpit just beyond the spring of an arch puts an
enormous strain on the preacher's voice.

The separation of the sexes has been rigidly preserved from
the first, the men being placed on the south side, and the
women on the north. At the Communion all the women receive first, the men afterwards, and only one railful is allowed
within the chancel gates at a time. Each communicant kneels
upon a separate cushion.

There is a font at the west end, but rather too much to one
side; it has a good cover of simple character worked by brass
chains. The priest stands facing north.

A fine screen of Renaissance character separates the nave from
the tower and supports the west gallery where the organ stands
(fig. 5). Above the organ a species of wooden tympanum covers
the apex of the tower-arch, and serves to display the Shirley arms
painted on an oval escutcheon. The whole composition is strangely
reminiscent of the medieval rood-screen with its loft and tympanum, although it is in reality more to be connected with the
pre-Reformation west galleries.

The gallery holds the choir and the very sweet-toned little
organ, without pedals, by Father Schmidt. This has been moved
eastwards at some time, possibly to give more room in the belfry,
but the organist and singers are now distinctly cramped. There

---

[1] Vol. i, 11.

Fig. 3. STAUNTON HAROLD CHAPEL : INTERIOR, LOOKING EAST

BEFORE THE REMOVAL OF THE PLASTER

is no question as to the genuineness of the organ. Mr. Francis Burgess, the well-known plainsong expert, wrote as follows after examining it ' The organ stands in its original case in the west gallery, and is now practically the same as when it left the builder's hands some two centuries and a half ago. It contains the usual specification of the period (Open and Stopped Diapasons, Principal, Fifteenth, and Sesquialtera), most of the stops being drawn in two halves, a convenient device for a one-manual instrument. The original pipes, entirely of wood, are somewhat the worse for wear, but they still show signs of the superb craftsmanship of their maker. The tone is "small", but by no means ineffective, as the organ is well placed in a splendidly resonant building.'

A verger in gown, carrying a wand, used to add to the dignity of the chapel and its services ; but the last occupant had held the post so long, and become so identified with it, that at his death no successor was appointed. The gown and wand are still in existence.

Before closing this paper one question arises—Where is the litany-desk ? Knowing what we do of the Caroline era, and knowing, too, that Sir Robert Shirley was the very embodiment of all that was best in the ideas of the time, it is hard to believe that what was then looked upon as so essential a piece of furniture could have been missing There are seventeenth-century litany-desks still existing in Durham Cathedral (the gift of Bishop Cosin) and the parish church of High Wycombe, Buckinghamshire, and it seems highly probable that there was one at Staunton Harold, which was removed during the eighteenth century or the early days of the nineteenth. There are signs that certain changes of questionable character took place about then—e.g. the space partitioned off for a vestry used to be at the east end of the *north* aisle, but was moved to the south aisle behind the pulpit , also, the writer is inclined to doubt whether the reading-desk was always used for reading Morning and Evening Prayer. The big Prayer Book now in use only dates from 1840, while the Bible is of 1660—there is not real room for both on the desk, there is no seat, and it does not seem built to kneel to; this is only possible by using a very high hassock, whereas by removing the hassock and placing only the Bible on the cushion, it can at once be seen how ideal it is for reading the Lessons.

The desk below, facing north, is furnished with a seat, and may well have been used by the chaplain, as there could not be a real clerk in a private chapel.

Posterity and present-day ecclesiologists owe a deep debt of gratitude to the Shirley family for the preservation of so much that is of value both in the building itself and its traditional customs."

Mr. Hope claimed a personal interest in the chapel inasmuch as his father baptized the last Lord Ferrers and had often officiated there. The building was of special interest as the only one erected during the Civil War; and it was curious that the Gothic tradition should have survived so long. There were similar unexpected Gothic details at Wadham College, Oxford, and the date was vouched for by documents. Peterhouse, Cambridge, was another case in point. The skinning of the walls was unfortunate as their present appearance was unpleasant, and it was a mistake to regard plaster as an invention of modern churchwardens. He had no doubt that the screen was Bakewell's work, and compared some work at All Saints', Derby; there was also a pair of gates to the old silk mills in that town by the same maker, as was proved by his name being stamped on them. The red colour on the western door he suggested might be lichen and not paint, and quoted a case at Fountains Abbey. One level throughout the church was an interesting feature that modern architects would regard as incorrect. The wonderful collection of plate was doubtless of the same date as the building, for an identical set by the same maker existed at Rochester, and a third at the Chapel Royal, St. James's. Still stronger Gothic influence was noticed on six sets in South Derbyshire, dating about 1640, which looked at first sight like sixteenth-century work. He inquired the date of the shelf placed above the altar, an arrangement which he thought would not have been tolerated in the seventeenth century.

Mr. Norman mentioned the church of Berwick-on-Tweed as another built during the Civil War, about 1645, but of much later appearance than Staunton Harold chapel. St. Catherine Cree in the City was a Laudian church with a Gothic plan, but otherwise debased Renaissance. There were many other churches in London that were built in debased Gothic style or added to during the seventeenth century, such as All Hallows, Barking; St. Alban, Wood Street; and St. Mary Aldermary.

Rev. E. E. Dorling was interested in the linen strip described as a corporas. At Wimborne Minster the altar-rails and wooden benches were always covered with cloths of white linen, and as that use of houseling-cloths had only survived in a few cases, he thought the linen strip might belong to that class of coverings.

Mr. E. P. Warren said the chapel followed an earlier type of Gothic than the staircase at Christ Church, Oxford, and was more Gothic than Wadham, which was forty years earlier. Staunton Harold showed no undue clinging to architectural

FIG. 4.   STAUNTON HAROLD CHAPEL : SEVENTEENTH-CENTURY PLATE

Reproduced by the courtesy of the proprietors of " Country Life "

tradition that might be expected in an elderly mason. He had seen no example of a small altar with its cloth spread out in that way except in Lutheran churches in Denmark, as in the small chapel at Frederiksborg Palace. At Durweston the altar had a shorter cloth of that kind simulated in oak, with the sacred monogram. It was intended to be covered and to throw out the angles of the cloth, the date being about 1800. He deplored the removal of the wall plaster, and quoted Groombridge chapel as a case of survival. It was built 1605–10, but had perpendicular windows at the east and west ends, an interesting Gothic porch with a Renaissance doorway, and a tablet referring to Prince Charles's return from Spain.

Mr. BAILDON cited as a parallel the chapel of Lincoln's Inn, which was built by Inigo Jones in 1625. Among other features might be mentioned the curious double or quadrangular arches, and a combination of pilasters reappearing in the crypt of Lincoln's Inn. The pulpits were similar in design, and the Inn had equally suffered the loss of its sounding-board, though it had since been recovered.

Mr. QUARRELL remarked that the name of the artist of the ceiling was well known in the neighbourhood. The paper had not touched on another matter connected with the name of Shirley, namely, the alabaster tombs at Bredon-on-the-Hill, dating from 1570–1 and 1591. The subject was worth following up, for Bredon lay in a backwater, and preserved many ancient features, including the oak pew of the Shirley family, also a sword, gauntlet, and helmet, though the last would not pass muster with an expert.

Mr. CRACE quoted Shifnal church with its timber roof as built late in the reign of James I, and referred to the altar of the church at present known as that of St. Charles the Martyr at Tunbridge Wells. He thought the beautiful outline and refined lines of the candlesticks showed they were not of the same date as the remainder of the church plate.

Mr. PEERS considered the chapel an extremely interesting example of architectural development, and pointed out that seventeenth-century Gothic was not a wilful mixture. In spite of the influence of Inigo Jones a Gothic style still survived that took its details from various models. Thus at St. John's, Peterborough, there were windows altered late in the eighteenth century with tracery like the east end of Staunton Harold. The latter church had perpendicular tracery in the tower, but

certain details showed that it was all of one date. The heads
of the upper lights were rounded in a peculiar way, but the
roll-moulding and fillet might have dated from William of
Wykeham's time. The work still retained the Jacobean feeling, with none of the severity of Inigo Jones, and was a pecu-
liarly English variety of Renaissance. The two stages of the
tower, though different, were probably the work of the same
mason. The screen under the organ gallery and the panels of
the gallery were Jacobean in style though dating from the time
of the Commonwealth. Windows at Bishop's Waltham, dated
1651, were built in a curious style that might be called vernacu-
lar Gothic, and the spire of Oundle church was a surprising work
for 1629.

Lord FERRERS replied that there was much truth in Mr. Peers's
remark that the chapel was built in that style because it was
the inevitable expression of contemporary feeling ; but it should
be observed that the earlier Gothic style was deliberately chosen
as a basis. There was a desire to reproduce something strictly
medieval, and the latest Gothic tradition was perhaps instinctively ignored. He had no theories about the worn strip of
linen that might have been a corporas. The author had not
intended to claim Staunton Harold as the only Gothic church
of the seventeenth century ; it was unique in being built during
the Civil War. He was still inclined to regard the red colour
as paint that had not been weathered by wind and rain, and had
a thin lime coating to preserve it. The altar-shelf seemed to
be contemporary with the other woodwork, but there had been
some slight additions on the top.

The PRESIDENT said the meeting had listened to what had
been in the truest sense an interesting paper, for which thanks
were due both to Mr. Borough and Earl Ferrers. England was
extremely rich in remains of that kind, and the present building
had in private hands happily escaped the ravages of time and
restoration. He had been specially attracted by the display of
church plate, and the covered paten reminded him of an ecclesiastical vessel exhibited to the Society twenty years ago that
had been called a font, but exactly resembled the lower part of
that paten. It bore an inscription, and had passed into the
possession of Lord Swaythling. A Gothic feeling was manifest
in all parts of the chapel except the woodwork, and it might be
that those craftsmen were more in touch with the spirit of the
time than the stone-masons.

S. HAZZLEDINE WARREN, Esq., F.G.S., exhibited portions of

Fig. 5.   STAUNTON HAROLD CHAPEL: INTERIOR, LOOKING WEST

two cinerary urns of the Early Iron Age found together at Deal, on which Mr. REGINALD SMITH read the following notes :

" The east coast of Kent is of all parts of England the most likely to contain relics of foreign origin, and attention has recently been called to pottery from Broadstairs (ten miles distant on the coast) similar to wares of the Champagne and Saxony.[1] The present exhibit adds two other items to the list; and Mr. Warren has shown his appreciation of their importance by handing over the fragments as a gift to the British Museum.

The first group of fragments, now accurately put together in plaster, is notable for the designs incised on the neck and shoulder, differing from indigenous vessels both of the Bronze and Early Iron Ages. Only a small portion is preserved (fig. 1),

Fig. 1.   FRAGMENTS OF URN FOUND AT DEAL, WITH RESTORATION.   D. 8 IN.

but enough to give the original form with the exception of the foot, the diameter being 8 in. and the height 7 in. The ware is thin, dark brown and slightly burnished, the pattern being traced with a rounded point before firing. On the neck is a step pattern derived from the Greek fret or key pattern, and furnishing a clue to the country of origin. Etruscan wares dating before the fifth century B.C. are considered to be the prototypes of step-pattern urns, ornamented by means of a toothed wheel, which occur on the Elbe banks, in Mecklenburg, Hanover, Lauenburg, and Holstein, also in Denmark (Lolland) and Bohemia.[2]

Later examples of the step or degenerate fret pattern are found in Southern Scandinavia [3] and are attributed to the early

---

[1] *Proceedings*, xxii, 509 ; xxv, 89.   Cf. *Archaeologia*, lii, pl. xii, figs. 1, 3.
[2] *Mémoires de la Société des Antiquaires du Nord*, 1896–1901, 372, 375, fig. 2.
[3] Cremation urn at Nybble, Vikingstad : *Meddelanden från Östergötlands Fornminnesforening*, 1912, p. 11.

Roman period of that region, that is, to the first or second century of our era; but the lines making up the design are dotted, not continuous, either in single or double rows. Dr. Sophus Müller [1] describes and illustrates Jutish urns of the same period, with lightly engraved lines in angular fret patterns, sometimes filled with hatching or dots, and one from Hanover on a contracted foot has a triple fret of dotted lines.

The step-pattern or simplified fret is generally called the meander on the Continent, though in English a wavy pattern is usually implied by that term. In a paper on meander urns Dr. Kossinna [2] of Berlin has summarized the known finds which are both East and West German, especially in the larger river valleys (Vistula, Oder, and Elbe). They are often associated with La Tène objects, and are classified as follows, in chronological order:

(a) Simple empty band of double lines;
(b) Band filled with hatching;
(c)   „   „   herring-bone pattern;
(d)   „   „   short longitudinal lines;
(e)   „   „   dots.

Various combinations of continuous and dotted lines are found, the latest being a single dotted line, produced at the beginning of the Roman Empire by the roulette. The period covered in North Germany is from the eighteenth century B.C. to the second century A.D. Specimens are illustrated by Voss and Stimming (*Vorgeschichtliche Alterthümer aus Brandenburg*, part v, plates 1, 4, 10, 12–14), and Beltz (*Vorgesch. Alt. Mecklenburg-Schwerins*, plate 60). The former series is from Westhavelland, and is decorated with double or triple discontinuous lines; and the latter shows a closer connexion with the Hallstatt period wares of South-west Germany.

Though the meander was a favourite and widespread form of decoration in North Germany, it was probably from the Celtic area of the Marne that the Deal specimens were derived. Apart from the Broadstairs examples, several features of the two fragments correspond to Gaulish wares in the Morel Collection (British Museum), and a few diagrams are given for comparison. Panels enclosing plain crosses are incised on the neck and shoulder of an elegant blackware vase (fig. 2) from Marson, Marne (Morel, *Album*, pl. xli, fig. 23), the design being filled with red. A red bowl from the same locality and probably the same cemetery (*Album*, pl. xli, fig. 12) has the design painted in a deeper colour, the simplified fret being on the neck and a step-

---

[1] *Nordische Altertumskunde*, ii, 60; *Urgeschichte Europas*, 168.
[2] *Correspondenzblatt* (*Archiv für Anthropologie*), 1907, 165; see also *Zeitschrift für Ethnologie*, xl (1908), 772.

pattern on the body (fig. 3). In the same collection is a vase
from Mesnil-les-Hurlus, Marne, with a triple step-pattern painted
on the neck in red on a black ground; and a tall urn from
Bussy-le-Château in the same Department (fig. 4) is interesting

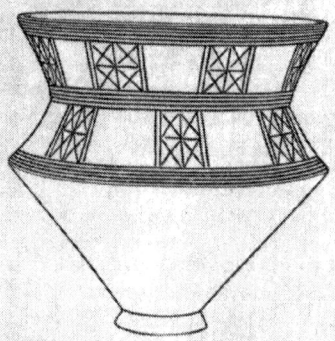

Fig. 2. BLACK URN WITH INCISED LINES RED, MARSON, MARNE. H. 6·8 IN.

Fig. 3. RED URN PAINTED, MARSON,   Fig. 4. URN WITH INCISED
MARNE. H. 4·5 IN.   ORNAMENT, BUSSY-LE-CHÂTEAU,
MARNE. H. 7·7 IN.

as showing the degeneration of the simplified fret into a double
horizontal scroll, obviously due to a careless rendering of the
angular pattern (*Album*, pl. xxxv, fig. 6). The panel separating
the scrolls recalls that of the Deal example, which with the
second fragment is evidently akin to a large urn from Mesnil-
les-Hurlus, Marne (*Album*, pl. xli, fig. 7). The decoration is
incised, and consists of a simplified fret on the neck and a double

row of chevrons running round the shoulder (fig. 5). The
latter design occurs on the second Deal fragment (fig. 6), the
outline of the completed urn being based on a plain specimen in

Fig. 5. URN WITH INCISED ORNAMENT, MESNIL-LES-HURLUS, MARNE.
H. 10·4 IN.

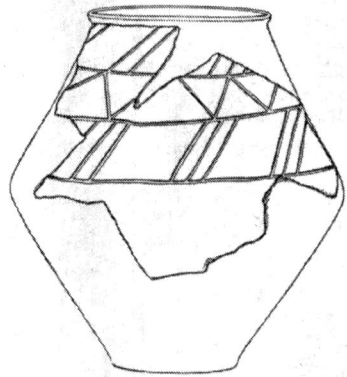

Fig. 6. FRAGMENT OF URN FOUND AT DEAL, WITH RESTORATION.
D. 13 IN.

the Morel Collection from Somme Bionne, Marne. The ware is
a reddish brown with minute white particles in the paste; and
the design consists of three incised zones on the shoulder containing groups of three sloping lines and plain chevrons. As

restored the height is about $10\frac{1}{2}$ in., that of the Somme Bionne urn being 8 in. in height and diameter. As the Marne cemetery is known to date from the fifth century B c. it is possible that the urn in question is of the same century; and if, as seems evident, the two Deal fragments are contemporary, that date is indicated on every ground, and a further addition made to the list of antiquities representing in Britain the earliest Iron Age or Hallstatt period of the Continent

A small fragment possibly of the same date as that from Deal, with a design still closer to the Greek fret, is in the possession of Mr. Montgomerie Bell, and was found in Oxford. It has long been regarded as unique in this country, but falls into its place beside the Deal specimens; and there now seems to be a clue to the foreign connexions of Kent in the dark centuries that succeeded the Bronze Age. Possibly there was commerce between the Remi and the Cantii, and if there was also a blood connexion, we may regard these fragments as signs of a Belgic invasion earlier than is generally recognized. That alluded to by Caesar may have brought us our first coinage in the second century B c , but there are now grounds for supposing that certain Belgae crossed into Kent two or three centuries earlier, and prepared the way for the culture of La Tène that was to have a splendid development on this side of the Channel."

L. A. LAWRENCE, Esq , F.S.A., exhibited a fragment of gold filigree from Selsey, on which Mr. REGINALD SMITH read the following notes :

"The shore between Selsey and Bognor has yielded an extraordinary amount of gold in minute fragments for many years past, but practically all date from the close of British independence under the local kings Tincommius, Verica, and Eppillus, all sons of Commius Specimens are in the British Museum and an account was published by Mr. Ernest Willett[1], whose father, the late Mr. Henry Willett, of Brighton, contributed largely to the collection and was formerly the owner of the fragment now exhibited. His son, Mr. Edgar Willett, gave it to Mr. Lawrence, with an assurance that it was found on the sandy shore from which so much of the same metal has been recovered.

It consists of a thin plate almost of butterfly form with the upper edges strengthened by an overlapping strip with filigree border in front, now much worn The triangular spaces in front are covered with a serpentine design in gold filigree, repeated but not pointing in the same direction. The serpentine coils are not continuous, the object being merely to fill the space

[1] *Numismatic Chronicle*, N S. xvii, 309 ; *Sussex Arch Collns* , xxiv, 72 and xxx, 1 , and Evans, *Coins of the Ancient Britons*, Supplement, 496

with an interlaced pattern, but the head is clear in both cases.
The interlacing is executed in triple filigree, the central line
being the stoutest of the three. A similar arrangement of roped
instead of beaded wires is seen on pieces in the Terslev hoard
near Praesto, Zealand, dated by coins about A.D. 950.[1]

The fragment probably belonged to a brooch or other piece of
personal jewellery, but it is not easy to place with any certainty.
Four-sided plates of filigree were commonly set in the ends of
penannular brooches (as the Tara brooch) dating from the best

FRAGMENT OF GOLD FILIGREE FROM SELSEY (⅔).

Irish period, which seems, from a comparison with the illuminated
manuscripts, to coincide with the eighth century ; and the present example shows a slight falling-off in design and workmanship. Some allowance must, however, be made on account of the
clumsiness of the medium when compared with contemporary
miniatures that attained such extraordinary perfection. Whatever its true purpose, this gold fragment must date from the
late Anglo-Saxon period, the design and method of execution
being equally characteristic. Though gold-work or any other
art-products of the time, apart from manuscripts, are rare in
England, the process of elimination justifies its attribution to
the first half of the ninth century. How it ever reached the
Sussex coast is a matter of conjecture, but it may be mentioned
that works of Irish art were then being pillaged and carried off
to Norway ; and some English treasure can hardly have escaped
a similar fate."

Thanks were ordered to be returned for these communications.

[1] K. F. Johansen, *Sölvskatten fra Terslev* (Copenhagen, 1913).

Thursday, 19th March, 1914.

The EARL OF CRAWFORD AND BALCARRES,
Vice-President, in the Chair.

The following gifts were announced, and thanks for the same ordered to be returned to the donors:

From Mrs. Arthur Cates :—
1. An account of Winfield Manor. By S. O. Addy and J. Croston. 4to. Derby, 1885.
2. Old and new Birmingham. By R. K. Dent. 8vo. Birmingham, 1880.
3. Two centuries of Soho. By Rev. J. H. Cardwell, etc. 8vo. London, 1898.
4. Old Glasgow: the place and the people. By Andrew Macgeorge. 3rd edit. 8vo. Glasgow, 1888.
5. Deerhurst, a parish of the Vale of Gloucester. By George Butterworth. 8vo. Tewkesbury, 1890.
6. A history of Tong, Shropshire, with notes on Boscobel. By George Griffiths. 2nd edit. 8vo. Newport, 1894.
7. The history of Torquay. By J. T. White. 8vo. Torquay, 1878.
8. Rambles round old Canterbury. By F. W. Cross and J. R. Hall. 8vo. London, 1884.

From George Hubbard, Esq., F.S.A.:—Plan of the site of the Globe Playhouse of Shakespeare.

The following were admitted Fellows:
> Jonathan Edward Hodgkin, Esq.
> Charles Harry St. John Hornby, Esq., B.A.

Charles ffoulkes, Esq. B.Litt., F.S.A., read a paper on a carved chest front at New College, Oxford, illustrating the Battle of Courtrai.

The chest is of Flemish workmanship of the early years of the fourteenth century. It is a particularly valuable record of the military equipment of the period, and is unique in that it contains the only known representation of the weapon used by the Flemish burghers, called by the chronicler Guiart the 'Godendag' or 'plançon à picot'. The heraldry displayed by the mounted men is somewhat difficult to elucidate, but the banners of the Trade Guilds are clearly shown and are of great interest as contemporary records. From these and other evidences the carving may be considered to be a graphic representation of the Battle of Courtrai in 1302, when the Flemish burghers, under Gui de Namur and Pierre Coninc, defeated the French under the Comte d'Artois with great slaughter. The arms of Pierre

Conine are shown on one of the banners and are found on no other records except on a seal in the archives of Bruges.

Mr. CLIFFORD SMITH hoped that the author would be able to pursue his studies in connexion with armorial chests and ivories. There was a famous chest at the Victoria and Albert Museum like that at York, but the subject was reversed, with the castle on the right hand. Chests in England were generally of uncertain origin, but most were probably Flemish, though Mr. Prior had suggested that the York example was the work of a local school of carving.

Mr. VALLANCE had seen the chest soon after it was acquired by New College and felt at the time that it had been shortened. The York example showed how it had been made up with upright standards at the ends. He congratulated the author on his clever elucidation of the heraldry.

The CHAIRMAN expressed a hope that a good photograph of the chest represented by the engraving would be obtained and submitted to the Society for an opinion. His own interest had been stimulated by the remark that Flemish antiquaries looked upon the New College chest as a forgery, and he would be glad to hear whether any evidence had been published to substantiate the charge. The uniformity of the figures of burghers in the second panel on the left was alien to the vivacity and spirit of the fourteenth century; and the parallel straight lines marking the waists recalled ivories of the eighth or ninth century in the Po valley. At the present day there were carpenter wood-carvers, to quote the author's term, but they did not exist about 1300. Every wood-carver was then an artist, and vice-versa; and the roughness of the style seemed to him to conflict with the evidence of authenticity. On the other hand, he thought the carver would not have been particular about the enemy's arms, and it would have been surprising to find the French heraldry correctly represented. Uniformity was again noticeable in the use of the left hand. Every figure moving towards the left was using his left hand. The possible cutting down of the panels was another point of interest, but the vertical sequence was proved by the correspondence of the feet and figures of the burghers carrying trade ensigns; and he did not think the top right-hand panel was imperfect at the end. It was a great achievement to establish the identity of the weapon called a Godendag.

Mr. FFOULKES wished, in replying, to exclude Pirenne from the Belgian antiquaries whose adverse opinion of the chest he had

criticized. As a body they had at once made up their minds on seeing the photograph that the carving was a forgery, and he could not understand such a prepossession.

Thanks were ordered to be returned for this communication, which will be printed in *Archaeologia*.

––––––––

Thursday, 26th March, 1914.

Sir CHARLES HERCULES READ, Knt., LL.D., President, in the Chair.

The following gifts were announced, and thanks for the same ordered to be returned to the donors:

From Harold Sands, Esq., F.S.A.:—
    1. A short history of the Royal Navy 1217–1815. By David Hannay. 2 vols. 8vo. London, 1898–1909.
    2. British castles. By C. H. Ashdown. 8vo. London, 1911.

From the Author:—Roman remains found at Barrington, Somerset. By H. St. George Gray. 8vo. n.p. n.d.

From the Author:—Three ballads illustrating the history of Holland. By C. H. Firth, F.S.A. 4to. Oxford, 1914.

Notice was given of the Anniversary Meeting for the election of President, Officers, and Council to be held on Thursday, April 23rd, St. George's Day, at 2 p.m.

ARTHUR BULLEID, Esq., F.S.A., read the following paper on Romano-British Potteries in Mid-Somerset:

"It should be clearly understood at the outset that the subject of my paper has no claim to be new archaeological matter, for the potteries have been known to antiquaries since the beginning of the nineteenth century. Owing to modern agricultural developments and peat-digging, an interesting and in some respects important collection of Roman antiquities is being gradually but surely swept away, and it was chiefly from the desire that there should be some detailed account of the sites before they are entirely lost that I undertook the examination of some mounds last autumn. The potteries are situated in the Brue district on the north side of the Polden range of hills, some eight miles WNW. of Glastonbury and four miles from the present coast-line. They extend for some three miles along the margin of what was at some time a swamp in the neighbourhood

of the Burtle sand beds, at a point where the peat begins to be
covered by beds of alluvial clay.   My attention was first drawn
to the pottery mounds by a short account of them written by the
late Mr. William Stradling in his little book entitled *A Description of the Priory of Chilton super Polden*, published in 1839.
The same account of the mounds with additional information was
incorporated in a paper on the Somerset Turbaries which appeared
in the first volume of the *Proc. Som. Arch. and Nat. Hist. Soc.*
in 1849.   Besides a short reference to the potteries by Professor
Haverfield in the *Victoria County History* taken from Stradling's
account, and a reference to them by Mr. John Morland in vol. xl
of the Somerset *Proceedings*, I am not aware of any other published notice.   In passing it may be noted that Mr. Stradling
was a friend of Sir Richard Colt Hoare and that the Priory about
which he writes had no connexion whatever with any religious
house, although built in the form of a church.   It was erected
by Stradling from architectural odds and ends collected from old
houses and probably church restorations in the neighbourhood,
and used by him as a museum.   The building was known locally
as Stradling's Folly.

Stradling's account of the potteries may be summarized as
follows: When a boy he was often taken to the Burtle villages
by a relative, who on the way pointed out to him a number of
mounds or barrows, as they were then considered by many. In the
year 1833 Stradling came to reside in the immediate neighbourhood of the mounds, and soon determined to make an examination
of some of them to find out their origin. He says the mounds are of
various sizes and composed of a mass of potsherds of black Roman
ware, many of the heaps containing several hundred loads of
fragments. He states his labours were soon rewarded, for at the
distance of a few yards from one of the mounds, at the depth of
18 in., a square platform of clay was found, around which were
several pieces of Roman ware mixed with rude brick, bearing marks
of straw. Upon making further search he adds that he was convinced that he was standing on what was once a Roman pottery,
and the bricks were for the purpose of keeping the rudely
formed pitchers, pipkins, vases, and a sort of patera, in position
during the process of burning. Stradling says the mounds were
very numerous, and concludes they were formed of the potsherds
of the different vessels broken whilst baking on the platforms of
clay which served for kilns. He states that the potteries were
sufficiently numerous to have supplied the country with the common black ware for a vast distance round, and adds, 'I found
afterwards on one of the kilns in the parish of Huntspill some
small pipkins which were perfect, until unfortunately cut through
by the peat scythe. Both peat and wood were used for fuel, as

Fig 2   FRAGMENTS OF WARE (1)

appears by pieces of charcoal. Scoriae of iron and pieces of coal were found in some places. Clay and sand were to be had at no great distance. After the process of burning all the perfect pieces were no doubt selected for package, and those with fire-flaws and other injuries were thrown by, and served to form those numerous and large heaps of potsherds' Stradling, unfortunately, does not give us an idea as to the exact number of mounds existing in his day, neither does he mention any details regarding kiln construction, nor the number of the mounds explored. The remaining information he gives about the potteries is with reference to a much-prized and nearly complete Roman jug which was found in one of the mounds (fig. 3, iii). This vessel is the only relic that has been preserved from his excavations, and is now in Taunton Museum.

My interest in the mounds dates from 1885, when, in conjunction with Mr. John Morland of Glastonbury, I saw one of the mounds (no. vi) opened (fig. 1). Subsequently a survey of the district was made by myself, also a plan showing the position of forty mounds. Last autumn I examined three mounds and went over the locality again, with the result that ten more sites were added to the list. Samples of pottery have been obtained from all the mounds with the exception of four, the origin of which should, therefore, for a time be considered doubtful. Although it was hoped to get more definite information regarding the kilns, the digging in this respect was a failure, inasmuch that only a clay floor was discovered similar to that described by Stradling. With reference to the shape and size of the mounds, the majority are roughly circular. two are crescent-shaped, and one or two are oval. The size ranges from 30 ft. to 100 ft. in diameter, and from 1 ft. to 5 ft. in height at the centre. The mounds consist of innumerable fragments of pottery, mingled with large quantities of briquetage, and fire ash. Looked at in section, a mound appears stratified, but upon tracing any given series of layers they are found to be restricted to a small area and do not run continuously through the whole diameter of the mound Samples of potsherds and briquetage from mounds vi, xxxviii, xxxix, xl are exhibited here to-night, and altogether about twelve distinct shapes are represented. These types of pottery for the most part are common to Roman sites. The shape found with greatest frequency is:

1. The olla, with over-bent rim, and rough band round the bulge of variable width (fig. 2, i, ix) The band is usually ornamented with latticed lines ; a considerable number of fragments of this shape are ornamented with a chevron design placed sideways with points to the right, and some with plain oblique lines (fig 2, ii, iii, v, vii). It will be observed that the shoulder and upper part of the body of some fragments have

been coated with a slip which with secondary firing has burnt
a different colour (fig. 3, i)   At Long Sutton, about thirteen
miles distant south-east from the potteries, two cremated burials
in vessels of this type were discovered in 1894 associated with
other Roman remains and coins dating from 250 to 300 A.D
In Devizes Museum is a cinerary urn of this form with band
of lattice-pattern $1\frac{3}{8}$ in wide, found at Westbury Ironworks,
Wilts., in 1881, containing burnt bones and a bronze coin of
Constantine I.   The mouth of the vessel was blocked by another
pot in such a way as to prevent the coin falling in after burial.
Mr. Thomas May tells me an example of the same type of vessel
from Hambledon also contained Constantine coins.

2   The straight-sided flanged bowl occurs next in frequency,
ornamented with overlapping curved lines (fig. 2, iv)   This is
a shape of common occurrence, and was found in large quantities
by General Pitt-Rivers in the Romano-British settlements of
Woodcuts and Rotherley, Wilts

3. The shallow dish with upright sides is also met with
frequently (fig 2, vi).

4 Vessels with wide overhanging rims of light red, or less
frequently of light grey, paste are common (fig. 3, vi).   The
ware is hard baked with light grey surfaces ornamented with
bands of a single waved line or a series of horizontal lines of a
darker shade of grey.

The following types occur less often

5. The vertically indented or fluted beaker of grey paste has
a peculiar form of ornament drawn with a blunt point, namely,
herring-bone with upright stem drawn through the middle of
the depression and ribs rising obliquely on either side (fig. 3, ii).
The ornament, I believe, is uncommon and recalls the painted
design on some of the New Forest ware

6. Narrow rimmed vessels or jugs with tapering necks, of light
grey paste, and dark grey surface tooled vertically and ornamented
with vertical lines (fig. 2, viii).

7. Vessels ornamented with waved lines, incised with a comb-
shaped tool, probably fragments of vessels similar to Stradling's
jug (fig 3, vii)

8. Fragments of vessels with close-set horizontal ribs or
grooves.

9. Fragments of red glazed ware   One of these is ornamented
with rouletted bands, and a second is part of a plain flanged
bowl.   These fragments are probably importations, whereas the
other types occurring more or less frequently may be regarded
as productions of the locality.

The briquetage consists of :

1. Thin rectangular tiles.

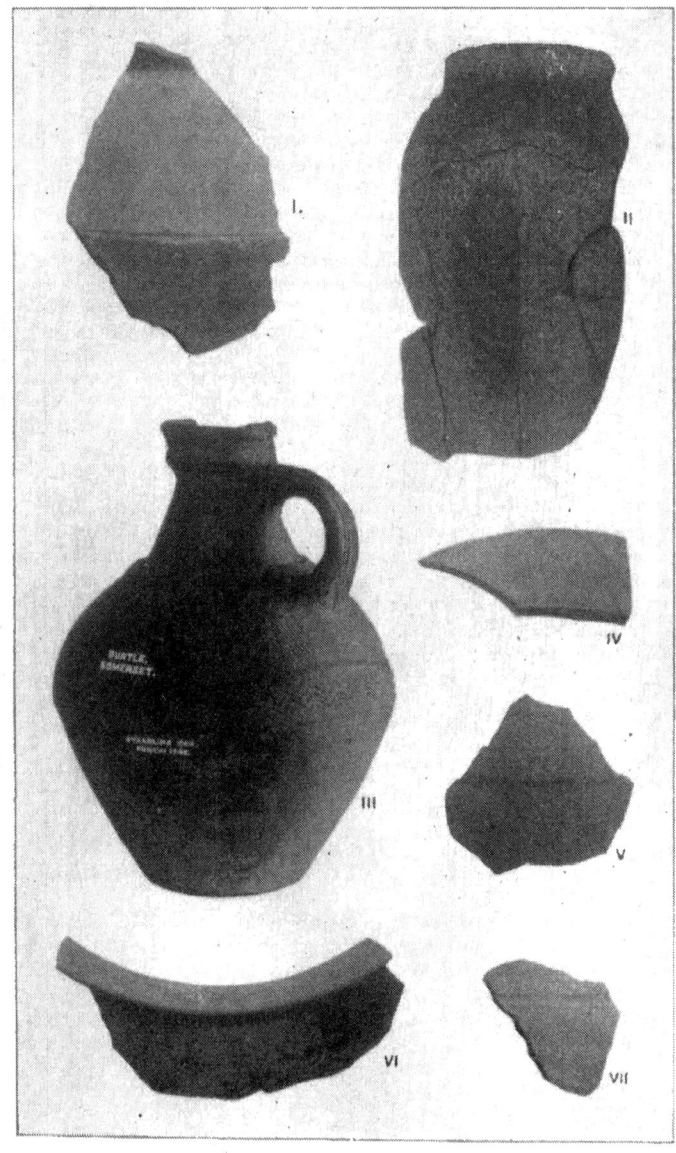

Fig. 3.   FRAGMENTS OF WARE (I) AND THE (I).

    2. Thick tiles or bricks.

    3. Bars.

    4. Fragments of moulded clay, probably parts of the kilns, or possibly seggars.

    5. Fragments of clay with finger imprints, luting.

    1. The thin tiles vary from $\frac{5}{8}$ in. to 1 in. in thickness, but as no specimen has been found complete the size is still a matter of uncertainty. It will be noticed that the upper surface is dotted over with shallow circular indentations, the under surface being marked with the impression of grass (fig 4, i-vii) The marginal surfaces in several instances are distinctly cut with a knife or some sharp tool. So far I have met with only one other instance of the circular indentation, and this occurs on the base of a vessel in the Pitt-Rivers collection.

    2. The thick tiles or bricks vary from $1\frac{1}{4}$ in. to $1\frac{7}{8}$ in. in thickness : the size is again uncertain. It will be noticed that several fragments have a rectangular notch cut at one corner (fig. 4, x, xi). The reason for this does not seem apparent, but if the notches of four bricks are fitted together, the space so formed corresponds roughly with the size of a bar.

    3. Bars occur in two forms, square and oblong in cross-section (fig. 5, i–vii, xii, xiii). The square bars vary from 1 in. to $1\frac{7}{8}$ in. in width and thickness, and about $13\frac{1}{2}$ in in length. The oblong vary from $1\frac{7}{8}$ in. to $2\frac{3}{8}$ in. in width, and $\frac{7}{8}$ in. to $1\frac{1}{2}$ in. in thickness ; the length is uncertain. In both varieties the upper end is pinched and flattened The lower end of the square bars is flat and in the oblong rounded. I have had no opportunity of comparing the Somerset bars with those from the Red-hills, Upchurch Marshes, or other pottery sites, so cannot say if there is anything in common between them. Neither have I been able to form an opinion as to the exact use and purpose of the two types which occur in about equal numbers in the mounds. The clay of which the bars are made is mixed with grass, badly baked and generally of a buff colour.

    4 Fragments of roughly moulded and badly baked clay are frequently met with (fig. 4, viii, ix), but it is a difficult matter to determine from the pieces whether they belong to the ovens or are parts of seggars, because no piece showing the angle-curve of the base of the latter has been found

    5. Fragments of luting occur in great variety with finger marks (fig. 5, viii–xi, xiv).

    Besides the above, pieces of slag, semi-fused potsherds and fragments of charcoal are found in varying quantities embedded in the fire ash.

    With reference to the process of firing, it is doubtful if more than the one method were employed—namely, the smother kiln. The fragments of buff and red-coloured pottery were probably due either to faulty firing or secondary burning after being thrown away on the heap.

There also arises the question of the date of the potteries, apart from the information to be gained from the pottery.

Stradling, writing in 1839, states 'that many years since a great many clay moulds for casting Roman coins were found in the parish of Chilton Polden; also upon August 26, 1835, almost adjoining one of the pottery mounds a large number of similar moulds was found a foot beneath the surface of the peat'. The moulds were made from coins dating apparently from 180 to 230 A. D. In the year 1838 'two small leather purses were discovered in a pottery mound, one containing the smallest kind of silver coins of the later Emperors', the other purse the smallest size bronze of the same era. Another hoard of coins was found early in the last century in a field belonging to the late Mr. Norris, adjoining some of the pottery mounds, but appears to be unrecorded by Stradling.

Mr. Norris's son has now forty-eight coins in his possession, forty-one of which are silver, and of these thirty-two belong to the fourth or very early fifth century These coins are presumably only part of the hoard found in a pot which was placed on a post and broken by workmen throwing stones at it. Some other finds of Roman date have been discovered in the neighbourhood of the Burtle potteries An upper quern-stone 18 in. in diameter was found in the field next to that containing the coins. On Aug 7th, 1868, a small hoard of coins, chiefly Constantine I and II, was found in the peat diggings about two miles distant from the potteries When digging for the foundations of a bridge near Highbridge, fragments of Roman pottery, moulds for casting coins, and pieces of small bricks such as were used for kiln-building were discovered in 1804.

I regret that the information regarding kiln-construction is so scanty, but as the excavations were only of a tentative character it is to be hoped that a site may be found disclosing the shape and size of the ovens at some future time. In the locality of the potteries about two-thirds of the fields have been disturbed by peat digging, so it is impossible to estimate the extent of the potteries, or the number of mounds that have been destroyed. The destruction was evidently taking place in the early part of last century, and it has been steadily going on since. During the last twelve years six sites have entirely disappeared. From the number of sites noted or still existing, it may be assumed that a very considerable industry was carried on in this out-of-the-way district of Somerset during the latter part of the Roman occupation of Britain, and that the trade was flourishing in 230 A. D. The locality is sparsely populated now, but at the

Fig. 4.   FRAGMENTS OF TILES AND BRIQUETAGE (⅓)

time the potteries were in full swing the number of inhabitants
was probably much greater. Some of the types of pottery are
of common occurrence wherever Roman remains exist, and it is
difficult, therefore, at this stage to say how far the Somerset ware
may have been distributed. It has been traced to North Somerset
in the neighbourhood of Bath. Mr. Thomas May has examined
some fragments and says the paste is not familiar; that being
the case, it should be possible to identify the ware in other districts. A vessel found at Westbury is a duplicate of Stradling's
jug, and it may at least be conjectured that the wares passed
beyond the confines of the present county into Wilts. It must
also be borne in mind that the potteries were near a navigable
river, and some of the ware may have been distributed by boat
to places more remote."

Mr. WILMER remarked that the Red-hills of Essex had been
referred to in the paper as pottery sites, and he only wished that
anything so definite could be said about them. They were
earlier than the Somerset site, the bulk of the pottery being Late-
Celtic, among which only one piece of Samian ware had been
found. He had been advised to concentrate his attention on
the Red-hills pottery, but experience in India prompted him to
take special note of the ' wasters ' that accompanied potsherds on
the sites of potteries. There were no wasters in the Red-hills,
and domestic pieces were so rare that the relics must have been
the utensils of some other industry. Riveted pottery pointed in
the same direction, as it would not have been worth while to
mend pottery where it was made. The cut clay was not the
same as the briquetage, and there was no clay of the sort in the
Red-hills. Considerable weight must be allowed to Mr. Reginald
Smith's theory that they were the sites of salt-works, in view
of the recent discoveries at La Seille, near Nancy. Another interesting feature was the porosity of the briquetage, which on
the theory just mentioned was designed to assist the efflorescence
of the salt. The same porosity was noticed in the Somerset
specimens, and might have been deliberate or accidental. Straw
was mixed with the clay in India to make bricks more weather-
proof, the increased porosity assisting in the drying process.
Similarly, sawdust was mixed with fire-clay to make kiln-supports
for enamels   The Somerset clay-products were inferior to those
of the Red-hills, but there was a general similarity; and in
spite of the difference in date, he thought both were the sites of
an industry requiring furnaces, fire-bars, and luting.

Mr. BUSHE-Fox thought the absence of 'wasters' (pieces
warped or stuck together in firing) showed that the remains did

not belong to pottery kilns in any form Some of the sherds had been re-fired, but that might easily occur if they were collected and embedded in the sides and roofs of ovens. The pottery told its own story and was not earlier than 200 A.D., much of it belonging to the fourth century. The wares were common and found in most places, but he was not familiar with two of the designs—the chevron and the fluted bars with leaf pattern.

The PRESIDENT agreed with what had been said with regard to the similarity of the Somerset and Essex sites, and thought Mr. Smith's suggested explanation of the Red-hills of special interest in the present circumstances. There seemed to have been on the western site two industries that might or might not have been contemporary, but he saw no reason why the pottery should not be of the same date as the briquetage. In a remote and unattractive district such as the Somerset marshland, primitive industries, like salt-making by the evaporation of sea-water, might have lingered on when elsewhere new processes had been introduced by the Romans. He agreed with Mr. Bushe-Fox's dating and felt convinced that the mounds had nothing to do with the manufacture of pottery. The absence of 'wasters', i. e. distorted or damaged pieces that were thrown aside as useless, seemed conclusive on that point To the present day the shardruck or waste-heap was a prominent feature of every pottery-works, adjoining the kiln, and sherds broken but not warped in firing were in themselves no evidence of a factory on the spot. Though something had already been published about the finds, enough had been learnt in the interval of eighty years to make the exhibition most welcome to the Society.

W. L HILDBURGH, Esq., M.A, Ph.D, exhibited a collection of Germanic Wafering-Irons of the sixteenth century, on which he read the following notes

" The irons which I am exhibiting were used for making very thin crisp cakes Such cakes, which are still made in many parts of Europe, usually bear some design upon their surfaces, partly because the hollows in the metal plates tend to retain the thin batter which might otherwise be driven away completely, in areas, from the space between the plates, partly because of the facility with which the batter used takes a sharp impression. In the irons used for making this kind of cake the major portions of the surface of the plates may be brought into actual contact when the instrument is empty, while the design sunk within one plate bears no definite relation to that within the other. The plates are hinged together, and each is provided with a long

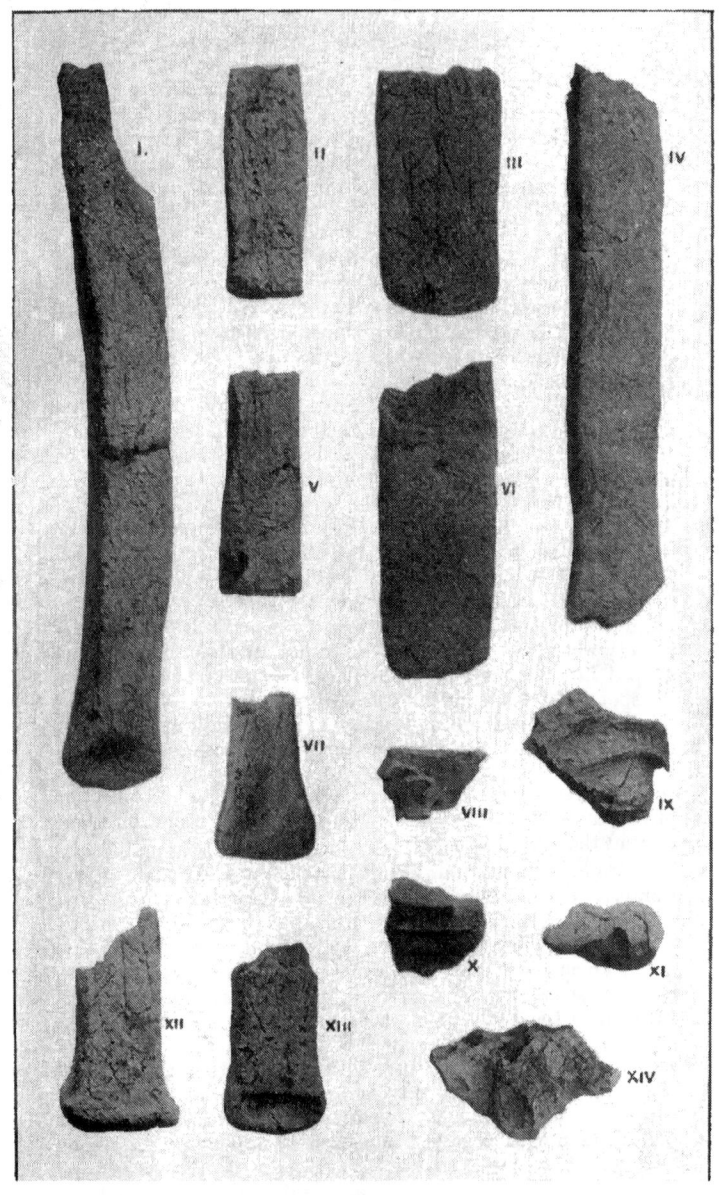

handle so that pressure may be brought to bear upon the batter. Irons of a similar kind have been used for many centuries for making holy wafers; irons of a different kind, in which projections from one plate fit into recesses in the other, and in which there is a small space between the two plates when the irons are closed, are used for making thin cakes of a related but somewhat different sort.

All the irons of the present series have been made, I think, for private use, and probably for use in the household, although the designs of some of them suggest that they may have been used for making wafers to be sold either at shops or, as is still commonly done with similar cakes on the Continent, at fairs. None of them is for ecclesiastical use, and none of them seems to have been made especially for the use of religious communities or guilds.

The designs of the irons of the present series, except for one deficiency, are fairly representative of those generally used. They consist of:—(a) The arms of private families, presumably those of the owners, together with crests, &c., some of these arms being genuinely heraldic, others suggesting that they have been adapted from merchants' marks. (b) The arms of great reigning families, employed seemingly as ornamental designs, the crudity of the workmanship which dates from a period when the technical excellence of objects intended for use by the wealthier classes was very high, and the occasional appearance of errors in the heraldic drawings, indicating that the irons upon which such arms occur were not intended for use by the families by whom the arms were borne. (c) Representations of sacred subjects, such as the Crucifixion, or the Martyrdom of St. Sebastian. (d) Purely fanciful or conventional designs. (e) Inscriptions, such as those referring to the family of the owner, or to the family of the ruler, or to the subject of the pictorial design, or to piety, or to eating or drinking, and dates. To these we should add (f) Representations of secular subjects, such as hunting scenes, of which there is no example in the present series.

The hollows within the plates, by which the designs are produced, may be regarded as being broadly of three kinds : (1) Lines, all of approximately uniform depth and width, which are used to form conventional designs, the outlines of objects or of borders, inscriptions, etc. Designs formed of lines of this kind are the simplest to produce, and, since they may be made by any one with sufficient skill and strength to use a cutting-tool and a hammer, vary from crude markings of no artistic value up to designs of a flowing and graceful character. The outlines formed by such lines may be filled in by finely scratched lines indicating solid surfaces, heraldic tincturings, etc. (2) Hollows individually of varying shape, area, and depth, whereby designs in varying relief are produced; these hollows may be made either by actually cutting the metal away, by driving it aside by means of suitable tools, or by cutting away a part and then finishing the hollows with blunt-ended tools. Since work of this kind can be produced only by a skilled workman, we generally find it good of its period. (3) Hollows produced by stamps. The stamps used are generally of small size, and each represents an object or a part of an object in the complete design which the cake is to bear; they may be used to represent animals, leaves, flowers, fruits, vases, portions of garlands, etc., or even merely square or circular dots of different sizes. They are generally in low relief, although sometimes the relief is quite high. The designs produced by the stamps may be regular, and divisible into a series of similar sections executed each with the same set of stamps used in the same order, or they may be irregular and executed by means of a series of stamps employed, according to the workman's fancy of the moment, to produce, for example, a hunting scene. In general the stamps employed for work of this kind are small as compared with the surfaces to be covered, so that when the workman had a considerable number of stamps at his disposal, as seems frequently to have been the case, he had opportunities for producing many delightful designs.

The decoration of the plates of a pair of irons may be by means of two or by all three of the types of hollows described. For example, a plate whose principal ornamentation consists of stampings or of a large intaglio figure may have a series of concentric lines, as a border, at some distance from the centre, or may bear an inscription; or a plate with stamped ornamentation and engraved lines as a border may have an intaglio heraldic or other device at the centre. The technical quality of some of the irons, and especially of some of the stamped or chased ones, is very high; not only is there shown a perfect sureness of hand and of eye, but the work seems sometimes to suggest by its character that the workman has tried, like his brother smiths in other departments, to show his mastery of his material by creating difficulties to be overcome.

The irons of the present series are all of Germanic origin, coming from Austria, Bavaria, and Switzerland, and illustrate all the types of workmanship to which I have referred. They show, however, the same tendency, exhibited by collections in those countries, towards engraved or chased decoration as distinguished from stamped. In the Historical Museum at Basel is the earliest iron for non-ecclesiastical use that I have noted; it is there ascribed to the fourteenth century, and it has each plate engraved with a central circle containing a figure and

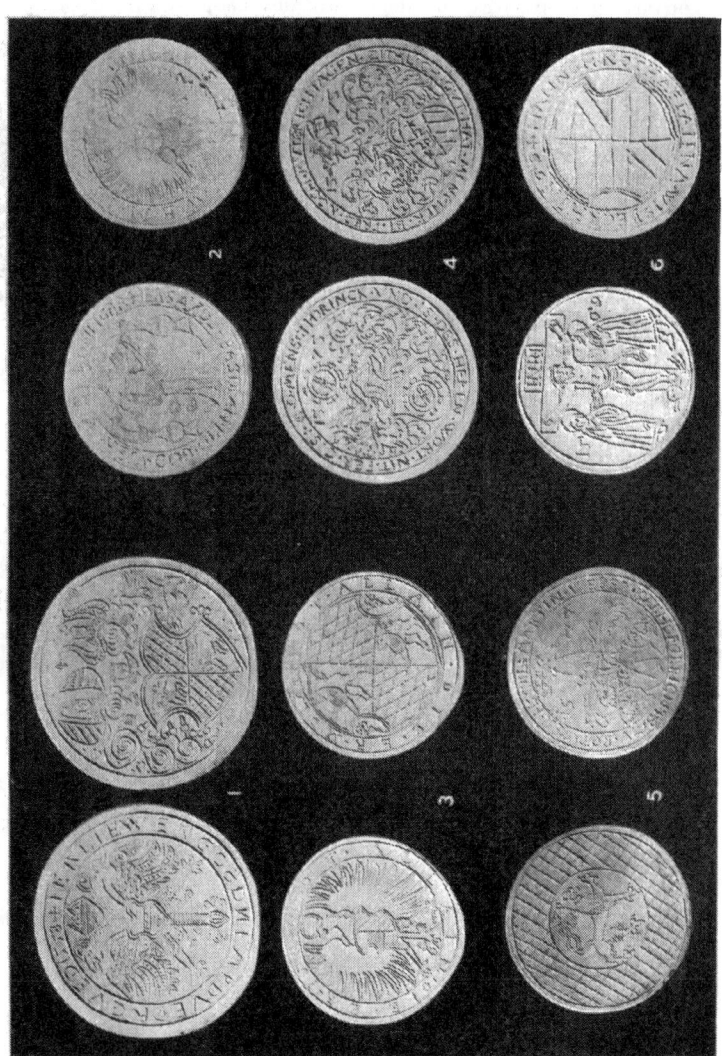

surrounded by a cross-hatched pattern, with an inscription round the edge of the plate.

In the latter half of the fifteenth century wafering-irons with stamped plates were made in Italy, dated specimens of which still exist, while there are others which show by their character that they, or at least the stamps for making them, are of the same period. Wafering-irons of this kind were made in Italy, as witnessed by the gradual changes in design, down to about the end of the sixteenth century—that is, through the period to which these Germanic irons belong—and perhaps later ; fifteenth or sixteenth century stamps may have been used at a later period, giving a fictitious character to plates made by their aid. During the period (to be conservative) of from about 1475 to 1600 almost all Italian wafering-irons—and large numbers must have been produced at that time—seem to have been stamped ; during the Baroque period irons engraved with purely linear designs expressive of the Baroque taste came into use.

But during the sixteenth century, just across the Alps, the ornamentation of the commonly used wafering-irons seems comparatively seldom to have been produced by stamping. In the collections of the National Museum at Munich, the Museum at Salzburg, the National Museum at Zurich, the Basel Historical Museum, and the various other art-historical or folk-museums in Germany, Austria, or Switzerland, the wafering-irons of the sixteenth century have mostly been produced by engraving or chasing. The Germanic stamped irons are characterized in general by less beauty of design than the Italian, and by, I believe, little or no adherence to the classical forms favoured in Italy. In boldness of execution, however, some of the Germanic stamped irons transcend, I think, even the best of the Italian that I have seen, while others excel in the delicacy of their treatment.

For assistance in working out the designs and the heraldry of some of the irons exhibited. I am indebted to Mr. Charles Bailey and Mr. A. Van de Put, of the Victoria and Albert Museum.

EXPLANATION OF THE PLATES.

Fig. 1. The plates of this pair of irons are rather large, being 7 in. in diameter. The decoration of both plates is entirely in the form of linear engraving, following the outlines of the objects represented, and is rather crude in character. On one plate are a double-headed eagle, with the arms of Austria, and an inscription, which seems to consist of poor German badly spelled, including the date 1558. The inscription reads .

+IERLIEWENGOƧDИEMPDVEDRGVED 1558.

I have not been able to translate this inscription, which may be an anagram ; it seems to me possibly to have some reference to an injunction to ' love God's name '.

On the other plate are the arms of the Palatinate and Bavaria quarterly, with crests, surrounded by various ornaments including a bird with a worm, a stag, and scrollwork with leaves and acorns.

Fig. 2. The plates of this pair are entirely engraved. Diameter, 6 in. On one plate is a representation of the Martyrdom of St. Sebastian and the German invocation, HEILIGER · HER · SAN SEBASDIAN · PID · GOD · VIER · VNS', ' Holy Lord St. Sebastian, pray God for us '. On the other plate is a double-headed eagle with the arms of Austria and Burgundy (ancient) and an inscription and date : + VER · THRAVSCHAV · WEM · 1559. The inscription is a rendering of a well-known German proverb, ' If you trust, look well in whom '.

Fig. 3. The plates of this pair (diameter, 5·8 in.) are entirely engraved ; the outlines are coarsely made, while parts, such as the wings of the eagle and the tincturings, are finely scratched. On one plate are a single-headed eagle with the arms of Austria and Burgundy (ancient), and a German inscription and date : GOT · ALLAIN · DIE · ER · 1564, ' To God alone the honour, 1564 '. On the second plate are the arms of the Palatinate quartering Bavaria, and the same inscription with the date written MDLX4'.

Fig. 4. The plates of this pair (diameter, 6·3 in.) are entirely engraved, the engraving, however, being more skilfully done than on any of the irons examined up to the present. On one plate are arms (a mill-wheel ; crest, a mill-wheel), the date 1575, and a rhymed German inscription : O · MENSCH · DRINCK · VND · IS · DES · HEREN · WORT · NIT · FER · GIS, ' O, Man, eat and drink, (but) forget not the Lord's Word '. On the other plate are arms, the date 1575, and a rhymed German inscription, RICHTAGEN · ZITHLICH · GUT · HAT · MENCHER · BI · FRED · NOCH · MUT, which seems to mean ' In rich days or temporary good times many a one has besides pleasure still courage '.

I have not obtained the name of the family for which this pair of irons was made ; the mill-wheel was borne by many families, and Mr. Van de Put has not found the arms which appear on the second plate.

Fig. 5. The decoration of the plates of this pair (diameter 5·7 in.) has been produced by engraving. One plate bears arms, a crest, the date 1577, and the inscription : MARTIN · WEBER · KAI · HOFGERICHTS : ZU · ROTWEIL · FISCAL, ' Martin Weber, Imperial Superior Court of Justice at Rotweil,

GERMANIC WAFERING-IRONS

Attorney-general' (or 'of the exchequer'). The arms are those of Weber, *silver, a deer's head, gules.* A Martin Weber was steward of the Landgraf of Klettgau in *c.* 1600.[1] The other plate bears a two-tailed lion surrounded by a coarse network of lines.

Fig. 6. The plates of this pair (diameter 4·2 in.) are entirely engraved, the outlines being in coarse cutting, the filling of the surfaces of the figures and the tincturing of the arms being in fine hatching. On one plate is Christ upon the Cross, between the Virgin Mary and St. John, with the date 1569. The other plate bears the arms of Nothaft, of Bavaria, quartering another coat, perhaps those of his wife, and an inscription · +HANNS·H·NOTHAFT·ANNA·WISPECKHIN 69. These irons were probably made for the purely personal use of a family; the arms and inscription suggest that perhaps they were a wedding-gift, or part of the gear brought by the bride at marriage. The plates are the smallest of the present series.

Fig. 7. The plates of this pair of irons (diameter 7 in.) are engraved somewhat crudely. One plate bears the arms, quarterly, of Bohemia, Hungary, Castile, and Leon (the fleur-de-lys is an heraldic inadvertence), and Austria impaling Arragon, the date '59', and an inscription: +FERDND·DG·ROM·VNG·BOE· DA·G REX, relating to Ferdinand I, King, by the Grace of God, of Rome, Hungary, Bohemia, Dacia, Germania. On the other plate is a single-headed eagle, with the arms of Austria, and a dated inscription · GOT·ALLAINDIE·ERR·1559.

Fig. 8. In this pair of irons (diameter of plates, 7 in.) we come to intaglio work which we may call chased; that is, the designs have been hammered into the iron, deeply and in various ways, by the aid of tools, possibly after cutting away some of the metal, the larger areas have not been engraved, as seals are engraved, by scooping away the material. On one plate is a figure of the Virgin Mary, with the Infant Jesus, about to be crowned by two angels; she stands upon a crescent moon, and has a background of rays; above her are the letters DER, being the last letters of the last word of the inscription. Round the edge of the plate runs the inscription: +OIVNKFRAW· MUETER·MARIA·BIT·GOT DEINGELIEBTEN SVN· IHESVM·CHRISTVM·FVR·VNS·ARM·SVN, 'O, Virgin Mother Mary, Pray God Thy Beloved Son Jesus Christ for us Poor Sinners'. On the other plate are arms, the date 1538, and the inscription: IOHAN·PIETENPERGER·LICEN·CAMER-MAISTER·ZV·SALZB·KIRCHHERR·ZV·LAVFFEN·VND· WAGING, 'Johan Pietenperger, Licentiate, Chamberlain at

[1] Siebmacher, *Burgerliches Wappenbuch*, iii, 17.

Salzburg, Patron of the Churches (? or Vicar) at Lauffen and Waging'.

Fig. 9. The plates of this pair of irons (diameter 6 in.) have been made in similar manner to those of Fig. 8, except that a few simple stamps have been used for the borders. The designs upon both plates consist of personal arms which I have not identified. This pair, which is undated, was probably made in the second half of the sixteenth century.

Fig. 10. We pass here to irons whose plates have been decorated principally by the aid of stamps. In the present pair of plates (diameter 4·9 in.) the stampings indicate the employment of only a few stamps, which were rather coarsely and simply made. These stamps appear to have been: a bird, a floral object, a crescent-shaped piece, and a straight piece. The two plates are similar to each other; they are undated, but belong perhaps to the late sixteenth century.

Fig. 11. In this pair of plates (diameter 4·5 in.) we find the principal method of decoration by stampings supplemented by a certain amount of engraving or chasing. The arms upon one of the plates, although similar to those of several other families, are perhaps those of Ehrenfels, of Switzerland, this being indicated by the final letter of the initials M : V : D : E : . The foliage and the border on this plate are stamped. On the other plate the whole of the decoration has been produced by means of small stamps, of whose marks I have found at least sixteen varieties; these stamps included several kinds of flowers and of leaves, a finial, an acorn, an urn, and some purely conventional designs. The plates appear to date from the late sixteenth, or the early seventeenth century.

Fig. 12. The plates of this pair of irons (diameter 6·4 in.) are remarkable for the technical excellence of their workmanship; practically the whole of their decoration has been produced by the employment of a comparatively few stamps used with great accuracy and, in some parts, penetrating to an unusual depth. At the centre of one of the plates are two shields, with the date 1574 and a five-petalled flower; round these is a design of acorns, each within a square of its own, ending in a border of small five-petalled flowers. The stamps employed appear to have been merely those for the acorns, a small ball, the two sizes of flowers, and, perhaps, a long-edged chisel for stamping a straight line. Where a portion only of an acorn has been impressed, the impression is not so deep as where the whole acorn is shown. The second plate is stamped deeply with a series of small five-petalled flowers (like those on the first plate), each within a square of its own, with a border of star-like five-petalled flowers.

Fig. 13. The decoration of the plates of this pair of irons

To face page 150

GERMANIC WAFERING-IRONS

(diameter 5·5 in.) has been produced principally by the use
of stamps. Here, however, the stamps have been impressed to
only a slight depth, and, in the feathers of the eagle especially,
sometimes with remarkable delicacy. The principal object
represented upon one plate is an eagle, portions of which are
engraved, portions stamped. Surrounding this eagle are bands
of ornament, produced by stamps, formed by lines of tassel-like
objects, a cord, balls, a cord, leaping hares, alternating with small
five-petalled flowers, a cord, balls, a cord, and tassel-like objects.
I think that only five figured stamps have been used for this plate,
those for the small feathers of the eagle, the tassel-like objects,
the balls, the leaping hares, and the flowers. On the second
plate the central design is a diapered one consisting of cords
forming a network each of whose meshes holds a cruciform
object; surrounding this are bands of ornament. I think that here
also five stamps have been used, two of them those employed
upon the first plate, while the cruciform object and two objects
of the borders are peculiar to this plate. The plates are undated,
but I think that we need not hesitate to ascribe them to a crafts-
man of the sixteenth century, working probably about the
third quarter. They are thoroughly Germanic in design and
treatment, yet I think that one may find in them an indefinable
Italian influence, connecting them with the Italian irons of the
same period and earlier, which seems to be absent in the other
irons of the present series, whether engraved, chased, or stamped."

The PRESIDENT referred to previous exhibitions of similar
specimens, though possibly not of German origin. He preferred
the English name wafering-irons to the French gauffering. It
was no doubt surprising to many present to see so many examples
in a private collection, but Dr. Hildburgh was an enthusiastic
collector of many other out-of-the-way things, and would perhaps
allow the Society on future occasions to become acquainted with
other groups of no less interest to antiquaries.

W. DE C. PRIDEAUX, Esq., F.S.A., exhibited a cast of the font
at Melbury Bubb, Dorset. The font appears to have originally
formed part of a cross shaft and to have been adapted as a font
later, but on this there is considerable difference of opinion.[1] It
may be classed with the fonts at Dolton, Devon and Wilne,
Derbyshire, and is like the cross shaft at Wolverhampton.[2]
The font is decorated with scenes from the Bestiaries.

[1] Bond, *Fonts and Font Covers*, 106, 138 ; Romilly Allen, *Early Christian
Symbolism*, 376.
[2] *Proceedings*, xxv, 158.

Mr. REGINALD SMITH thought the carving deserved fuller treatment than the late Mr. Romilly Allen had given it, but the subject involved a close study of the medieval bestiaries, which were not too familiar. The interlacing in the field was often a prolongation of the tail or limbs of an animal (as on a fragment in the wall of Wroxeter Church), not a serpent complete in itself; and the date of the original work was in all probability the first half of the eleventh century.

Mr. DRUCE had gone to Melbury Bubb in search of an alleged crocodile on the font, and had taken the photographs reproduced on the screen. The hostility of the stag and dragon was one of the subjects represented, and went back as far as Pliny. A stag biting a serpent was to be seen in Durham Castle, and the style of the animals on the font reminded him of the Scotch crosses. He shared the view that the font had once formed part of a cross shaft, and would like to know something more of its history.

ALABASTER FIGURE OF ST. JOHN BAPTIST ($\frac{1}{4}$).

Sir GEORGE SITWELL, F.S.A., exhibited an alabaster effigy of St. John Baptist which he had recently acquired in Italy. The figure is of English work, and represents St. John wearing a chasuble-like cloak, below which can be seen the coat of hair. In his right hand he holds a book on which is seated the lamb but without the staff and pennon. The figure, which has been cut off below the knees, now measures $11\frac{1}{4}$ in. in height. No traces of colour remain.

Canon BEANLANDS, F.S.A., exhibited an Elizabethan Com-

COPPER-GILT ELIZABETHAN COMMUNION CUP : ABOUT ⅔

munion Cup of copper-gilt. The cup is of a type common between the years 1575 and 1620, but beyond the material of which
it is made, it is peculiar owing to the excessive trumpet shape of
the lip, the curious flattened moulding above the stem, and the
little dog-tooth punching of the base moulding.

With regard to the metal of which the cup is made, chalices
of metal other than gold and silver were forbidden before the
Reformation ; and after the Reformation in England only two
cases can be found suggesting the permissive use of 'some other
pure metal'. One of these instances is Bancroft's Canterbury
Visitation of 1605, and the other is as late as 1638, when perhaps pewter was becoming recognized as a suitable material for
sacramental vessels in poor parishes.

The cup shows signs of having been withdrawn from use at an
early period, and presumably was superseded by a silver chalice
after a few years of use.

The PRESIDENT pointed out the difference between the specimen exhibited and silver com-
munion-cups of the same period,
about 1570–1580: it was more
slender and elegant, but had
features that might be found on
other cups of the same date. It
had had a reversible paten as a
cover. Metal chalices not of gold
or silver were then very unusual,
but many of that date and earlier
had the foot of base metal and
the bowl of silver.

W. PAGE, Esq., F.S.A., exhibited a fragment of a bone pax
of the fourteenth or fifteenth century, representing the Crucifixion,
sent to him by Mr. F. H. Cheetham.
It was found under the floor of the
vestry of the Church of St. Michael

PORTION OF A BONE PAX (⅓).

on Wyre, North Lancashire, and is now in the possession of
Mr. Hugh Phipps Hornby of that place, who keeps it in his
private museum.

The PRESIDENT remarked that the pax was of interest to the
student of ivory-carvings as belonging to a class which had by
some been regarded as false.[1] Among characteristics of this

[1] See British Museum *Catalogue of Ivory Carvings*, Introduction,
p. xlvii.

group regarded as particularly suspicious, were the hatched backgrounds, and the appearance of the sun and moon as radiate semicircles at the sides of the panels. Both these features were found in the present example; and if the conditions of its discovery showed that it was in the place where it was found before the beginning of the nineteenth century, that might be regarded as so much evidence in favour of the genuineness of the whole group.

Thanks were ordered to be returned for these communications and exhibitions.

Thursday, 2nd April, 1914.

Sir CHARLES HERCULES READ, Knt., LL.D., President, in the Chair.

The following gifts were announced, and thanks for the same ordered to be returned to the donors:

From the Corporation of the City of London:—Calendar of coroners' rolls of the City of London, 1300–1378. Edited by R. R. Sharpe. 8vo. London, 1913.

From Harold Sands, Esq., F.S.A.:—
1. Medals and decorations of the British army and navy. By J. H. Mayo. 2 vols. 8vo. Westminster, 1897.
2. Greater London. By Edward Walford. 2 vols. 4to. London. n.d.

Arthur William Gould, Esq., was admitted a Fellow.

Notice was again given of the Anniversary Meeting to be held on Thursday, April 23rd, St. George's Day, at 2 p.m., and lists were read of the Fellows proposed as President, Council, and Officers for the ensuing year.

The Report of the Auditors of the Society's accounts for 1913 was read (pp. 156–61), and thanks were voted to the Auditors for their trouble and to the Treasurer for his good and faithful services.

REGINALD A. SMITH, Esq., F.S.A., and HENRY DEWEY, Esq., F.G.S., read a paper on the High Terrace of the Thames; being the report on Excavations at Greenhithe and Crayford made in 1913 on behalf of the British Museum and H.M. Geological Survey.

Since the last Report was presented in April, 1913,[1] work on the 100-ft. terrace of the lower Thames has been continued on eighteen days under the same conditions. A few sections remained to be verified at Swanscombe, and finds in an adjoining pit show the St. Acheul horizon, which is absent or practically barren at Barnfield.

At Ingress Vale, about a quarter of a mile north-west of that site and on the other side of a small valley, is the deposit known for several years as the Greenhithe Shell-bed, and noted for well-preserved specimens of *Neritina grateloupiana* and a fauna with Pliocene affinities. Eight days' work on this site produced not a single flint implement, but about 500 good flakes exactly resembling those of the Lower Gravel at Barnfield and at exactly the same height. The conclusion arrived at is that the two beds are contemporary and were once continuous, forming the earliest known deposit of the 100 ft. terrace. The industry may be classed as pre-Chelles and previous to a glaciation ; and the white implements of St. Acheul type recovered years ago from the Shell-bed may belong to a later deposit that has superficially disturbed the earlier.

A week was also spent at Wansunt gravel-pit, south of Crayford Station and at the north end of Dartford Heath, between the valleys of the Cray and Darenth. A recent paper by Messrs. Leach and Chandler on finds in the loams capping the gravel here [2] raised the question of a transverse channel on the brow of the hill (about 100 ft. o.d.), unworn flint implements found at the base of the clay having presumably been dropped there by people living on the bank. The occurrence of late Drift implements was confirmed, but the authors were disposed to regard the deposits overlying the gravel as the upper members of the terrace, and to attribute their presence to the action of the main river.

Mr. W. M. NEWTON described his exhibit, which comprised some remarkably large pointed palaeoliths from a Dartford pit that he had been working for some years solely for purposes of research. One was found 16 ft. in the gravel and 2 ft. above the chalk. His shell-bed specimens had been obtained from an employé of the Cement Company who passed the site every morning and made inquiries regularly when excavation was going on there. In his own mind there was no doubt as to the authenticity of the implements. A digger in the Wansunt pit had procured him some specimens there, but the gravel was evidently barren, as he had had a man working there for five years without success.

[1] *Archaeologia*, lxiv, 177.
[2] *Proc. Geol. Assoc.*, xxiii, 102.

INCOME AND EXPENDITURE ACCOUNT

INCOME.

	£ s. d.	£ s. d.
Subscriptions	1935 3 0	
„ unpaid (7 Fellows) . . .	22 1 0	
		1957 4 0
Admissions	273 0 0	
Less ½ to Research Fund . . .	54 12 0	
		218 8 0
Dividends	843 10 4	
„ from Court of Chancery . . .	122 6 1	
		965 16 5
Sale of Publications :		
General	198 19 6	
Catalogue of Alabaster Exhibition . .	44 18 9	
		243 18 3
Sundry Receipts :		
Income-tax repaid	79 6 11	
Interest on deposit	32 9 6	
Anniversary dinner receipts . .	26 5 0	
Wroxeter and Old Sarum Funds . .	22 0 0	
Sundries	32 9 0	
		192 10 5

£3577 17 1

FOR THE YEAR ENDING 31st DECEMBER, 1913.

EXPENDITURE.

	£ s. d.	£ s. d.
Publications :		
General	1116 10 3	
Catalogue of Alabaster Exhibition	117 16 0	
		1234 6 3
Library :		
Books	127 13 6	
Binding	92 0 11	
Subject catalogue	98 18 7	
		318 13 0
Subscriptions to Societies		50 10 6
Franks Scholarship		54 0 0
Salaries, Wages, Allowances, Pension :		
Secretary	50 0 0	
„ assistant	250 0 0	
Clerk and Librarian	250 0 0	
„ allowances	20 10 0	
Porter	141 0 0	
„ allowances	19 18 0	
Wages	149 2 0	
Pension, W. H. St. John Hope	250 0 0	
Income-tax and insurances on above	30 12 9	
		1161 2 9
Repairs :		
General	108 8 10	
Electric light alterations	77 7 0	
		185 15 10
House Expenditure :		
Insurance	26 4 0	
Lighting	50 6 4	
Fuel	22 4 0	
Tea at Meetings	20 19 2	
Cleaning	75 4 2	
Clock winding	2 2 0	
		196 19 8
Official Expenditure :		
Printing	132 15 9	
Postage	17 0 11	
Stationery	43 4 9	
Telephone	9 0 0	
		202 1 5
Sundry Payments :		
Legacy duty and costs	16 10 0	
Auditors	24 3 0	
Anniversary dinner	35 2 0	
Various subscriptions	14 3 0	
Inventory of furniture	13 6 0	
Wroxeter and Old Sarum	22 0 0	
Sundries	44 12 5	
		169 16 5
Balance, carried to Balance Sheet		4 11 3
		£3577 17 1

BALANCE SHEET,

LIABILITIES.

	£ s. d.	£ s. d.
Sundry Creditors		1116 3 4
Owen Fund		39 7 5
Balance, 31st December, 1912 . .	30899 8 0	
Less creditor omitted 1912 . 113 3 3		
Less two Fellows amoved . 5 5 0	118 8 3	
	30780 19 9	
Balance from Income and Expenditure Account	4 11 3	
		30785 11 0

£31941 1 9

31st DECEMBER, 1913.

ASSETS.

Investments—General :

	£	s.	d.	£	s.	d.
£10583 19s. 7d. Metropolitan 3 per cent.[1]	11060	5	2			
£1010 1s. Metropolitan Water Board 3 per cent. " B " Stock[2]	1000	0	0			
Ditto—Stevenson bequest :						
£2128 9s. 6d. Bank Stock[1] . . .	7162	6	4			
£2725 Great Northern 4 per cent. Perpetual Preference Stock[1]	3692	7	6			
£2757 London and North Western 4 per cent. Guaranteed[1]	3763	6	1			
£2761 North Eastern 4 per cent. Guaranteed[1]	3741	3	1			
£592 5s. 10d. Midland 2½ per cent. Consolidated Perpetual Preference[1] . . .	494	11	3			
				30913	19	5
Sundry debtors :						
Subscriptions	22	1	0			
Publications	158	7	3			
Sundries	2	2	0			
				182	10	3
Cash :						
Deposit account	800	0	0			
Current account	31	13	8			
In hand	12	18	5			
				844	12	1
				£31941	1	9

[1] Valued at Stock Exchange List prices on 31st December, 1899.
[2] Valued at cost, as when purchased in 1905.

We have examined the above Income and Expenditure Account and Balance Sheet with the Books and Vouchers and certify them to be correct. We have inspected the Certificates representing the Investments, except the Inscribed Stocks, for which we have seen Certificates from the Banks in whose books they are inscribed. The value of the Library, Antiquities, Furniture, and other property of the Society is not taken credit for in the Balance Sheet.

HAROLD SANDS.	FRANCIS W. PIXLEY.
HORACE WILMER.	CECIL TENNANT.

RESEARCH FUND—

RECEIPTS.

	£	s.	d.
Balance in hand, 31st December, 1912	31	4	3
Dividends	125	5	0
Grant from General Account, part admission fees . .	54	12	0
Donations and Subscriptions	80	3	0
Donation on account of Old Sarum Excavation Fund . .	2	0	0
	£293	4	3

STOCKS AND INVESTMENTS,

	Amount of Stock.			Value, 31st December, 1913.		
	£	s.	d.	£	s.	d.
Metropolitan 3 per cent.	10583	19	7	8784	14	0
Bank Stock	2128	9	6	4991	5	2
Great Northern Railway Consolidated 4 per cent. Perpetual Preference . . .	2725	0	0	2616	0	0
London and North Western Railway 4 per cent. Guaranteed	2757	0	0	2757	0	0
North Eastern Railway 4 per cent. Guaranteed	2761	0	0	2733	7	9
Midland Railway 2½ per cent. Consolidated Perpetual Preference	592	5	10	358	6	9
Metropolitan Water Board 3 per cent. "B" Stock	1010	1	0	752	9	9
	£22557	15	11	£22993	3	5

OWEN FUND.

2½ per cent. Consols	300	0	0	215	5	0

RESEARCH FUND.

India 3½ per cent. . . .	1805	13	4	1534	16	4
J. Dickinson & Co., Ltd. 5 per cent. Preference	500	0	0	500	0	0
Victoria 3 per cent. Consolidated Inscribed .	527	13	0	401	0	3
Metropolitan Water Board 3 per cent. "B" Stock	966	4	2	719	16	6
	£3799	10	6	£3155	13	1

SUMMARY OF CASH ACCOUNT.

PAYMENTS.

	£ s. d.	£ s. d.
Byzantine Research Fund		10 0 0
St. Augustine's College, Canterbury, Excavation Fund		5 0 0
Glastonbury Abbey Excavation Fund . .		4 4 0
Meare Village Excavation Fund . .		2 2 0
Maumbury Rings Excavation Fund . .		2 2 0
Kenchester Excavation Fund . . .		2 2 0
Slack Excavation Fund		2 2 0
Old Sarum Excavation Fund . . .		100 0 0
Wroxeter Excavation Fund . . .		100 0 0
Corbridge Excavation Fund . . .		20 0 0
Balance, 31st December, 1913 . . .	43 12 3	
Balance due to Old Sarum Excavation Fund .	2 0 0	
		45 12 3
		£293 4 3

Audited and found correct :

HAROLD SANDS.
HORACE WILMER.
FRANCIS W. PIXLEY.
CECIL TENNANT.

31st DECEMBER, 1913.

Amount of
Stock.
£ s. d.

In the High Court of Justice, Chancery Division.
In the suit of Thornton v. Stevenson.
The Stocks remaining in Court to the credit of this cause are as
follows, viz. :

Great Western Railway 5 per cent. Guaranteed . .	8894 0 0
Midland Railway 2½ per cent. Perpetual Preference .	14992 8 5
	£23886 8 5

After payment of certain annuities, now amounting to £300 per annum, the
Society is entitled to one-fourth share of the residue of the income of the above
fund.

WILLIAM MINET,
Treas. S. A.

Dr. STRAHAN said the purpose of the excavations was to determine what types of implements occurred in the various deposits, and to decide whether they could be utilized as zone-fossils. Some points were already settled, as the horizons of certain specimens had been certified by the excavators. But he confessed to some doubt as to the distinction of one bed from another, and thought that the gravels, sands, and clays all belonged together and were deposited in one period. They appeared to shade off one into another, and were probably not persistent. He was not satisfied that they marked different periods, and last year's work had revealed an inexplicable mixture of types. The lowest bed at Barnfield was of special interest, as the industry was homogeneous and the fauna well represented, but unfortunately no implements had occurred at that level, whereas in the Shell-bed the same flakes occurred with definite implements considered to be of much later date. Disturbance of an older bed by ice or some other natural agency was an unsatisfactory explanation, and the occurrence of St. Acheul forms at that level was disastrous to the theory advanced. There was a great deal still to be done, but he could make no promises as to future participation, though it seemed a pity to interrupt an investigation that had begun so well.

Professor McKENNY HUGHES was not familiar with the pits examined, but had mapped gravels beyond. There was a similar sequence near Cambridge, different horizons being characterized by *Elephas antiquus* and *E. primigenius*, and no intermingling had yet been noticed there. He put forward the theory of arrested surface-soils, and thought the flints had acquired their characteristic patina before being buried.

Mr. DALE referred to the lowest gravel deposit of the 100 ft. terrace. When the previous report was presented, the meeting was assured that only flakes had been found at that horizon, but implements from a corresponding bed were now exhibited. The flakes showed no secondary working, only the bulb of percussion, and yet a pre-Chelles industry had been mentioned, with a Pliocene fauna. He concluded with a note of caution as to classification and dating.

Mr. RICE dwelt on the difficulty collectors had in getting details from the workmen, and found that the most careful excavation did not suffice to solve the problems that arose. Though a satisfactory conclusion had not been reached, he regarded the undertaking as a move in the right direction; and both archaeologists and geologists owed a good deal to the excavators, who had provided much food for thought.

Mr. CLEMENT REID thought there was evidence of an alternation of warm and cold faunas, and suggested that there was a similar alternation of the population. There might have been two parallel sequences, originating in the north and south respectively, the civilization and the fauna changing from time to time on the same spot. The implements might in that case represent not an advance in general culture, but alternating phases of culture due to successive occupations of the area in question by immigrants from different directions.

Mr. REGINALD SMITH replied that if the St. Acheul implements of the Shell-bed were in their original position, it would be much more difficult to explain the presence of a fauna with Pliocene affinities, as the implements were late in the Drift series. If the twist were involuntarily produced in handling the flint during manufacture, it became necessary to explain the greater proportion of straight-edged implements. A glaciation had not been invented to explain a disturbance of the Shell-bed. Many leading geologists who knew something of archaeology recognized a change to severe cold after the St. Acheul period; and, however described, such a change would be adequate for the purpose. All but a few acknowledged one or more glaciations in the Pleistocene, and the fauna alone was sufficient evidence. Archaeologically the strata at Swanscombe were quite distinct, whether the geologists rolled them into one or not; and the cave-deposits at any rate proved frequent and considerable changes of fashion in palaeolithic implements. It was difficult to believe that Drift man used every type throughout, without any change. From the very nature of the matrix, finds in gravel were frequently of mixed character, but an attempt had been made to find and examine an undisturbed bed with a homogeneous series of flints. The flint flakes found in the Shell-bed last year agreed in quantity and quality with those of the lowest gravel at Barnfield, but differed widely in character and patination from the white twisted St. Acheul implements exhibited; and the authors were not inclined to associate the two groups without further evidence.

The PRESIDENT stated that the report was the second presented to the Society on official excavations undertaken with a view to determining with greater precision the different horizons of the gravels and the implements characteristic of them. For the last sixty or seventy years collectors had been satisfied with the information given by workmen with regard to the occurrence of flint implements, but the example set by Professor Commont was having its effect in England, and an attempt was being made to study the stratification of Pleistocene deposits from various standpoints. In England there was as good a field as in France, if not better; and with the sanction of the British Museum Trustees and the Director of the Geological Survey two seasons' work had been done in the lower Thames valley, the investigators having been chosen so as to concentrate attention on the archaeological and geological aspects of the excavations. He was glad to think that the work had been continued, and hoped that nothing would interfere with it in other parts of the country, as the exploration of one spot was not enough to prove the sequence of types and horizons. The exhibits were very welcome in illustration of the report, and thanks were due to those who had contributed from their private collections. The undertaking was rather a novelty in England, and much was expected from the alliance between geology and archaeology. Specimens taken out of the gravels under close supervision were classical pieces, and might well rank as zone-fossils, which should lead to a more hopeful view of the Pleistocene deposits. Hitherto the conflicting views of geologists had had nothing but a depressing effect on those interested in pre-history; and if the logic of geology were to control excavations, no one would venture to open any superficial deposit at all. There was, however, comfort in the thought that geological criticisms were mutually destructive; and the discussion of such pressing problems as glaciation and patination could not be barred for ever. The action of ice and change of climate were invoked by some and ridiculed by others; and a comparatively simple case of patination, the counterchanged flints of the Egyptian desert, still remained a mystery. But a beginning had been made on sound lines, and Messrs. Smith and Dewey merited the thanks of the meeting for a clear exposition of the points involved.

Thanks were ordered to be returned for this communication, which will be printed in *Archaeologia*.

ANNIVERSARY.

THURSDAY, 23rd APRIL, 1914.

St. George's Day.

WILLIAM MINET, Esq., M.A., Treasurer, and afterwards Sir CHARLES HERCULES READ, Knt., LL.D., President, in the Chair.

Robert Garraway Rice, Esq., and Wilfrid James Hemp, Esq., were appointed Scrutators of the Ballot.

Colonel Sir Clement Molyneux Royds, C.B., was admitted a Fellow.

The PRESIDENT proceeded to deliver the following Address:

"GENTLEMEN,

I am happy, in meeting you again on St. George's Day, to be able to record a prosperous year. Although it has not been marked by any outstanding events, we have pursued our even course usefully, I think, and may regard our present position with a fair amount of satisfaction.

Our losses by death have been about normal.

The names of the deceased Fellows are as follows:

Ordinary Fellows:
*John, Baron Avebury. 28th May, 1913.
Rev. Arthur Henry Sanxay Barwell. 15th November, 1913.
Colonel Alessandro Palma di Cesnola. 24th February, 1914.
William Henry Duignan. 27th March, 1914.
Frederick Royston Fairbank, M.D. 3rd October, 1913.
William Younger Fletcher. 17th November, 1913.
Rev. Frederick Charles Hipkins. 8th January, 1914.
Sir Hubert Edward Henry Jerningham, K.C.M.G. 3rd April, 1914.
Edward Laws. 25th July, 1913.
Isaac Saunders Leadam. 18th December, 1913.
Arthur Russell Malden. 22nd October, 1913.
Frank Johnstone Mitchell. 11th October, 1913.
Rev. Morgan Thomas Pearman. 15th June, 1913.
Rev. Frederick Walker Preston-Joy, D.D. 1st October, 1913.
Sir Augustus Prevost, Bart. 6th December, 1913.
William Henry Hamilton Rogers. 20th November, 1913.

*John Oldrid Scott. 30th May, 1913.
Eugène Edward Street. 9th October, 1913.
*John William Trist. 24th October, 1913.
George Troyte-Chafyn-Grove. 27th September, 1913.
Sidney Young. 10th March, 1914.

Honorary Fellows:
Dr. Hans Hildebrand.
Professor Johann Rudolf Rahn.

The following has resigned:
Thomas Foster Shattock.

The following have been elected:
Robert Bagster.
Arthur Thomas Bolton.
William Alexander Cater.
Rev. John Frederick Chanter, M.A.
Alfred William Clapham.
Rev. Philip Thomas Byard Clayton, M.A.
Captain Charles Walter Cottrell-Dormer.
Major Algernon Tudor Craig.
William Vandeleur Crake, B.A.
Archibald Campbell Dickie.
Robert Copp Fowler, B.A.
Arthur William Gould.
Jonathan Edward Hodgkin.
Charles Henry Hopwood.
Charles Harry St. John Hornby, B.A.
Rev. Henry Arnold Hudson, M.A.
Montagu Edward Hughes-Hughes.
Major Francis Fane Lambarde.
Henry William Lewer.
William Blake Odgers, M.A., LL.D., K.C.
Henry Oppenheimer.
Charles William Dyson Perrins.
Charles George James Port.
William de Courcy Prideaux.
Maurice Rosenheim.
Colonel Sir Clement Molyneux Royds, C.B.
Frank Simpson.
Henry Vassall, M.A.
Cuthbert Wilfrid Whitaker, M.A.

One of the events of the past year, which affects not only our
Society but in a greater degree the world at large, is the death
of my predecessor in the Chair, Lord AVEBURY. A man of the

* Compounders.

widest interests, of many gifts, among which I think the most
useful to the world at large was the extraordinary power of
application to the study which interested him at the moment, he
has left a blank which, as far as one can see, is not likely to be
filled.   During his four years' occupancy of the Presidential Chair
he unfortunately had but few opportunities of bringing to bear
upon our business the wide erudition which he possessed.   With
the claims of the House of Lords, of the business of the bank, and
of the more strictly scientific pursuits which have been both the
solace of his leisure and have largely contributed to the instruction of his contemporaries, but little time was left for the
avocations that belong to the office I now hold.   It is perhaps
unfortunate for the Society that Lord Avebury did not occupy
the post of our President at an earlier period of his career when
his tastes were more definitely antiquarian.   At an early age,
when he was, in fact, thirty-five, he produced a volume entitled
Prehistoric Times, a work not only remarkable as summarizing
the whole of prehistoric knowledge at that time, but which
attained such a popularity as to have survived the enormous
advance that has taken place in this branch of science.   It is
said, and I believe with truth, that in order to master the literature of the subject, he learnt more than one of the Scandinavian
languages, a feat which would be remarkable in almost any one,
but which for a man of his absorbing occupation as a banker is
something that is given to very few to be able to compass.

It is hardly necessary for me in this place to attempt a
biography of Lord Avebury: all that seems needful is to give
such an appreciation of his standing in the world of Science and
Letters as may form for posterity some kind of idea of the relation that he bore to us.   While it is true that his earlier studies
were devoted to the archaeological side of science, yet there can
be no question that his heart was infinitely more bound by the
ties of popular science, and it is in this direction that he shines
the most.   The study of landscape as related to geology, devo-
tion to the various sides of natural history, close observation of
the habits and lives of bees, ants, and other small creatures, all
gave him more entertainment in his leisure at High Elms than
probably would be found in the more abstruse antiquarian problems that have arisen and been discussed during his long and
useful life.   As most of the Fellows know, his home was within
a stone's throw of that of the great Charles Darwin, and to that
propinquity must certainly be attributed his bent for the pursuit
of natural science.   The intimacy of the friendship between
Lubbock and Darwin was deep and constant, and it can hardly
be doubted that this friendship incited him to study the problems of animal and insect life.   It is always difficult to foresee

in what light the future will regard men whom we call great, but in my view it can hardly be questioned that posterity will be grateful to Lord Avebury for presenting to them the wonders of science in a guise that can easily be grasped. This is not the place in which to enlarge upon his useful work as the originator of bank holidays; but here again he has earned the gratitude of a vast number among the more humble of his fellow countrymen. His interest in the hours of shop assistants also appeals to a class with whom one might think he had little in common; but in point of fact one outstanding feature in Lord Avebury's character was the intense sympathy that he had with working-men's clubs and the desire for knowledge of the class who frequented them. Even less is it my business to deal with his professional occupation as a banker; but from what I know, it is admitted that the common sense and commercial sanity which were two of his best-known features led to his being regarded in the City as a man of weight, and as one on whose judgement reliance could be placed.

There remains little for me to add. Through my friendship with Sir Wollaston Franks I made Lord Avebury's acquaintance in the early 'seventies, and from that time onward we had been on the most intimate terms; he was always kindness itself, not only to me, but to everybody with whom he came in contact. An additional bond between us was formed by his marriage with the daughter of another great friend of mine, General Pitt-Rivers, and it may be of interest to record in this place that the General shortly before his death arranged with Lord Avebury and myself that we should be the trustees of the various museums and other collections that General Pitt-Rivers had gathered together at his seat in Dorsetshire. But the law stepped in and prevented the fulfilment of General Pitt-Rivers's desires. I think that this is greatly to be deplored, for I am sure that his purpose was that these collections should be maintained as a museum for the public good. Unfortunately, their present legal condition is that they may be dispersed to the four winds at any moment.

Another great character, who, although not a Fellow of the Society, it yet seems fitting that I should notice here, is Sir JONATHAN HUTCHINSON, the eminent surgeon, especially known for his investigation of leprosy, who died on the 23rd June last. His professional life, like that of Lord Avebury, although of great public advantage and distinguished in many directions, has but little concern with our Society; but as a hobby in his later years he took a keen interest in education, and in the possibility of making museums useful in that direction. During the last year or two, as we all know, this has taken a lively form in London at the British Museum, and other public institutions have followed

the example first set through the enthusiasm of Lord Sudeley.
But Sir Jonathan Hutchinson's ideas were that local museums
might be made of definite educational value if the objects gathered
together were arranged on proper lines; and with these views he
built and partly endowed a museum at Haslemere, near his own
house, and gave a vast deal of thought and attention to the means
by which this institution could be rendered of permanent utility to
those living in the neighbourhood. This museum still exists, and
I trust will continue to exist; but it must be confessed that unless
a greater amount of local enthusiasm and public liberality is
forthcoming in order to provide a fitting endowment for it, there
is a chance that it may suffer extinction, and the public will be
a loser. England is fortunate, not only in the attainments of her
scientific men, but perhaps more in their character, and men
like Sir Jonathan Hutchinson, who have great and distinctly useful
ideals, deserve the support of the intelligence of their fellows.
Recent experience has shown with what intensity the ordinary
frequenter of museums accepts the more educational side of
such institutions, and it would be a lasting pity if Sir Jonathan
Hutchinson's museum at Haslemere were to come to a premature
end for want of the public support which it so eminently deserves.

Although Monsieur Louis MARC SOLON was not only not a
Fellow of the Society but would have deprecated being called
an Antiquary, yet his tastes were of such a character as to bring
him within our purview. An artist to his finger-tips, he started
life as an etcher and entered the studio of Monsieur Lecoq at an
early age, and produced in due course some very charming etchings of decorative subjects. But he only found his real vocation
when he obtained a post in the Imperial Porcelain Factory at
Sèvres, where he took up the charming craft of which afterwards
he became the chief exponent. This was a technical process
known as 'pâte sur pâte', in which a fine porcelain paste is
applied in varying thicknesses upon a base of the same material,
so that when it has passed through the furnace it comes out
resembling a cameo. No other artist of his time has ever
approached the perfection with which Solon handled his own
peculiar method. But for the Franco-German War no doubt
Louis Solon would have remained one of the chief ornaments of
the manufactory at Sèvres to this day, but being in poor health
he elected to leave France at that time and formed friendships
with the chiefs of Minton's Works at Stoke. He entered their
service, and from that time until within a few years of his death
he continued to practise his beautiful art under their auspices.
Although this was his main business in life, his claims for recognition in this Society are due to the fact that his amusement
consisted in collecting the indigenous wares of the Staffordshire

potters of the seventeenth and eighteenth centuries, and of these he made a singularly fine collection, which was dispersed shortly before his death. Works of art of all kinds have appreciated in value vastly during the last thirty years, but hardly anything has risen to so high a pitch both in price and public appreciation as the naïve but artistic productions of the old English potter. It is a singular thing that the man who was the master of the ultimate of refinement of the art of the potter should have taken pleasure in collecting some of his most primitive products. Not only did he collect them, but he published sumptuous works, illustrated with his own etchings, both on *The Art of the English Potter* and on the analogous wares of the Rhine. In addition to the actual products of the various factories, he made also an exhaustive collection of works on the subject and produced a catalogue of this remarkable library. He was born in the year 1835, and until his sight failed shortly before his death it may be said that he was constantly at work, and although he lived in England for forty years, he remained essentially a Frenchman to the day of his death.

Mr. WILLIAM YOUNGER FLETCHER, who died on the 18th November last, was an old colleague of mine at the Museum for many years. Born on the 12th July, 1830, he entered the Department of Printed Books in 1849, where he was usefully employed until he retired in the year 1895. His chief interest and employment during his maturer years was in connexion with the old book-bindings in his Department, and on these he wrote some useful works and was a recognized authority. He belonged to the old school of British Museum officials and was among the most genial and urbane of men; his retirement was generally regretted among his colleagues in the Museum.

Although Sir HUBERT JERNINGHAM but seldom appeared at our meetings, yet, as a very old friend of my own, and an agreeable personality in the diplomatic and literary world, I can hardly pass him by without a few words of appreciation. He was born on the 18th October, 1842, at Painswick in Gloucestershire. His early education was entirely French, and to that he owed the facility with which he spoke that language, a tongue essential in diplomacy. He was an attaché in Paris, then at Constantinople, and proceeded later to Carlsruhe and Darmstadt, rising in the profession until he became Second Secretary and acted as Chargé d'Affaires. After filling other diplomatic and consular posts, he entered Parliament, and represented Berwick-on-Tweed, near which his country house was situated, from 1881 to 1885. In 1887 he was appointed Colonial Secretary of British Honduras, and afterwards Lieutenant-Governor of Mauritius and Governor of Trinidad and Tobago. On his retirement from public life, he spent a good deal of time in England, both in town and at his country seat, Longridge, and occupied his leisure in producing various books, *The Reminiscences of an Attaché*, *The History of Norham Castle*, and sundry books of travel. In appearance he was striking, and he possessed to the full the urbane and courteous demeanour that is associated with the Diplomatic Service. His interest in antiquarian pursuits was always strong, and but for the demands of society upon his time and energies, he might have produced work that would have placed him in an assured position in the archaeological world. He died after a short illness on the 3rd of the present month.

The Rev. ARTHUR HENRY SANXAY BARWELL, Canon of Chichester, died on the 15th November last. He was born on the 13th July, 1834, at Goetteville, in Normandy, and he afterwards lived with his parents at the Chateau d'Omonville, near Dieppe. He was educated first at Rouen, and later at a school at Maidstone. His father, uncle, and two brothers were all in the Army, and family feeling all ran in that direction, so that Canon Barwell at the age of 18 was gazetted to the Bombay Army, and in the following year obtained a commission in the Bombay Native Infantry, while his two elder brothers were in the Madras Native Infantry and in the 84th Regiment, both of them serving later in command of corps of Bashi-bazouks in the Crimean War—a somewhat odd setting for a man who was afterwards to become an ideal country parson and a canon. His heart, however, was much more strongly inclined towards his ultimate career than towards the Army, and after three years he resigned and came home to read for Orders. In 1855 he became a pensioner at Trinity College, Cambridge, matriculated in the following year, and took his degree in 1860. He held various cures, and finally, in 1873, he settled as rector at the charming village of Clapham on the shoulder of the downs behind Ferring, in Sussex. Here he lived an ideal life as a country parson until the year 1904, when his apparently vigorous health gave way, and he retired from active work to Blechingley, and there lived contentedly, but by no means idle, until his death last year. This is a simple and it may seem a very commonplace story, but those who knew Canon Barwell can readily testify to the fact that he was anything but a commonplace man. His energy and thoroughness in the conduct of his apparently small cure, joined to a hard common-sense and a most uncompromising honesty, would alone have lifted him out of the mass of clergymen of this country. It was fortunate for me that he possessed one quality that brought him within my sphere, viz. his passion for the enamels of Limoges. To this taste that he had in common with myself, I owe a long friendship which was to me during its whole course of inestimable value. As the Society is aware, he left to the British Museum practically the whole of his magnificent collection, the best of the kind in private hands in Europe, and in the Museum they will always remain as a witness of his admirable taste. To the Society he bequeathed the choice of such books from his library as were needed, and in this way we have considerably enriched our shelves.

In my experience characters such as Canon Barwell's are of rare occurrence. There is hardly any situation in which a man may run to seed more easily than in the conduct of a small country parish. His duties and responsibilities, beyond a very limited area, are practically what he chooses to make them, and freedom from any financial anxiety, which was Canon Barwell's case, is hardly likely to add to his energies in the duties of his cure. The width of his interests both in artistic and more general matters prevented anything like stagnation, while intercourse with a fairly large circle of friends brought the echoes of the great world into the quiet parish on the Downs, with a grateful influence for both sides.

A highly picturesque personality is gone from the ranks of the Society in Colonel ALESSANDRO PALMA DI CESNOLA, who died in Florence on 24th February in his seventy-fourth year. His life is so full of picturesque and dramatic elements that, although it is only partly concerned with archaeological matters, a brief summary may be interesting. At the age of fifteen he enrolled in a battalion of Bersaglieri, and volunteered for the Crimean War, where he was present at the battles of Tchernaia and Sebastopol. In 1859 he engaged in the War of Independence, in which he distinguished himself at Palestro and San Martino. Again, in 1866, he joined the forces of the Nationalists, and was present at the famous battle of Lissa. Finding no outlet for his energies at home, he went in 1870 to Rio de Janeiro, and in that year fitted out an expedition to explore the interior of the Argentine, reached the sources of the Rio de la Plata, and travelled through Paraguay, where he found the capital in ruins as the result of another War of Independence. Further explorations in Brazil among the Indian tribes brought him into conflict with his own countrymen and the newspapers. Returning to relative civilization at Buenos Aires, he fell upon a yellow-fever epidemic. Taking up nursing the victims of this deadly disease, he himself succumbed to it. He recovered, however, and found himself sound in health but without money, so proceeding to Montevideo, he took the post of Captain of the National Mobilized Guards in that city, and finally, at the termination of the revolution, became a Major in the Republican army. This exciting South American episode occupied just three years, for in 1873 he left South America for New York, a voyage that occupied no less than three months. Here he joined his brother Luigi, a General in the United States Army. The latter having been made U.S. Consul for Cyprus, the two left for that island, and Alessandro, our late Fellow, was nominated U.S. Vice-Consul at Paphos.

At this stage begins what may be called his archaeological life. The two brothers started diggings on the fruitful ancient sites, and were able to gather a vast collection of antiquities, the great part of which were destined for the Metropolitan Museum at New York, where, on arrival, they produced a vast amount of controversy and recrimination. Alessandro was finally left to work alone in Cyprus, the brother being appointed Director of the Museum in New York, and continued excavation for Mr. E. H. Lawrence, whose daughter he afterwards married. He gathered together a vast series of antique glass and jewellery, which I remember well in my early days. The British occupation of the island brought his aspirations to an end. Cesnola published a volume on his investigations at Salamis, called *Salaminia*, and an album of illustrations. It was at about this time (1882) that he was elected a Fellow, and from that time onward he has lived a more or less retired life in his native country. It is but seldom that so variegated a career is to be found in the annals of our Society, and it seems to me worthy of record.

Three years ago in my address I alluded to a suggestion that had been made for the establishment in this country of a Ministry of Fine Arts. My view then was that such a step should only be taken after very serious consideration, if at all. I am not sure that my views have changed. In the meanwhile, however, I understand that a Society has been formed to support the appointment of a Minister, and for putting before the Government of the country the arguments that may be found useful in its promotion. There are one or two fundamental considerations that, in my judgement, should not be overlooked in this matter. In the first place, I think it is not unfair to assume that it is the existence of such a Ministry in France which has led to the suggestion that we should possess one; but it is well to remember that the conditions of the Fine Arts in England and France are radically different. In France, or more precisely in Paris and in the great cities, there is unquestionably a widespread feeling for Art and an everlasting desire on the part of the citizens to learn more and see more in connexion with it, as well as a critical appreciation, more or less instructed, of the great works of art which are exhibited in the galleries, museums, and in other parts of the country. I wish I could say that such a feeling or such a desire

exists in England. But it is a common experience with almost
every one to discover that the ordinary person that one meets in
everyday life has hardly ever been inside the National Gallery,
and is profoundly ignorant as to the contents, and even of the
functions, of our great public museums. One or other such institution may be a fashionable craze for a few months, but it soon falls
into line as one of the things that are realized, but hardly ever
visited. It is hardly necessary for me to insist on the importance
and value of the contents of our London galleries and museums,
and if they are neglected by our modern public, the reason can
only be that the public is not interested. Therefore, and this
is my point, the difference between the functions of a Fine Art
Minister in France and in England is fundamental. In France
he is engaged in the control of a powerful stream of public taste
and public opinion, perhaps more vigorous and rapid than he
would desire, and the effects of his guidance may be destructive
or beneficent as with other streams. But I take it that the existence of a strong body of artistic opinion in France is not likely
to be denied. While, therefore, the French Minister finds his
hands full with control and guidance, what will be the duties of
his English *confrère*? He cannot guide a thing that has no
existence, and his chief business will therefore of necessity be
constructive, and it will be his duty to gather round him a body
of men who can be trusted as guides for an uninstructed nation,
and thus, by transforming their ideas into acts, to evolve from
the present chaos of unreason and parrot-like repetition some
intelligent standards of artistic understanding. There are at the
present time evident tendencies in this direction, and one of them
is seen in the invitation to certain bodies like ourselves, who have
no concern with the Government or with politics, to bear our
share in the specialized work of the Government departments.
The Advisory Board under the Ancient Monuments Act of last
year is a case in point. Here we and the other societies who
work with us can bear a useful part and bring our influence to
control public opinion so as to raise the standard of national
taste.

With our party system of government it is, of course, inevitable
that the Minister to be appointed shall be a supporter of the
Government of the day, a grave defect, inasmuch as it might rule
out the man who is clearly best for the post. But, being inevitable,
we must needs accept it, and do our work with the only tools we
can get. Our successors will hardly bless us if we sit with folded
hands as a protest against methods that fall short of the ideal.
If therefore we are to have the opportunity of experimenting with
a Minister of Fine Arts, let us wish him well and see to it that
our influence is usefully present in all matters that fall within
our province.

It is two years ago that I had the pleasure of calling the attention of the Society to the opening of the London Museum, which had then just been installed in a suite of rooms in Kensington Palace. It was obvious then, and became increasingly clear as time went on, that the limited amount of space available in the Palace would call for some drastic changes if the Museum was to be a living organism. A combination of circumstances and a good deal of generosity have provided a solution, which, though by no means ideal, will yet serve to postpone for some time the consideration of the final habitat of the collections. When the Duke of Sutherland gave up his splendid mansion the remainder of the lease was bought by Sir William Lever, and he, with a public-spirited generosity that is fortunately not rare with us, presented it to the Trustees of the London Museum. The collections were transferred to their new home with praiseworthy promptitude, and thrown open to the public on the 23rd March last. Although Stafford House is by no means ill suited for such a use, it has, perhaps, more of the attributes of a palace than was the case at Kensington, and gorgeous as the rooms are, as well as admirably lighted, it is self-evident that a palace can hardly be expected to serve as a museum without great sacrifices on the one side or the other. Of this there can hardly be a better example than the Museum of the Louvre. The danger of fire, to instance only one point of view, must necessarily be greater in elaborately decorated saloons, innocent of what is optimistically called fire-proof construction, than in a building in which such a necessity is kept in view throughout every stage of its building. I have no doubt, however, that those responsible for the collections have given earnest thought to this and other similar matters.

It cannot be denied that as they stand now the contents of the Museum present a very attractive appearance, and it can hardly be doubted that in their new environment they will be even more popular than they were at Kensington. The most has been made of the very handsome setting, and the arrangement reflects great credit on the very limited staff.

As an old museum official, I feel that it is perhaps a duty for me to say a few words on the principles that should be held in respect in the formation of such a museum. The initiation of a new museum is always difficult, and no one knows better than I how many pitfalls lie open for the unwary feet of even the most cautious of enthusiastic directors. It is almost impossible to foresee with precision how the best-laid schemes will work out in practice. One has only to think for a moment of the innumerable interests that belong to the history of a city like London over a period of two thousand years. Relics of places or persons, documents, prints, drawings relating to people, places, or things, the history of the ever-changing topography, the many thousands of works of art, many of them quite insignificant in themselves, but as reproducing the daily life of old London of inestimable value, all demand a place. If one adds to all this a library of books relating to London, contemporary paintings of the vanishing city, either of which would be quite in keeping, it will be seen that Stafford House, capacious as it may seem, would hardly suffice to contain the collections that may reasonably be expected to accrue. In carrying out the formation of such a museum the difficulties of a director are surely great enough ; but he is met almost inevitably by the generous donor offering valuable gifts eminently desirable in themselves, but obviously as unsuitable for such a museum.

For all these reasons, but in the main for reasons of space, I would strongly urge that the collections at the London Museum should be strictly confined within the historical period. In fact, that it should be limited to the time when London existed, and exclude the remains of the mammoth hunter on the terraces of the Thames. To illustrate historical London is a gigantic enterprise, vast enough for the energies of any museum, while the interest of the exhibits remains coherent and consecutive, being based on their historical sequence. Once go beyond the limits of history, the interest and importance of the objects are not only of an entirely different kind, and demand a totally new standpoint, but they have nothing to do with London because London did not exist.

It is my duty on occasions of this kind to make some reference to the explorations that the Society has in hand. I need not remind the Fellows, for I have often done so on previous occasions, of the important obligations which we owe to ourselves and to the world in the proper accomplishment of our explorations at Wroxeter and Old Sarum. There has been no question that they are in thoroughly competent hands, and that, with the guidance of the Research Committee, the work of each season will be well done. The yearly cost of these two undertakings is about £1,500, and although we obtain handsome contributions from the local societies and from others outside our body, yet it cannot be too strongly impressed upon the Fellows of this Society that they, through the Council, have made themselves responsible for the efficient performance of these contracts. Some of our friends in the Society have been very generous in their contributions, and the appeals for subscriptions are a necessary though an ungrateful task for the officers, but I think there is nothing that comes within our scope that is more worthy of the support

of the Fellows of the Society, or where their contributions would
be more gratefully received and well expended. The responsi-
bility of such undertakings is by no means at an end when the
excavations are complete. It is of little use to make explorations
without adequate publication of the results. Here again the
expense is by no means small, but I am sure that no one within
the Society grudges this most appropriate expenditure of its
income; the ideal position would be that our Research Fund
should attain to such dimensions that the income would suffice
to defray about half of the annual expenses of these explorations ;
we could then appeal with a better face for outside help. At
present our Research Fund produces only a negligible income,
and practically all the expense of these particular works is defrayed by voluntary contributions. What we really require is
a few generous gifts or, in an extreme case, legacies, so that the
capital of our Research Fund may be sensibly increased. Until
some such condition is attained, a great deal of very ungrateful
labour will necessarily be imposed on the officers of this Society.

Every Fellow will have received, during the last week or two,
a circular from me on this subject, inviting them to give orders
to their bankers for a very modest annual contribution towards
research. The minimum sum there mentioned is, I think, well
within the means of every Fellow, but it is my duty to emphasize
here that we confidently hope that a large number of our Fellows
will feel themselves bound to contribute on a more generous
scale, and thus secure a very much larger average annual subsidy
towards our explorations.

A suggestion that I hope may be borne in mind by my successors in this chair is the propriety of making an appeal in due
course for a grant from the Government towards our Research
Fund. It is a most proper and reasonable expenditure of public
money, and the amount would in any case be relatively small.
The action of the Government in passing the Ancient Monuments Act shows that archaeology as related to the history of
the country is recognized as having a legitimate place in the
national budget. Further, the utility of the public collections,
as factors in the educational system, is now commonly accepted
and acted upon. If it were made a condition of a Government
grant that all remains discovered by its aid should be permanently
preserved in a properly constituted museum, there could then be
no question as to the propriety of voting money for the purpose
of exploration. The museums would not only be definitely enriched, but the added treasures would be of far greater historical
value from the fact that they had been brought to light under
scientific conditions. With even £2,000 or £3,000 a year what
a vast amount of useful work could be done, and how effectively

the reconstruction of the history of the country could be achieved. In this respect no body could take action with more effect or with greater propriety than the Society of Antiquaries.

An argument of an indirect kind may be found in the foundation of the Franks Scholarship by the Society. That at least demonstrates that we do not forget that, while we deal with the past, we yet look to the future in relation to archaeological studies, and are ourselves not neglectful of our own side of education.

Some years ago I referred to the question of the administration of the law of treasure-trove and to the fact that the Council had appointed a Committee to consider what action the Society might well take in placing suggestions on the subject before the Lords of the Treasury. As I then informed you, this Committee held several meetings and discussed the matter in all its aspects from the archaeological point of view. This report of the Committee was in due course sent to the Treasury, but no action has since been taken. The delay was partly due to conversations that I had with officers of the Treasury, who were strongly of opinion that the Report as it stood could not be accepted by the Government. This decision hardly surprised me, but I took no further steps at the time, for two reasons. One was the retirement from the Treasury of Sir George Murray and the subsequent appointment of two other gentlemen to take his place, neither of whom I knew; and secondly, because these steps brought me so near my retirement from the Presidential Chair that I felt it would be futile for me to initiate a policy which I should certainly be unable to see to an end. The matter, therefore, must rest in the hands of my successor, and I feel sure that the experience of your President and of the Committee on Treasure Trove will amply suffice to place before the Government the matured views of the Society in regard to this matter. In my previous reference to the law of treasure-trove I came to the conclusion that it would be better to endeavour to ameliorate the present conditions rather than to try for the abolition of the law: further experience and consideration make me doubt whether this is the best course to pursue. I am rather inclined now to believe that the Society would stand a better chance of success if it could represent to the Government the benefit that might result from the entire disappearance of the law of treasure-trove from the Statute Book. In this, I must confess, I am adopting rather what is expedient than what might be called ideal from the scientific standpoint. As I pointed out before, the Crown, while it has the right to claim treasure-trove, is on the side of archaeology, inasmuch as the more precise the evidence of dis-

covery can be made, the better the chance of the Crown to establish its case. Such records are, of course, of the highest importance
for us, and if the rights of the Crown with regard to treasure-
trove be abolished, there will be no official inquiry as to the
circumstances of the discovery of the objects. It is common
knowledge that the law is constantly evaded; compromises are
often made with regard to it, and of this a recent instance
occurring in London is an admirable example. There can be
little question that the whole procedure belongs to a past time,
and is practically obsolete, and but for the fact that the precious
metals are concerned and become the prize when the law is put
into operation, the whole statute would long ago have passed
into oblivion. This Society, however, is more or less the official
custodian of archaeological tradition, and it is its duty to perform
the functions appertaining to this office for the benefit of the
community at large, and to fight for what it considers the proper
course, no matter who the opponent may be.

I have once or twice alluded to the difficulties which have beset
me personally from the fact that I am an officer of the British
Museum while I occupy this chair. I feel that I owe an apology
to the Society for what may have seemed to be an apathetic
attitude towards some of its affairs. I have, however, felt very
strongly that as a servant of the Government there are functions
appertaining to the proceedings of this Society which I could
hardly perform in my own person. It is a common practice in
laying before the Government the opinions of the Society upon
specific matters to send a deputation to a Minister of the Crown,
and in the case of a Society such as ours, it is but natural that
the President should take his proper place as the leader and
spokesman. It is easy to imagine that the views of the Society
might be diametrically opposed to that of the Government on
some archaeological points, and it would then become the duty
of the spokesman of the Society to use forcible language in
presenting the Society's case to the Minister. The difficulty in
my own case hardly needs to be pointed out, and I have steadily
refrained from taking any active part in such deputations, not
from any want of feeling in the matter, but from my conviction
that a Government servant is bound to let his position as such
take the first place to the exclusion of other, and what must be
secondary, interests. Another result of my holding this dual
position is that a distinction that falls upon the President of this
Society upon election has in my own person been somewhat of
a dead-letter. I refer to the fact that the President is *ex officio*
a Trustee of the British Museum. I cannot speak too strongly
of the kindness with which the proposition that I should stand

as President of this Society was received by the Standing Committee of the Trustees of the British Museum some six years ago. I was not only permitted to stand, and thus necessarily become a Trustee of the Museum, but many of the Trustees congratulated me very warmly upon the honour it was proposed to bestow upon me; nothing, in fact, could have been more agreeable than the relations between myself and the other Trustees. As a matter of fact, however, it is of very little avail to belong to the general body of Trustees; it is undoubtedly an honour, but it has no serious duties, the only section of the Trustees who take active part in the government of the Museum being the Standing Committee, and it is very evident that it would have been an impossible position for me to have sat upon that body, and thus have helped in framing the regulations that governed my own conduct and that of my colleagues at the Museum. In order to preserve continuity I did attend one meeting of the Trustees at the Prime Minister's house. I trust that it may be the good fortune of my successor to be elected to the Standing Committee of Trustees; he at any rate will not suffer from the same disqualification as myself, and the presence of the President of the Society on the Standing Committee cannot fail to be of great advantage both to himself and to me and my colleagues on the archaeological side of the Museum.

It is almost inevitable that in the course of this my last address, I should attempt a brief review of the events of my Presidency. Looking back is of necessity a somewhat sad business, and signal gaps have been made in our ranks during the past six years. Many names of distinction and of men for whom we all felt a sincere regard have disappeared from our list, but I feel confident that the process of renewal that is always going on will keep the status of the Society up to the level becoming its ancient dignity and modern position. It is at any rate the duty of every Fellow to use his best efforts towards this end.

A few years ago saw the completion of the exploration of the city of Silchester, though its cemetery has yet to be located and explored. This allowed the Society to begin the long-promised attack on the Roman city at Wroxeter, as well as that on the interesting many-sided site of Old Sarum. These two are now well begun, and the Fellows may feel assured of the quality of the work at both places. The gentlemen in immediate charge of the work are both competent and experienced, and are acting in harmony with the Research Committee, in whose hands the Council has placed the direction of these two undertakings. Our late Treasurer, Mr. Norman, has during some years past given a great deal of time and attention to London archaeology, in collaboration with Mr. Reader, and has gained the position that he eminently deserves as one of the leading authorities on the subject.

Without question, the most signal advance in Government recognition of archaeology has been the appointment of the three Royal Commissions for the Survey of Ancient and Historical Monuments for England, Scotland, and Wales, and a fourth to deal with the custody of Public Records. Of equal importance is the Ancient Monuments Act, for which the Society, with other bodies, has a representative on the Advisory Board. Recent events have shown that this type of legislation has come none too soon. It is greatly to be regretted that ecclesiastical buildings were inevitably omitted from its scope. It is little less than a scandal that the most important buildings in the country should be practically the freehold of those whom chance has placed in temporary control without any safeguard but what is provided by public opinion. It is not generally enough realized that cathedral churches are extra diocesan, and that for alterations or for selling their property they do not require the sanction of a faculty, as is fortunately necessary elsewhere. I am regrettably debarred from alluding to a recent instance where the merest chance prevented the alienation of some of the pre-Reformation plate of one of our cathedrals. The mere recital of it would demonstrate effectually the need for safeguards, and these I hope legislation may eventually provide.

During my occupancy of the Chair I think we may congratulate ourselves on the high average of the attendances at the evening meetings, and I think, though I am not sure about it, that there has been some slight increase in the amount of discussion following the papers. There have been times when the discussion has added very considerably to our knowledge and to the interest of the communications.

During the last few years, as some of the Fellows may have observed, these discussions have been uniformly reported in *Proceedings*. But I am not so sure that the Society is aware that this innovation is entirely due to the voluntary good offices of my friend Mr. Reginald Smith. He is one of the most regular attendants, and has put us all under an obligation in this way as well as in rearranging our museum and superintending the proper labelling of the contents. For these, as well as for other services, we owe him our thanks.

I alluded last year to the new scheme of lighting in our meeting-room; in the interval this new method has been put into operation, and I think is an unqualified success. Some care will no doubt be necessary to maintain the high standard that has been set at its inception, but, for agreeable qualities and adequate lighting, it is hard to see in what way it could be improved.

I now come, Gentlemen, to the end of my long address to you; it is only natural that in arriving at this point I feel, as I think any of you would do in my place, that there is a tinge of pathos in it. No one can knowingly do any important thing for the last time without a slight feeling of sadness; it is something like a parting, a farewell to a known past and the putting of one's foot on the threshold of an unknown future.

During the past six years I have experienced very much kindness from the Society as a whole and so many friendly actions from individuals that I must naturally feel a keen regret at parting from you in my present capacity. In speaking of a parting, however, I need hardly say that it is merely nominal; I hope for a good many years yet to take a full share in your deliberations, and I need hardly assure you that, after twenty-two years continuously spent in the active service of the Society, I am not likely to give up the habits formed during that time, and, so far as my official duties will permit, I shall be always at your service. I take pleasure in thanking you all for your constant kindness to me at the meetings and on all occasions when we have met together in consultation, and I shall always cherish the memory of our friendly relations. I especially desire to express my gratitude to my brother officers who have so ably seconded my efforts in the conduct of the Society. I have already been able to pay a tribute to the loyalty and goodfellowship of our former Treasurer, Mr. Philip Norman. His successor, Mr. Minet, though young as our Treasurer, is a very old friend of mine, and I know of no one who could more efficiently perform the duties of his office. Mr. Peers, our Secretary, I have also known for a good many years, but I cannot speak too highly of the enthusiasm and good sense that he has brought to bear upon the affairs of the Society. He has of late greatly increased his responsibilities by the competent way in which he has directed the Inspectorship of Ancient Monuments, an office which makes him doubly valuable to the Society; and although it may not allow him to devote so much of his time as he would like to our affairs, he has in that direction secured for himself a status in the archaeological world of no small dignity, and the Society should be proud in having a man of his attainments in its service. My other friend, our Director, Sir Edward Brabrook, is known to all of you, and it is hardly necessary for me to say anything in commendation of him as one of our officers. He is rapidly attaining, if he has not already attained, the proud and honourable position of the Father of the Society, and for urbanity and goodfellowship it is

hard to find any one in the Society who can claim to be his equal.
In the same way, I think I can safely leave Mr. Kingsford to the
judgement of the Society; he undoubtedly comes into closer
contact with the Fellows than the majority of the officers. So
far as my relations with him have been concerned, I can only feel
the most entire satisfaction at having been largely instrumental
in securing him as our Assistant Secretary. He has by this time
a wide experience of the duties of such a post, and performs them
in the most competent and satisfactory way. Of Mr. Clinch I can
speak with confidence, and here again I have the satisfaction of
thinking that I was a party to his being appointed to his post in
the Society; he has, in my opinion, more than justified all that
I was able to say about him as an applicant, and his intimate
knowledge of our library and the obliging way in which he makes
this knowledge free to the Fellows of the Society make him very
valuable to us in his office of Librarian.

In these very competent hands, then, Gentlemen, I leave you,
and I am very sure that under the guidance of the President
whom you have just elected, the future of the Society should be
assured."

The following resolution was thereupon proposed by the Earl
of Crawford and Balcarres, seconded by Lt.-Colonel Sir Arthur
Leetham, and carried unanimously:

"That the best thanks of the meeting be given to the President for his address, and that he be requested to allow it to be
printed."

The PRESIDENT signified his assent.

The Scrutators having handed in their report, the following
were declared elected as Officers and Council for the ensuing
year:

Eleven Members from the Old Council.

William Minet, Esq., M.A., *Treasurer.*
Sir Edward William Brabrook, Knt., C.B., *Director.*
Charles Reed Peers, Esq., M.A., *Secretary.*
David, Earl of Crawford and Balcarres, LL.D.
Montague Spencer Giuseppi, Esq.
David George Hogarth, Esq., M.A.
Philip Norman, Esq., LL.D.
Sir Charles Hercules Read, Knt., LL.D.
Harold Sands, Esq.
Harold Clifford Smith, Esq., M.A.
Horace Wilmer, Esq.

Ten Members of the New Council.

Sir Arthur John Evans, Knt., M.A., D.Litt., F.R.S., *President.*
Oswald Barron, Esq.
Reginald Blomfield, Esq., M.A., R.A.
Ralph Griffin, Esq.
William Martin, Esq., M.A., LL.D.
William Page, Esq.
Francis William Pixley, Esq.
D'Arcy Power, Esq., M.A.
Horace William Sandars, Esq.
Cecil Arthur Tennant, Esq., B.A.

THURSDAY, 7th MAY, 1914.

Sir ARTHUR JOHN EVANS, Knt., M.A., D.Litt., F.R.S.,
President, in the Chair.

The following gifts were announced, and thanks for the same ordered to be returned to the donors:

From William Page, Esq., F.S.A.:—
  1. Monastic Schools in the Middle Ages. By G. G. Coulton. 8vo. London, 1913.
  2. Architectural Association Sketch Book, Vols. 6–11, 1872–1878. Analytical Index, Vols. 5-8. Sketch Book, New Series, Vols. 4–5.

From the Author:—The medical education and qualifications of Oliver Goldsmith. By Sir Ernest Clarke, F.S.A. 8vo. London, 1914.

From the Author:—St. Margaret's, Westminster. The church of the House of Commons. By Rev. H. F. Westlake. 8vo. London, 1914.

From Harold Sands, Esq., F.S.A.:—
  1. A history of the dress of the British soldier. By Lt.-Col. John Luard. 8vo. London, 1852.
  2. The Tower of London. By Richard Davey. 8vo. London, 1910.
  3. Genesis of Lancaster, or the three reigns of Edward II, Edward III, and Richard II, 1307–1399. 2 vols. By Sir James Ramsay. 8vo. Oxford, 1913.
  4. Fore and Aft: the story of the fore-and-aft rig from the earliest times to the present day. By E. K. Chatterton. 8vo. London, 1912.
  5. Sailing ships: the story of their development from the earliest times to the present day. By E. K. Chatterton. 8vo. London, 1909.

6. Mediaeval military architecture in England. 2 vols. By G. T. Clark. 8vo. London, 1884.
7. Regesta Regum Anglo-Normannorum 1066–1154. Vol. I. Edited by H. W. C. Davis and R. J. Whitwell. 8vo. Oxford, 1913.
8. History of marine architecture. By J. Charnock. 3 vols. 8vo. London, 1800-2.

A special vote of thanks was passed to Mr. Harold Sands for his gift of Charnock's *Marine Architecture* to the Library.

Arthur Thomas Bolton, Esq., was admitted a Fellow.

The PRESIDENT announced that he had appointed the following to be Vice-Presidents of the Society:

David, Earl of Crawford and Balcarres, LL.D.
David George Hogarth, Esq., M.A.
Philip Norman, Esq., LL.D.
Sir Charles Hercules Read, Knt., LL.D.

Professor HAVERFIELD, LL.D., D.Litt., F.S.A., read the following paper on the excavations at Corbridge in 1913:

"In previous reports to our Society I have remarked that the Corbridge excavations have given us a surprise, and indeed a different form of surprise, every year. They have been true to their nature in 1913, though the new feature with which they have presented us is not quite what we wanted. Last year was the first in the series of excavations of this site which has failed to yield some really important group of discoveries, whether of buildings or of coins or other small objects. The area selected for trenching in 1913 lay to the north-east of that previously explored, and, as it seems, on the north-east or north of the entire site. Like the area excavated in 1909, it extended up to the lane which leads from Corbridge towards Hexham Bridge, and it somewhat resembled that area; it was, however, even less full of well-preserved buildings which might be thought once to have possessed a definite character. Across the north of it ran a continuation of the north ditch found in 1909, which formed during part of the Roman occupation the northern limit of Corstopitum. Near its eastern edge ran a continuation of the north-and-south street found in 1910. On either side of this street were buildings, but they were for the most part even fewer and less important than those found along the southern part of its course (Sites XXI–XXV). At its northern end this road crossed the ditch and apparently proceeded northwards, so that it must have very shortly fallen in with the still visible remains of the Dere Street which ran over Stagshaw Bank towards Scotland.

This suggests that the line of this road, close to Corstopitum, ran a few yards east of the cart-track with which it has been generally identified, but the question is one of little more than strictly local moment. The road was equipped with gutters, and, like the main east-and-west road, showed three periods of construction.

Some little distance west of this road was the one large building which Mr. Forster was able to discover (Site LVI). This was a very long buttressed building, with a central wall down the middle of at least its southern end; it measured 30 ft. in width and probably 150 ft. in length, though its northern end was somewhat obscure. Apparently this northern end overlay and was later than the north ditch just mentioned. The southern end, on the other hand, seems to have been destroyed at some time within the Roman period, and a later Roman building planted over it. Very little pottery was found in it; what there was seemed to belong to the middle or the latter half of the second century. The whole structure most resembles a granary, though the surviving foundations do not show the usual ventilating windows or passages. Mr. Forster has conjectured that it was a granary of later date and worse masonry than the granaries found on the main east-and-west street (Sites VII and X), and that, while these date from the middle of the second century in their origin, this one may have been added in connexion with the campaigns of Septimius Severus. Indeed—though this may be an accident—a coin of that Emperor was found at a low level in the gravel lying against the foundations.

If this building is disappointing in the poorness of its masonry and the obscurity of its character, the smaller finds were hardly more encouraging. The principal discovery was the top of a small altar (figs. 1–4), extracted at the very end of the excavations from one of the ventilation passages of the East Granary on the main east-and-west street (Site VII). A good many late third and early fourth-century coins were found in these passages, but they do not appear to afford any clue to the date of the altar; that must have been broken up intentionally to be used as repairing-material, and thus the top of it got into this granary, while the bottom, if it survives at all, may be anywhere. The altar bears on the front, above the cornice, two letters, of which the second is F, and the first is either B or P or R. We might think that it represented an abbreviation of *Bonae Fortunae* or *Reduci Fortunae*, if it were worth guessing on such scanty evidence. Below the cornice, on the shaft of the altar, is the beginning of a neatly cut inscription, of which the first two lines '*Deae Pantheae*' alone survive. It seems that the goddess to whom the altar was dedicated, whose name no doubt followed in the

Figs. 1–4. INSCRIPTION AND CARVINGS ON FRAGMENTARY ROMAN ALTAR
FOUND AT CORBRIDGE, 1913

(From photographs by Mr. R. H. Forster)

third line, was given by her worshipper the epithet 'Panthea', which was used occasionally, both in Italy and even in the provinces, and which apparently meant that the god who was worshipped was regarded as for the moment possessing the attributes of all the gods. It was a curious inverted pantheism which does not seem to have spread very far, and about which there is probably not much to know. The goddess most frequently honoured with this appellation on other altars seems to be Fortuna.

The other three sides of this altar-top contain the upper parts of three figures of which only the heads survive. One is obviously a head of Mercury. The other two heads, which lean over on to the shoulder and are covered with Phrygian caps, are less certain. Our Fellow Professor P. Gardner, and our President, Sir A. Evans, agree in suggesting that they represent the two figures which we see on Mithraic monuments, and indeed also on tombstones, wearing Phrygian caps and carrying torches. The Mithraic figures, however, do not appear to lean their heads over in the fashion of our altar; for that, we must go to the tombstones bearing the figure of 'Attis'. It seems useless to speculate on the connexion of these figures and of Mercury with the nameless goddess who bore the epithet Panthea.

Other finds demand shorter notice. They include a rude figure of Jupiter with his thunderbolt (18 in. high, feet lost), a rude figure of Mercury, a curious head surmounted by circular scale-work which suggests either a Caryatid or a corbel, and—in pottery—another fragment of what may be called the Corbridge 'appliqué' ware, which was struck from a mould almost, but not quite, identical with the mould generally known as 'Harry Lauder'. This ware seems to be a rough local imitation of the more refined Samian and the Castor work in the 'appliqué' style; from the number of pieces which have now been found, we may perhaps think that it was not an isolated venture, but that several pieces of this class were made in Corbridge.

Noteworthy, lastly, is a small bronze head, hollow inside, obviously the head of a barbarian with appropriate moustachios, and with the hair dressed in what I am told is the Numidian fashion. It seems to have had a lid and arrangements for suspension, and must be classed with other similar objects which are sometimes called 'balsamaria'. Its interest lies mainly in the character of the face, which seems to be neither African nor Gaulish, nor indeed to agree with any known barbarian type.

This is a brief list of finds. I trust that when Mr. Forster opens the ninth year of the Corbridge excavations in July, 1914, surprises will greet him of a more agreeable and important character."

Mr. FORSTER admitted it was a lean year when compared with past seasons, but the Corbridge standard was high; and even if there were nothing novel, the mass of finds would do credit to any other site, and served to confirm former discoveries. The new road-section corrected certain details of McLauchlan's survey. At the north end of the field the road crossed marshy ground, and a section showed a foundation of roughly dressed stones, but farther south a bed of large cobbles. On the plan could be seen an empty space between the road with its buildings and the long buttressed building, and the conclusion arrived at was that the space had once been marshy ground, connected with that found farther west in 1909. It had been partly filled in but never enough for buildings to be erected on it. During the latter part of the Roman occupation, Corstopitum was in a state of decay. The buttressed building was 150 ft. long and over 25 ft. wide, the largest yet found, with the exception of the Forum; it dated probably from the time when Severus was organizing the conquest of Caledonia. It was of inferior construction, and served in all probability as a store-house for grain. At the north end the masonry was missing and the clay foundation ended in a straight line. There was no trace of a raised floor as in other granaries. The buttresses enabled walls to be run up of less breadth, thus saving time and material; and there would have been temporary pressure at that particular date. In connexion with the Dea Panthea, he cited the inscription at Carvoran or Magna (*C.I.L.*, vii, no. 759).

Mr. BUSHE-FOX said that sensational finds were not always the most useful. The season's work showed that the early occupation did not reach the area excavated, as the early pottery was missing. What there was confirmed the theory that the long building dated from Severus. Corbridge was the site most likely to throw light on the dark period of Trajan, when a whole legion disappeared. It was curious that no traces of fortification had been found, and he wondered if the large masses of stone were the foundations of a gateway at the north end of the town.

The PRESIDENT congratulated the excavators of Corbridge on advancing the knowledge of Roman Britain. Great accuracy had now been obtained in dating by the pottery, and the long building might well have been the stores and base of Severus. The Carvoran parallel had occurred to himself, and he mentioned the blending of attributes, not on the official coins, but on signets and other personal ornaments about A.D. 200. This tendency reflected the philosophic struggle with Christianity in the fourth century. The figures on the sides of the altar with leaning heads probably bore reversed and upright torches, as in the Mithraic sculptures.

A. Hamilton Thompson, Esq., M.A., F.S.A., read the following paper on 'Visitations of Religious Houses by William Alnwick, Bishop of Lincoln 1436–49':

"The manuscript record of Bishop Alnwick's visitations of the religious houses of his diocese, among the episcopal muniments at Lincoln, consists of 133 leaves of foolscap paper, closely written upon both sides in the minute hand of the bishop's registrar, Thomas Colstone. These leaves, long unbound, have suffered much in time past from neglect and damp, and a well-meaning mender in comparatively recent times has preserved their tattered edges by pasting strips of nearly opaque paper over them, regardless of the writing beneath. Workers for the *Victoria History of the Counties of England* have briefly summarized the contents of the manuscript so far as they relate to the Buckinghamshire, Lincolnshire, and Oxfordshire houses; and a full transcript of the whole manuscript has been made, and will shortly be published with a translation by the Lincoln Record Society. It is obvious that such a record, dealing with a diocese which embraced eight English counties and part of a ninth, is of peculiar value to students of the religious life in England during the later Middle Ages. While, however, any detailed examination of its evidence with regard to individual religious houses must be reserved until the publication of the text renders it available for general study, the composition of the visitation minutes and of the injunctions which in several cases follow them provides information of a very definite kind, which may be submitted in this place as throwing much needed light upon a certain class of medieval document.

The foundations visited were sixty-nine in number—six abbeys and four priories of Benedictine monks,[1] two abbeys and seven priories of Benedictine nuns, seven priories of Cistercian nuns, nine abbeys and twenty-one priories of Austin canons, one abbey and four priories of Austin nuns, seven colleges of secular clergy, and one hospital.[2] Naturally, there is no information with regard to houses of exempt Orders; but every important house of the Orders mentioned above is represented, and of Bardney and Peterborough abbeys and St. Michael's priory, Stamford, there are three visitations each, and of Dorchester abbey and the

[1] In addition to these, visitations of the cells of Frieston, Oxney, and St. Ives are included in those of their respective mother houses, Croyland, Peterborough, and Ramsey.

[2] There is also a cancelled notice of a visitation of St. John's Hospital, Northampton.

college of Fotheringhay two. Although dates are carefully given, the minutes follow no chronological order. They extend over a period from the end of 1437 to the middle of 1447. To the end of 1439 belongs the visitation of the chief houses in the archdeaconry of Huntingdon. The reports for the archdeaconries of Lincoln and Stow in 1440, of Leicester in 1440 and 1442, of Northampton in 1442, of Bedford in 1443, and of Oxford in 1445, are fairly complete. Buckingham received very little attention.[1] The registrar kept the sheets of minutes by him and entered a visitation wherever he found a blank leaf. Occasionally he left a blank space to be filled up with injunctions or the continuation of some process which delayed the conclusion of the visitation, and did not complete his work. It is therefore probable that a large number of visitations held by Alnwick or his commissaries remain unrecorded, and minutes of his primary visitation in particular seem to be wanting save in the case of a few houses. Unfortunately, the dates in his official register, which was carelessly kept and posted up only at long intervals, afford little additional information as to his movements and are sometimes inaccurate.

Each set of minutes begins with a heading containing the name of the house and the precise date of visitation. No account is given of the formal reception of the bishop, which is frequently noted with some detail in the book of Norwich visitations edited by the late Dr. Jessopp.[2] The account of the proceedings begins in the chapter-house, where the bishop, *sedens iudicialiter pro tribunali*, listened with the assembled convent to a sermon preached by one of his clerks or, in the larger houses, by one of the more learned brethren. The head of the house was then called upon to return his or her certificate of the notice of visitation and to show the titles of their incumbency, viz. certificates of election, confirmation, and installation, the foundation charter of the house, and its current balance-sheet (*status domus*). The chapter-house was then cleared, and the individual members of the house were examined privately by the bishop and his assessors. Their evidence, taken down in summary form, was known collectively as the *detecta*—i.e. the matters discovered *to* the visitor; and from a sifting of these, the results of the preparatory inquiry, the *comperta*, or matters discovered *by* the visitor, were established.[3] In the case of serious individual

[1] Only two houses, Ankerwyke Priory and Nutley Abbey, appear.
[2] *Visitations of the Diocese of Norwich, A.D. 1492-1532*, ed. A. Jessopp, D.D., F.S.A. (Camden Soc.). There is a very full and elaborate account of the proceedings at a visitation of Lincoln Cathedral in 1432 in Lincoln Epis. Reg. Gray, ff. 121 sqq.
[3] The distinction between the *detecta* and *comperta* is sometimes overlooked. It is clearly shown, however, in the elaborate injunctions to

faults, where a member of the house was definitely accused
(*diffamatus* or *notatus*) of a crime or noteworthy breach of rule,
he was summoned before the bishop and articles were laid against
him. If he pleaded not guilty, he was given a term, usually till
the afternoon of the same day, to find compurgators. Occasionally a case or cases of this kind involved an adjournment of the
visitation, especially where an apostate member of the house had
to be sought out and brought to the bar. Some visitations in
this way dragged on at intervals for months, and the processes
thus recorded are of the greatest interest. But, as a rule, the
bishop was able to conclude his visitation, after attending to
individual cases, on the same day or the next morning. On
leaving, he made a summary publication of the *detecta* and *comperta*, and issued certain verbal injunctions, usually in a brief
form, which were supplemented, often within the next few days,
by a series of written injunctions.

The Alnwick MS. provides full reports of the *detecta* produced
at each visitation. In order to facilitate reference, the name or
office of the person to whose default each *detectum* points is frequently written against it in the margin.[1] Occasionally a
deponent presented a written schedule which was abstracted in
the text. In a few cases the schedule itself has been preserved.[2]
The *detecta* are followed by notes relating to the conclusion or
adjournment of the visitation. In several instances the minutes
end here. Sometimes everything was satisfactory and the bishop
saw no need to issue new injunctions ; in one case, at Bourne, he
merely confirmed Bishop Flemyng's injunctions with one slight
addition. The procedure, however, where more than this was
necessary is illustrated at the visitation of Gracedieu priory
in 1440–1.[3] A list of twenty-three *comperta*, chiefly reflecting
upon the prioress's misrule, follows the minutes of the evidence,

---

Ramsey Abbey (ff. 48 sqq. of the MS.), e. g. 'quia per inquisicionem
diligentem et sollertem per nos in huiusmodi visitacione factam *comperimus*
nonnulla puritati religionis inimica et contraria indies committi', etc. ;
'item quia *comperimus nobis simili modo detectum*', etc. ; 'quia *detectum
simili modo inuenimus et delatum*', etc. *Reperire, inuenire* are used as
synonyms for *comperire ; deferre* as equivalent to *detegere*.

[1] The *detecta* printed in Bradshaw and Wordsworth, *Lincoln Cathedral
Statutes*, ii, 366 sqq., illustrate this method.

[2] e. g. the schedule presented by a prior at Peterborough in 1437, and
the *gravamina* laid against the abbot by a canon of Dorchester in 1445.

[3] The nunnery has some celebrity owing to the literary charm with
which Cardinal Gasquet has drawn a picture of its internal life founded
upon domestic accounts kept some twenty-five years before Alnwick's
visitation (*English Monastic Life*, 1904, pp. 158–76). Some of the evidence in 1440–1 throws a light upon the financial state of the convent
at that very period, which proves that account-books provide an unsafe
basis for general inferences as to monastic life.

and is supplemented by further *comperta* respecting other members of the house and one of the chaplains ; after which come the written injunctions. Similarly at Ramsey the *detecta* are followed by a list of *comperta*, between which and the written injunctions is inserted the text of the verbal injunctions left by the bishop.

The language in which the written injunctions were couched was founded upon traditional precedents, and the student of episcopal registers soon becomes familiar with the characteristic phraseology of such documents.[1] So often are similar injunctions repeated in almost similar terms, from the thirteenth century onwards, that there is a natural temptation to regard their contents as merely formal pieces of advice, bearing no direct reference to facts, but intended to enforce rules which, if slackened in any way, might become a dead letter. This view has been encouraged by writers whose object is to defend the monastic life of the Middle Ages against the attacks of zealots. It has gained credence because hitherto there has been no means of studying a long series of carefully composed injunctions side by side with the minutes of the visitations which they followed.[2]

The fact, however, that a large number of injunctions with a close family likeness are included in a single register would be pointless if they were nothing more than repetitions of common forms without reference to definite facts. An episcopal register is primarily a collection of precedents. The comparative poverty of documents in the later registers—for example at York, and even at Lincoln—is due to the fact that few new precedents were by that time needed. The earlier registers contained enough and to spare. If injunctions sent to religious houses were merely polite circulars, a few common forms would be

---

[1] For printed series, see especially *Registrum Epistolarum fratris Johannis Peckham Archiepiscopi Cantuariensis* (Rolls ser., no. 77), ed. C. T. Martin, F.S.A., 1882-5 ; *Registrum Radulphi Baldock*, etc., *Episcoporum Londoniensium* (Cant. and York Soc.), ed. R. C. Fowler, F.S.A., 1911 ; and the York Registers (Giffard, Wickwane, and John le Romeyn), ed. W. Brown, F.S.A. (Surtees Soc.). Some English injunctions from Longland's register at Lincoln were contributed to *Archaeologia*, vol. xlvii, by E. Peacock, F.S.A., and a volume of injunctions from the registers of Bishops Flemyng and Gray at Lincoln is now in the press for the Lincoln Record Soc.

[2] The need of such an opportunity is shown by the note of a writer in *V. C. H. Lincoln*, ii, 173 : 'It is impossible, without the actual visitation report, to say how far injunctions are merely formal or meet actual difficulties.' A certain number of injunctions occur in Dr. Jessopp's volume of Norwich visitations ; but these are for the most part brief notes, like those already mentioned in Alnwick's visitations of Ramsey and Gracedieu, or the verbal injunctions issued by Bishops Goldwell and Nykke.

enough, and these could be easily found in earlier books. A whole quire of injunctions in a fifteenth-century register such as Gray's at Lincoln, would be a piece of wasted labour. Their presence is explained only upon the hypothesis that each was a special decree, issued as a permanent and binding addition to the statutes of the house which it concerns. In the archiepiscopal registers at York the ordinary marginal description of a set of injunctions is *decretum*.[1] In the registers of any diocese they will be found referred to under four terms, practically synonymous but often bracketed together for the sake of emphasis, *injunctiones, ordinationes, mandata*, and *statuta*. Each item is constantly introduced by such phrases as *Statuimus et iniungimus, iniungimus et mandamus, mandamus districtius iniungendo*, and other variations which effectually preclude the idea that it is merely a pious counsel. The last clause is usually a triple and peremptory admonition, enjoining the observance of the injunctions and the exaction of the penalties defined in them under pain of the greater excommunication. They are ordered to be read in public a certain number of times in the year and to be fastened up in some conspicuous place in the dorter, so that no one may be able to plead ignorance of their purport. Their language therefore, although chosen with regard to general facts, had to be drawn up in the form of general rules for future consultation; and thus it may occasionally cover in its general terms breaches of rule of which the visitation afforded no positive evidence, but the risk of which made their inclusion desirable. Gross faults affecting individuals, as has been noted already, were dealt with separately; and sometimes, where a whole house was contaminated by grave failings, a bishop was willing to spare it open shame by dispatching separate sealed injunctions relating to the more serious *comperta*.[2] It sometimes happens, however, that the ordinary injunctions contain detailed references to actual facts and the names of individuals; and such instances distinctly imply that there was urgent necessity for calling attention to facts which applied to more than one particular case.[3]

This theory of the composition and meaning of episcopal in-

[1] See e. g. *Reg. Romeyn*, ed. Brown (Surtees Soc.), i, 317, 'Decretum super visitacione de Novo Loco in Schirewode'; Reg. Thoresby, fo. 241 and *d*, 'Decretum de Fellay', etc.

[2] This was the course adopted by Bishop Gray in his visitations of Lincoln Cathedral and Ramsey Abbey in 1432 (Linc. Epis. Reg. Gray, ff. 124 and *d*, 196 *d*), and Alnwick did not spare the feelings of the monks of Ramsey so readily.

[3] It may be noted that, out of thirty-one sets of injunctions in the Alnwick MS., only one, addressed to Bourne Abbey, is a mere endorsement of previous injunctions the text of which may be found in Linc.

junctions must suggest itself to any one who studies and collates their contents with the necessary care and attention. Its proof is supplied by the condition of the written injunctions as they exist in the Alnwick MS. These documents are rough copies, full of erasures, interlineations and marginal additions, and have been manifestly composed as a result of a painstaking collation of the *detecta* and *comperta*. The paragraphs in many cases are numbered, and in some of these cases the *detecta* are actually furnished with marginal reference-numbers corresponding to those of the injunctions which cover them.[1]   The composition was entrusted to Thomas Colstone, who, modelling his language upon the common forms with which he had been familiar through nearly half a century of service under successive bishops, adapted these to the relative severity or mildness of tone which the *detecta* required.[2]   For houses of monks or canons and secular colleges he wrote in Latin, for nunneries in an English which is a close translation of the Latin forms in which he thought. After they had been composed and revised, they were submitted to the bishop for correction, and, while many of the erasures and substitutions are Colstone's own, there are many alterations and notes in a different hand which may be that either of the bishop himself or of one of his household clerks. The injunctions were then copied out and dispatched, and the rough copy was kept to be copied into the permanent register.[3]

In the transcript of the manuscript about to be published, all interlineations and marginal additions in the text have been clearly marked, and all cancelled words and passages, which it is

Epis. Reg. Flemyng, fo. 234 d. To this endorsement, however, is added a special injunction requiring the recall of an apostate canon, who had assumed a secular habit. He had obtained the office of *secundarius a decano* in St. Mary's, Warwick, and had been recognized there by some Bourne people who were going on pilgrimage to Hayles Abbey in Gloucestershire.

[1] This is the case, e. g., with the injunctions for the abbey and the ' new college ' at Leicester.

[2] This is a striking characteristic of Peckham's injunctions, in which, although there is naturally much similarity of phrase, it is obvious that each set was specially composed for the house to which it was sent. Mr. Fowler, in his introduction to *Reg. Rad. Baldock*, etc., p. iii, notes of the injunctions contained in the volume : ' The differentiation of the orders to various houses shows clearly that they were in no sense mere formalities, but aimed at definite evils.' See also the learned article by Mr. G. G. Coulton upon *The Interpretation of Visitation Documents* (Eng. Hist. Review, Jan. 1914).

[3] There is no trace of these fair copies in Alnwick's register, which, as noted above, was unsatisfactorily kept. The only set of injunctions in the register is addressed to Bardney Abbey (fo. 37, 1 April, 1440), and of these no rough copy remains. The preservation of the visitation MS. is possibly due to the delay in copying.

generally easy to read beneath the single lines of the pen which struck them out, have been restored as far as possible, so as to give the student a full opportunity of following the method of composition for himself and drawing his own inferences. It is sufficient here to illustrate the present writer's conclusions by drawing attention to a few instances connected with one very common type of injunction, which, perhaps more than any other, might be taken as favouring the theory of the polite circular.

Finance appears at no time to have been the strongest point in the monastic economy; but the difficulty of making both ends meet, if it was occasionally due to extravagance, was also the result of necessary expenses and outgoings which were very considerable. Constant hospitality to strangers and pilgrims was a severe drain upon the resources even of the wealthier houses, where such hospitality naturally increased in proportion to their importance. The habitual excuse pleaded for the appropriation of parish churches was the drain on the resources of the monastery caused by the recourse of strangers and the neighbourhood of the king's highway, while on the other hand its rents were in arrear and the value of its property had been lowered by fire, flood, and pestilence.[1] A house was frequently burdened, moreover, with external charges the nature of which is well known. The founders and patrons claimed the right of pensioning off poor relations or old servants upon the convent, who supplied them with doles or corrodies of bread and beer, or a money-payment in commutation, out of the common goods. As time went on, it became common for the convent to sell corrodies, annual pensions, and other doles for ready money to applicants, often for the term of their lives and sometimes with remainder to their heirs; and it is obvious that the advantage gained by the transaction was not so permanent as the yearly disbursement incurred.[2] An injunction common to the large majority of such documents forbids such sales without licence from the bishop and without the consent of the more and sounder part of the convent, and couples with them the equally imprudent habit of cutting down and selling timber for the immediate needs of the convent.

It might fairly be argued, with such injunctions by themselves to guide us, that this was merely a precautionary piece of advice.

---

[1] Instances are very numerous. Two may be mentioned from York Archiepis. Reg. Zouche, ff. 71 d, 145, viz. the appropriations of Great Ouseburn Church to the Abbot and Convent of Eggleston (23 May, 1348) and of Cotham Church, Notts., to the Prior and Convent of Thurgarton (1 Dec., 1350). The preambles to these decrees are full of interesting matter.

[2] See Dr. Kitchin's remarks on *Compotus Rolls of the Obedientiaries of St. Swithun's Priory, Winchester* (Hants Rec. Soc.), pp. 23-5.

Let us take. however, a few examples and compare them with the *detecta* which they follow.

In the English injunctions to Harrold priory, a house of Austin nuns in Bedfordshire, which Alnwick visited on 16th January, 1442/3, the injunction referred to is given in two separate parts, which may be quoted as a specimen of the customary forms :

> ' Also we enioyne yow prioresse and your successours vndere payne of pryuacyone and perpetuelle amocyone fro your and thaire astate and dygnyte that fro hense forthe ye ne thai selle graunte ne gyfe to ony persone what euer thai be any corrodye, lyverye, pensyone or anuyte to terme of lyve certeyn tyme or perpetuelly but if ye or thai fyrste declare the cause to vs or to our successours bysshoppes of Lincolne and in that case have our specyalle licence or of our saide successours and also the fulle assent of the more hole parte of your couent.
>
> ' Also we enioyne yow prioresse and your successours vndere the payne of prinacyone afore saide that ye ne thai selle gyfe alyeue ne felle no grete wode or tymbere saue to necessary reparacyone of your place and your tenaundryes but if ye and thai hafe specyalle licence ther to of vs or our successours bysshoppes of Lincolne and the cause declared to vs or our successours.'

Turning to the *detecta* for definite evidence, we find among certain complaints presented by dame Thomasine Courteney :

> ' Item dicit quod sunt ibidem duo corrodiarii vnus de tempore nunc et alius de tempore alterius priorisse.'

She made no specific allusion to the felling and selling of timber, but at the end of her evidence is the petition

> ' Fiat prouisio de nemoribus non vendendis vel alienandis ',

upon which the special injunction was founded.[1]

Another set of English injunctions, addressed to the Cistercian nunnery of Heynings, belongs to the class in which summaries of special *detecta* or *comperta* are prefixed to the various clauses : [2]

> ' Also for as muche as hit is detecte to hus that here a fore ther has been grete parcelles of your wodes felled and sold we charge yow pryoresse undere payn of pryuacyone of your dygnytee that fro hense ye neyther felle ne selle . . .[3] but to your necessary fewelle and beldyng ne that ye graunte ne gyfe corrodye lyvery ne annuytee wythe owte our leve or our successours asked and had and expresse assent of your couent.'

In this case the second part of the injunction is added merely

---

[1] The reference to the present numbering of the leaves of the MS. is ff. 113 d, 114. The visitation took place on Jan. 16 ; the injunctions were dispatched two days later from Newnham Priory.

[2] Sets of injunctions in which this method is freely used are those for Croyland Abbey (June 1440), Newarke College, Leicester (Dec. 1440), Newnham Priory (Jan. 1442-3), Nutley Abbey (Aug. 1447), Ramsey Abbey (June 1439), Thornton Abbey (July 1440).

[3] This portion of the injunction is now illegible.

as a corollary to the first. The actual *detectum* comes from the evidence of dame Alice Portere :

> 'Item dicit quod priorissa prosternit grossas arbores extra casum necessitatis.'

This the prioress denied :

> 'Ad hec dicit quod nullas prosterni fecit nisi ab euidente, etc., vtilitate et de expresso consensu conuentus.'

Whether, however, this was true or not, the bishop found it advisable to make an injunction against the usual improvident means of raising ready money.[1]

On July 15, 1442, bishop Alnwick visited the priory of Daventry, a house originally Cluniac, over which the bishops of Lincoln had acquired the right of visitation at an early date. Bishop Gray had visited the monastery in 1433 and had delivered injunctions, one of which dealt with the question of granting corrodies, coupled with the allied contingencies of felling timber and pawning valuables.[2] Alnwick's injunction concerns the first two of these points :

> 'Item iniungimus vobis priori qui nunc estis et qui vobis succedent in futurum sub pena amocionis et finalis priuacionis vestri et sui ab officio statu et dignitate huiusmodi ne aliqua feoda corrodia liberatas aut annuales redditus quibuscunque personis ad certum tempus terminum vite vel imperpetuum concedatis vendatis vel donetis nec nemora vel grossas arbores quouismodo vendatis aut prosternatis nisi solum ad focalia necessaria et reparaciones necessarias faciendas absque nostri vel successorum nostrorum episcoporum Lincolniensium licencia petita et obtenta et eciam de consensu maioris et sanioris partis conuentus predicti.'

Here again the second part of the injunction is added as a corollary to the first. It appears that the prior had wasted the goods of the house to such an extent that the bishop found it necessary to assign the temporalities in commission to the subprior and another monk ; but there is no direct statement that he had felled timber. The need for the injunction, however, appears from the revelations of the sacrist, William Daventre, to which the prior's answers are appended :

> 'Item dicit quod prior concessit sub sigillo suo cuidam Johanni West de Dauentre vuum censum annuum xx solidorum et vnam

---

[1] Ff. 22, 23. The visitation was on April 7, 1440 : the injunctions are not dated.

[2] Linc. Epis. Reg. Gray, fo. 199. The preamble to Gray's injunctions was that which he used for Huntingdon Priory, and could have been sent only to a house in a state of utter decay : 'Heu prothdolor religio periit caritas exulat obseruancie regulares . . . quasi obliuiscuntur . . . Non est hic aliud nisi ebrietas et crapula sompnoleucia non dicimus incontinencia sed torpor et omne aliud quod in malum declinat et hominem trahit ad gehennam.'

togam de liberata domus absque consensu conuentus cum in nullo
sciat aut possit prodesse prioratui. Negat concessionem.

'Item prior concessit Johanni Horne de Dauentre vnum annuum
censum v marcarum vt staret pro monasterio in agendo et tamen
pocius contra prioratum quam cum domo. Fatetur pactum cum
eodem Johanne tamen non est sibi solutum.'[1]

At Dorchester abbey in 1441 the convent was generally in a
bad state: the abbot was guilty of immorality and dilapidation,
and the temporal government had fallen into the hands of a lay-
man, who lived in the monastery with his servants at the common
expense.   There is no further evidence in the *detecta* as to the
corrodies and pensions which this irregular state of things probably involved; but there is an injunction in the usual terms.
This, however, is not a mere wanton or formal addition to the
document; for at the end of the *detecta* comes the special note
that the abbot was enjoined in virtue of obedience and under
pain of excommunication and deprivation, to grant no corrody,
pension, etc., in perpetuity, etc., without the advice, consent, and
licence of the diocesan and patron asked and had. It is impossible
to doubt that such an injunction, evidently the verbal injunction
made at the visitation, was founded on good cause, and that the
written injunction was not composed without consideration.[2]

The injunctions (July 1440) for the small Benedictine abbey
of Humberstone, near Grimsby, originally an offshoot of the
Tironensian abbey of Hambye in the diocese of Coutances,[3] contain a clause forbidding the granting of corrodies, couched in the
usual terms, but without the addition of the clause against felling
timber. The evidence of Thomas Fressheneye upon this point is
very detailed, and is interlineated with the abbot's answers.

'Item dicit quod abbas isto absente vendidit vnum corrodium
cuidam Wyldbore pro quo recepit c marcas et valet fere per annum x
marcas (*fatetur de consensu*); et aliud vendidit Willelmo Paincharde
pro quo recepit x libras et valet per annum xxxiij s. iiij d. (*fatetur de
consensu tamen conuentus*); et aliud Johanni Hoise pro quo recepit xx
libras et valuit per annum quatuor marcas; et aliud Roberto Howet
de Normanby pro xx libris et valuit quatuor marcas per annum
(*fatetur de consensu*); et aliud Roberto Howet sargeaunt portere isto
existente apud Molycourt pro viij marcis et valet v nobilia per annum
(*fatetur*); et aliud Ricardo Bekeryng botylere pro xx marcis et valet
xlvj s. viij d. per annum (*fatetur*); et quod actum est de istis receptis
nescitur nisi de xvij marcis receptis de Ricardo Botylere cum quibus
Anderby tunc cellerarius soluit debita abbatis.'

That is to say, the abbot, for ready money amounting to

---

[1] Ff. 88 *d*-90. The injunctions bear date from Daventry Priory, July 17.
[2] Ff. 111-113. The visitation was on March 27, 1441; the injunctions
bear no date.
[3] This is noted in the injunctions delivered by Flemyng in 1422-3
(Linc. Epis. Reg. Flemyng, fo. 234). In the heading of Alnwick's
visitation the monastery is said to be *ordinis Turonensis* (*sic*).

£135 6s. 8d., had committed the convent to yearly charges
amounting to £17 13s. 4d.; while of the sum received only
£11 6s. 8d. had been properly accounted for.[1]

The abbey of St. Mary of the Meadows at Leicester, the most
important house of Austin canons in the diocese, was visited by
Alnwick in December 1440.   One of the elaborately composed
injunctions forbids the granting of corrodies and felling of timber,
with the following additional clause :

> 'quodque nec quenquam extraneum de bonis communibus mona-
> sterii sustentetis aut tali aliter quam vt hospiti transeunti alimoniam
> de hiisdem bonis quouismodo ministretis seu ministrari faciatis aut
> permittatis nisi in hoc aliter processeritis de expresso consensu et
> assensu conuentus predicti aut sanioris et maioris partis eiusdem.'

In this case the injunctions are for the most part directed against
the abbot, William Sadyngton, whose masterful control of the
common funds and ill temper had alienated a generally well-
conducted body of canons.[2] All money passed through his hands :
the cellarer and treasurer had only a nominal tenure of offices
which he usurped.   The accusation of felling timber is covered
by the complaint that he had employed the common sources of
income in unauthorized building expenses, and took all the credit
to himself, as if he had paid out of his own pocket.   William
Coventre, the guest-master, said :

> 'quod abbas habet in manu sua officia thesaurarii et cellerarii et
> quando vltimo computauit dixit quod melius foret vt non computaret
> quia pocius foret sibi conuentus indebitatus quam ipse conuentui ; et
> semper recipit arreragia compotorum ministrorum et de hiis receptis
> nullum reddit compotum ; et dicit quod omnia edificia monasterii de
> nouo facta sunt expensis communibus et elemosinis et tamen abbas
> dicit quod ipse fecit hec omnia.'

John Sadyngton, the cellarer, supplied the reason for the injunction against corrodies and the amplifying clause by which the
maintenance of strangers was forbidden :

> 'Item dicit quod sunt duo qui sustentantur de bonis communibus
> domus per abbatem vnus clericus et alter laicus sed nescit qualiter
> vel quando venerunt in monasterium.'

These, as other *detecta* show, were suspected of practising the art
of 'multiplying' with the abbot, who, in his zeal for money-
getting, had traffic with professors of the black art and used
charms and incantations.   Henry Gysley laid information :

> 'de quodam hospitato iuxta portas monasterii ad sumptus mona-
> sterii per quod credit fratres peius valere cuius nomen ignorat.'

---

[1] Ff. 69, 70, 74 d. The visitation was on 6 July, 1440 : the injunctions
were dispatched from Wellow Abbey on 8 July.

[2] John Whytley deposed ' quod abbas in correctione non est modestus
sed rigorosus et crudelis et si quis canonicus sibi displiceat inhumaniter
reprehendit eos eciam opprobriose ac contumeliose in eorum scandalum '.

Two of the *detecta* furnished by William Coventre have marginal numbers pointing to this injunction:

> 'Item dicit de multiplicatore vt supra nominato Roberto et seruiente suo Thoma vt supra et dicit quod sic diuulgatum est in partibus et timet quod per hoc dampnificabitur monasterium per ministros regis.
>
> 'Item dicit quod sunt infra monasterium lij seruientes seculares et in verneyerde [*sic*] xviij quorum plures sunt nedum inutiles sed dampnosi monasterio.'

Coventre also added:

> 'quod abbas habet plures tales seculares ignotos sibi adherentes quibus vltimate fauet.'

William Buttrc, the sub-chanter, dealt with the last point in fuller detail:

> 'Item dicit quod abbas multum extraneat se a confratribus et multum dedignanter et torno vultu respicit eos nolens eis loqui sed preteriens indignanter; et cum sederint secum in mensa tempore minucionum non est affabilis inter eos nec communicat cum eis in mensa sed tantum cum secularibus sibi seruientibus et sic non tractat eos ut fratres aut filios sed tanquam forent sibi ignoti vel alieni.'[1]

Two final examples may be taken from houses of Austin canons in north Lincolnshire. There is an injunction to Thornholm priory (April 1440) closely similar to the Leicester injunction and divided into three parts in the same way. The last clause, however, is confined to the maintenance of one particular type of outsider:

> 'quodque non sustineatis quoscunque de parentela vestra sumptibus domus,' etc.

William Lincolne said:

> 'quod prior vendidit cuidam Edwardo vnum corrodium pro quo recepit xx.li. quod stat in vj panibus certi ... melioris ponderis ... et conuentus[2] et totidem lagenas [*sic*] et vnam domum pro habitacione sua certum focale nescit quantum vnum porcum pro lardaria et vnum modium pro farina.
>
> 'Item vendidit aliud corrodium Johanni Cutylere ad terminum vite et coniugis sue ipso mortuo ad medietatem pro xx marcis quod consistit in sua habitacione ad reparacionem prioris septem similibus panibus et vij lagenis ceruisie.
>
> 'Et preter ista sunt v alia corrodia antiquitus vendita.'

Richard Burstalle's evidence gives the reason for the last part of the injunction:

> 'Item dicit quod prior expensis domus sustentat fratrem suum naturalem et eius filium et sustentauit per biennium et in nullo prosunt domui.
>
> 'Item dicit quod in prioratu sunt sex corrodiarii quorum quilibet valet annuatim ad minus xls. et duo sunt ad extra.'

[1] Ff. 104-106. The visitation took place on 3 December, 1440: the injunctions were dispatched later in the month from Liddington, Rutland.

[2] This passage is illegible, but the change of case in the rest of the paragraph appears to be a mere piece of carelessness.

Simon Lincolne, a canon in the infirmary, corroborated Burstalle's evidence about the prior's relations, and stated further :

> ' quod prior recipit ad mensam filios generosorum et nichil recipit ab eisdem non obstante quod prioratus oneratur ere alieno et aliis grauibus.'

The sale of timber was mentioned by William Asshendone :

> ' Item dicit quod prior vendidit diuersas grossas arbores per se : videatur igitur si precium earum contineatur in billa ministrata per priorem.'

This was repeated by Simon Lincolne, while Burstalle complained that the sale had been effected to the detriment of necessary repairs to the buildings :

> ' Item dicit quod pecunie recepte pro boscis venditis per priorem extendunt se ad c. marcas et quod edificia propter non reparacionem deteriorantur ad xl. li. in defectu prioris, et istud dampnum euenit tempore istius prioris propter ipsius incuriam.' [1]

The ninth injunction to Wellow abbey, close to Great Grimsby, concerns corrodies only, without further additions. The evidence comes from the deposition of John Tolsone :

> ' Item dicit quod abbas vendidit vnum corrodium Johanni Mathewe pro l marcis de consensu conuentus : non stat in tanto quantum percipient [sic] duo canonici in esculentis et poculentis et stetit in eo x annis et amplius.' [2]

Only one type of injunction has been examined here, and that of the most general and inclusive character, and the examples have been purposely selected without any attempt to present the conclusions of the present writer in a designedly favourable light. The examination, however, of others in the same way produces the same results.[3] Cases in which an injunction apparently bears no reference to the depositions are extremely rare ; and in such instances it would appear that the compiler had reason for thinking that such an injunction might be useful, and so inserted it. Now and then he certainly wrote down an injunction which he or the bishop, comparing it with the evidence, thought unnecessary and crossed out.[4] Secondly, it is not uncommon to find an injunction modelled upon a time-honoured form, of which

---

[1] Ff. 86 d-88. The date of the visitation was 12 April, 1440 : the injunctions were not issued until 4 August following, from Sleaford Castle.

[2] Ff. 71, 77 d. The visitation was held on 7 July : the injunctions bear no date.

[3] e. g. an injunction against *potaciones post completorium* occurs in 15 out of the 31 sets of injunctions, and is borne out in every case by the *detecta*.

[4] The injunctions to Dorchester Abbey in 1440 are a case in point. Two injunctions, forbidding the keeping of hounds in the monastery and ordering a careful survey of buildings, were cancelled : one, forbidding the access of women to the cloister, was added as an afterthought.

a part only is supported by the *detecta*. Yet here the common form has been built up on a recognition of the similarity of the practices which it denounces : one affords suspicion of or actually implies another. There is, therefore, good reason for applying the common form in a wider sense than the evidence at first sight appears to warrant. But there are also the numerous cases in which the text of an injunction, modelled upon a common form, is modified or amplified either to exclude or to emphasize the *detecta*. Sometimes only part of the common form is used : sometimes it is left out altogether. At other times it is given in full with special alterations and additions. The same variety is found in injunctions of which the visitation records are lost : Flemyng's and Gray's in their fair copies show differences the only explanation of which is that they are founded directly upon a conscientious examination of the *detecta*, and consequently contain historical evidence as to the contemporary state of the monasteries to which they refer, which cannot be overlooked or treated lightly.

It is undoubtedly true that Alnwick's visitations cannot lead the candid student to very favourable conclusions as to the state of the religious houses of his diocese in the fifteenth century. Carelessness in the observance of the rule was almost universal. Money matters were unsatisfactory. Divisions and quarrelling were very general : the abbot or prior, as at Leicester abbey, sometimes was at war with the whole house : sometimes he had his party, while one of the obedientiaries led another.[1] The buildings, as at Bardney, were sometimes ruinous, and no steps were taken to repair them.[2] There was a general tendency, especially in nunneries, for religious to abandon the common life and occupy private rooms, where parties of friends had their meals together instead of in the frater. There was much intercourse with lay-folk and superfluous entertainment, which wasted the alms of the house. There was also a lowering of the moral standard, of which, though it very seldom extended to the whole convent, there are individual instances in a very large number of

---

[1] This happened, e. g., at Gracedieu Priory, where the prioress favoured some of the young nuns, calling them her *discipule* and encouraging them to spy upon their sisters.

[2] Architectural references are neither numerous nor definite ; but a visitation of Nun Cotham, a priory of Cistercian nuns, supplies evidence for the division of Cistercian fraters into upper and lower stories, the lower being used as the misericord. Dame Ellen Frost, the sub-prioress, besought ' quod refectorium seruetur omni die cum sit vnum refectorium superius in quo vescuntur piscibus et lacticiniis et aliud inferius in quo ex gracia vescuntur carnibus ', etc. This arrangement clearly existed during the fifteenth century in several Cistercian abbeys, e. g. Jervaulx, Kirkstall, and Ford ; but hitherto documentary evidence for it appears to have been wanting.

the houses visited. These facts, however, reflect discredit upon
the weakness of human nature, not upon the monastic ideal, and,
before they are made the basis of an attack upon the monastic
system, it is well to consider how far we ourselves would have been
able to live up to its stern requirements. The close examination
of such documents serves to bring us closer to the truth of a
problem which is still often hotly disputed, and to raise its discussion above the inaccuracies of partisan statement."

Thanks were ordered to be returned for these communications.

Thursday, 14th May, 1914.

Sir ARTHUR JOHN EVANS, Knt., M.A., D.Litt., F.R.S.,
President, in the Chair.

The following gifts were announced, and thanks for the same
ordered to be returned to the donors :

From J. E. Pritchard, Esq., F.S.A. :—A sketch of the early history of
Bathford and its neighbourhood. By H. D. Skrine. 12mo. Bath,
1871.

From the Author :—The development of London, and the London Building Acts. By W. R. Davidge. 4to. London, 1914.

From Lawrence Weaver, Esq., F.S.A. :—The gilds and companies of
London. By George Unwin. 8vo. London, 1908.

The Rev. Philip Thomas Byard Clayton, M.A., was admitted
a Fellow.

Notice was given of a ballot for the election of Fellows on
Thursday, June 11, 1914, and the list of the candidates to be
put to the ballot was read.

The Marquess of Northampton exhibited the Clephane horn,
upon which O. M. Dalton, Esq., M.A., F.S.A., read a paper
which will be printed in *Archaeologia*.

The medieval oliphant, known as the Clephane horn, was
long preserved by the family of that name at Carslogie Castle
in Fife, and presumably passed into the possession of the Mar-
quesses of Northampton after the marriage of the second
Marquess with Miss Clephane in 1815. It was published by
Sir Walter Scott in his *Border Antiquities* in 1814 ; and was

shown at the Manchester Art Treasures Exhibition in 1857,
and at South Kensington in 1862. It has been variously regarded as late-antique, Carolingian, and Romanesque; but a
comparison with other oliphants, with designs in illuminated
manuscripts and with frescoes, seems to show that it should be
ascribed to the province of Byzantine art, and that it probably
belongs to the eleventh century. Though considerably damaged,
it is in some respects the most remarkable of all known oliphants; and its rich figure-decoration, illustrating the contests
of the amphitheatre, lends it an exceptional importance to
archaeology.

Professor BOYD DAWKINS hazarded the suggestion that the
word oliphant was derived from the Greek word for ivory.

The PRESIDENT said the absence of criticism was a tribute to
the thoroughness of Mr. Dalton's researches. He was himself
inclined to accept a Byzantine origin, but saw one or two difficulties; some decorative elements in that style did not appear
on the Clephane horn, and there was a certain reticence in the
handling of the foliage that suggested an earlier date. It was
interesting to find so much left of the classical spirit in the
eleventh century, such as the amphitheatre, the wrestling, and
other contests. The dress of the wrestlers was that usually
associated with gladiatorial shows. One would gladly know
how such things reached Constantinople and western Europe;
and it was tempting to regard the horn as one used in the
amphitheatre and depicted on certain examples. There were
remarkable vases in Crete resembling a straight horn, and dating
about 1600 B.C. They were not only an early form of the
rhyton but were divided into zones representing divisions of
metal plates, and the subjects depicted were curiously like those
on the oliphants. Was it possible to trace the use of the horn
from Carlovingian times back to Minoan Crete? The Clephane
horn seemed to preserve the classical tradition in an early and
simple form, but he was not prepared to dispute Mr. Dalton's
chronology.

Mr. DALTON replied that the style in fact closely followed
classical tradition, but there were features later than the sixth
century; and as the wars of Heraclius and the iconoclastic
troubles compelled us to overleap two or three hundred years,
it seemed necessary to assign the horn to the revival which
followed the close of the ninth century.

G. B. GRUNDY, Esq., D.Litt., communicated the following
note on the so-called Ryknield or Riknild Street:

" The general course of this road from Littleover, near Derby, to a point at Weston-sub-Edge, near Broadway in Worcestershire, is fairly well known. The course from Weston to the place where the road met the Foss Way has always been a matter of conjecture.

This conjectural part of it passed over the Cotswold Hills.

Professor Haverfield in his article on Roman Worcestershire in the *Victoria County History,* and Mr. Codrington in his book on Roman roads suggest that, after passing Weston, it followed the line of the west boundary of the parishes of Weston and Chipping Campden up to the road from Broadway to Stow-on-the-Wold, which is here called the Five Mile Drive. This parish boundary is straight; and the tendency of parish boundaries to follow the line of a Roman road is well known. After crossing the Drive the boundary becomes a county boundary between Gloucestershire and Worcestershire as well as a parish boundary. For about a third of a mile after crossing the Drive it continues in the same straight line. It then bends through an angle of about fifteen degrees, and runs south by east along a green road which is now no more than a cart-track. After crossing the road from Chipping Campden to Snowshill it enters the private grounds of the late Major Knox of Spring Hill, and passes for nearly a mile through a line of plantations, some of which are of recent planting. The boundary runs parallel to, and from ten to twenty yards east of, a private road locally known as the Switchback, up to a point about a quarter of a mile north-east of the house at Spring Hill. It then continues, partly through the garden, partly along the east edge of it, down into a valley to the south-east of the house. At that point the county boundary turns west at right angles, and becomes, of course, of no further interest as a conjectural line of the road; but if the line of the straight piece of the county boundary be produced southwards, it is taken up, after an interval of two and a half miles, by a straight piece of road running from the north to the village of Condicote. Just north of the village it diverges from the line to enter the village; but immediately south of the village the line is taken up again by an absolutely straight but little used lane which runs from Condicote for about two miles as far as the road from Stow-on-the-Wold to Cheltenham. This point is about two miles from the Foss Way. If the line of this lane were continued to the Foss Way it would meet that road at a point about a mile due north of Bourton-on-the-Water.

By the kind hospitality of the late Major Knox of Spring Hill I was recently able to explore this conjectural line of road at that part of it which is supposed to coincide with the county boundary; and with his help I gathered some evidence which may be useful in determining the course of the road.

From the Five Mile Drive to the road from Chipping Campden to Snowshill the county boundary follows what has evidently been a broad balk dividing the plough-lands of one parish from those of the other. It has already been said that the line bends through an angle of about fifteen degrees in this part of its course; and the object of this bend is evidently to carry the line round the head of a deep steep-sided combe known as Tilbury Hollow. It is a combe which even a Roman road would seek to avoid, if it could do so without too great a divergence from the straight line. Along the balks, as is usually the case with the broad balks which divide the plough-lands of neighbouring village communities from one another, a cart track and right-of-way have developed. The boundary wall is on the west side of the balk. Running along the balk beside the wall for practically the whole distance of a mile is an agger such as is associated with the remains of Roman roads in this country. It rises from a foot to eighteen inches above the general surface of the balk. The modern cart track has in some places cut into it, but has for the most part avoided it, keeping along the east side of the balk, i.e. on the side opposite to the wall. The present breadth of the agger is from twelve to fourteen feet; but it is obvious that its original breadth has been diminished by the cutting of a ditch along the side of the wall. In the plantations on Major Knox's estate there is what looks like the line of an agger, which is more or less clearly traceable until you come to the garden. There it has disappeared. But it appears again just below the gate where the drive leaves the garden, and extends for a few hundred yards into the small valley to the south of the house. But in this part it has been much cut up by the making of a ditch and bank. On the far or south slope of the valley the agger is not apparent; and beyond that point ploughed fields extend as far as the eye can see—in fact, the land is not of such a nature as to hold out any hope of the agger of a Roman road having survived upon it.

After examining this line I chose two places, one on the balk, and one in the woodland, at which to make a section of the apparent agger. That in the woodland known as the Central Wood I made first. It did not appear very promising, because the soil had been much disturbed by the roots, not merely of the present trees, but of old trees which have stood upon the same ground. What I found was as follows: the top layer for about nine inches deep in the centre, and about six inches deep at the sides, consisted of what was probably leaf-mould, with a certain admixture, not very noticeable, of fine broken

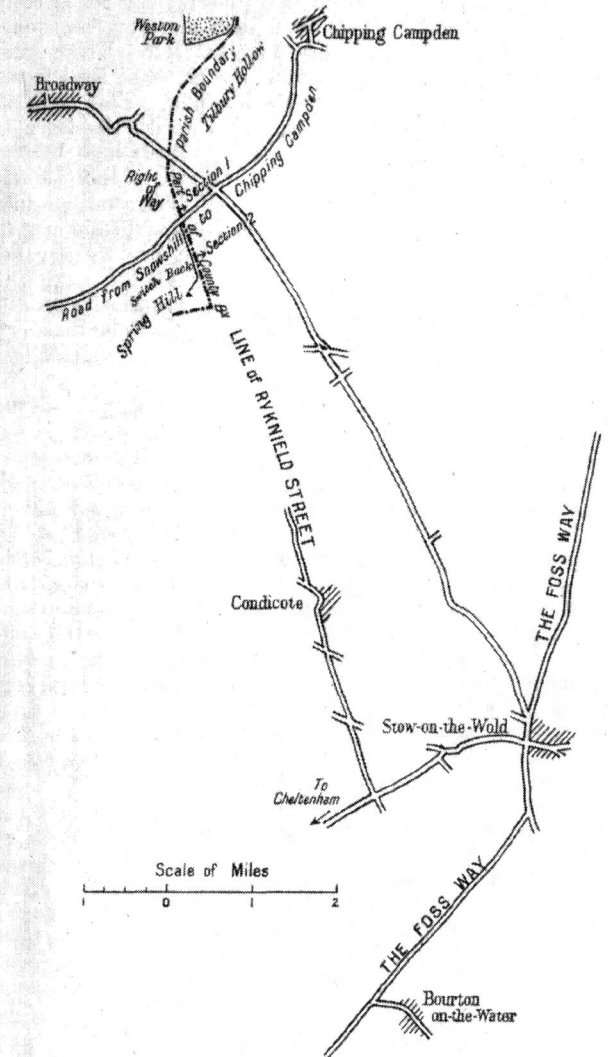

SKETCH-MAP SHOWING THE COURSE OF RYKNIELD STREET BETWEEN WESTON
AND THE FOSS WAY.

stones. Underneath that came a distinctly marked layer of stones in the shape of rough slabs of a more or less square shape, and from twelve to eighteen inches' side. These were the slabs which are easily split from the plentiful local stone, and are now largely used in wall building. This layer of stones was about six inches thick. Underneath the layer of stones was a layer of earth which had obviously been beaten. It was of quite a different nature to the soil of this country when in its ordinary condition; but was in that condition into which it is reduced by, for instance, the continual trampling of animals. Beneath this was the rock which lies so near the surface in the Cotswold country.

So far the investigation had not led to any conclusive results. The structure was such as might be suspected to be that of a road; but it was not that of any Roman road of which I had previously taken a section.

The second section was made on the balk, a little more than a hundred yards north of the Chipping Campden and Snowshill road. There the apparent agger was much more marked than in the wood. The surface in this case was covered with a layer of turf. When the turf was removed a layer of small broken stones and earth was disclosed. In this instance the stone largely preponderated in quantity over the earth. Underneath this came a layer of flags or flat stones similar to those found in the same relative position in the wood. This was about six inches thick. Underneath that came the same beaten earth which had been noticed in the previous section; but in this case it was deeper. After that came the local rock of the country.

My own impression is that this is the actual line of road. The small stone of what I believe to have been the original surface of the road corresponds to that which Professor Haverfield and I found on the surface of the Akeman Street in Blenheim Park. Underneath the structure is different to what we found on the Akeman Street. In the present instance the layer of slabs seems to have been designed to prevent the small surface-stones from being trodden into the earth; and the beaten earth is intended to form a solid foundation for the road, and, at the same time, to raise the roadway well above the surface of the adjacent ground level. In the case of the Akeman Street the same precaution was taken, but in a more elaborate way, against the possibility of the surface-stones being trodden in."

The PRESIDENT, on behalf of E. H. BINNEY, Esq., M.A., communicated the following note on Roman Pottery, etc., found at Nythe Farm, Wilts. :

"Near Nythe Farm, Stratton St. Margaret, Wilts., at a spot about 3 miles east of Swindon Station, on Ermine Street, the Ordnance Map marks 'Nidum, Roman Station'. Visiting the place so marked in April last I found that the ground being covered with pasture in that neighbourhood showed nothing on the surface (except some irregularities in the level close to 'Covingham Farm'), but in a large field belonging to Nythe Farm, about 200 yards farther north (on the west side of the road), a great number of holes had been dug to a depth of about 3 ft., apparently to receive posts for new railings.

Those along the side of the road, forming a line parallel with the hedge and about 2 yds. within it, and the holes along the two sides leading to the road (to a distance of some 50 yds. from it) yielded black earth containing a large quantity of fragments of pottery, mostly grey and black ware of varying degrees of coarseness, a few pieces being large enough to indicate roughly the size and shape of the vessels to which they belonged. There were a fair number of pieces of 'Samian' ware, a number of iron nails, and an iron spiked implement with a socket. Two fragments of glass were found, one of them being a piece of the hollow rim of a flat-sided vessel. I found one bronze coin, and obtained another from a workman who had found it in digging foundations for a new cottage adjoining the north side of the field, but both were so corroded as to be difficult to identify.

In the holes near the road the black earth extended to a depth of nearly 3 ft., below which was clay. As one receded from the road the clay was found nearer the surface, and at 50 yds. from the road there was very little of the black earth below the turf."

Professor BOYD DAWKINS referred to maps on which Ryknield Street could be distinctly traced. From Chipping Campden there was a long straight piece of Roman road that he thought came due south from Alcester; and south of Chipping Campden there were small sections that could be picked out on the map, indicating its course till it reached the Foss Way. It was a good instance of Roman point-to-point road-making, as contrasted with the pre-Roman roads that were mostly ridgeways. In this case the older road, 'Buckle Street' (1 in. contour Ordnance Map, sheet 217), occupies the divide on the west and makes for the Foss Way, near Bourton-on-the-Water, taking the line of least resistance. He had endeavoured to make out a scheme of pre-Roman roads, and many were clear in Hants, Wilts., and Somerset. The Romans found them not straight enough and in some cases modified the earlier course. Bronze Age camps were linked together by those early trackways, which were also marked by tumuli; and in many cases the Roman and British roads might be compared to a bowstring and a bent bow.

Mr. J. G. Wood referred to the utilization and straightening of British roads by the Romans. The Foss Way south of Cirencester went straight, and the earlier road went round by Tetbury, making a bow. If the line from Honeybourne to Weston were produced south, it would coincide with a stretch between Condicote and the Foss Way, but between Weston and Condicote there was a gap. The reason why the Roman road did not run straight there was that it would have had to cross the Midford sands, which were water-bearing. A diversion was therefore made to the west. There was a spur to carry the road at Springhill where the fragments occurred, and that arrangement showed the ingenuity of the Roman engineers. The discovery was of much interest, and he inquired whether the stone used for paving was of local origin.

Mr. Peers said the road was composed of three layers—earth with small stones, flags, and a layer of beaten earth. He had lately taken over officially a mile and a half of a Roman road in Goathland parish, North Riding, Yorks., parts of which had been quarried by the farmers. The simplest course was to expose it, and that had been done. It was a paved way, 12 ft. to 14 ft. wide, with irregular kerbing. The section was visible where streams had cut through. A bed of clay had been laid in a trench. Stone slabs were set on this, and earth or clay placed above them to make a level surface. There was a curious resemblance to the road described in the paper, which could only have been intended for light traffic.

Mr. Reginald Smith inquired whether it was possible to determine the relation of the burials or cemetery mentioned in Mr. Binney's paper to the line of the Roman road near Swindon. The main roads were often flanked by burials, and an examination of the pottery, coins, and other objects from the graves might give a limiting date for the construction of one of the chief Roman roads in Britain.

The President was aware that Professor Boyd Dawkins had proved in many districts the adaptation of older tracks by the Romans. Mr. Grundy was investigating other points on the Berkshire Downs, and a new chapter in the history of Roman Britain would probably be opened. Certain roads had been too hastily condemned by specialists in the Roman period.

Thanks were ordered to be returned for these communications.

THURSDAY, 28th MAY, 1914.

Sir ARTHUR JOHN EVANS, Kut., M.A., D.Litt., F.R.S.,
President, in the Chair.

The following gifts were announced, and thanks for the same
ordered to be returned to the donors :

From the Author :—St. Nicholas's Church, Liverpool : its architectural
history. By Henry Peet, F.S.A. 8vo. Edinburgh, 1913.

From the Author :—Portraiture of our Stuart monarchs from their coins
and medals. Part V. William III. By Helen Farquhar. 8vo.
London, 1913.

From Harold Sands, Esq., F.S.A.:—Mast and sail in Europe and Asia.
By H. Warington Smyth. 8vo. London, 1906.

From the Brighton and Hove Archaeological Club :— Brighton and Hove
Archaeologist. Vol. I, 1914. 8vo. Hove, 1914.

Frank Simpson, Esq., was admitted a Fellow.

Notice was again given of the ballot for the election of Fellows
to be held on Thursday, June 11th, and the list of the candidates
to be put to the ballot was again read.

A. L. RADFORD, Esq., F.S.A., exhibited a small collection of
English regal heraldic stained glass, mostly of the early sixteenth
century, consisting of the following pieces : shield of arms of
Richard I, from Lichfield Cathedral, temp. Edward I ; two blue
and white Lancastrian roses, temp. Henry V ; one white rose,
temp. Edward IV ; quarries with the crowned R and boar's-head
badge of Richard III ; portrait of one of the daughters of
Edward IV, from the Becket window, Canterbury Cathedral ;
crowned red rose of Henry VII ; arms of Henry VIII and Jane
Seymour in a Gothic wreath composed of red and white roses ;
another piece, but smaller, with the same arms ; arms of Henry
VIII in a wreath, with the initials H.K.P., being the initials of
Henry and Katherine Parr ; monogram H.K.P.,in a classic wreath
divided by bands of red and white roses ; the badge of Jane
Seymour, in the form of a signet ring ; arms of Henry VIII in
a Gothic wreath of red and white roses ; arms of Edward VI
in a wreath of amorini ; Prince of Wales's feathers, with initials
E.P. and motto HIC DEIN in a wreath of amorini ; small coat
of arms of Henry VIII, with initials H.R. and date 1532 ; arms
of Edward VI, with prince's crown, in wreath of amorini ; red
and white Tudor rose and crown, temp. Edward VI.

The bulk of the collection was formed by the late Richard
Cockle Lucas, the sculptor, and was acquired twenty-six years

ago, from his son, by the present owner. The two last pieces were obtained later, and were formerly in Cowick priory, near Exeter.

J. P. BUSHE-FOX, Esq., read a report on the excavations undertaken at Hengistbury Head in 1912–13:

Hengistbury Head is situated to the east of Bournemouth, and south of Christchurch Harbour. In prehistoric times it had been converted into a promontory fort by the throwing up of large earthworks. The area actually explored amounted to about forty-two acres. Three barrows, two of them 100 feet in diameter, were also dug; these yielded fine examples of Bronze Age pottery. With one of the burials was an incense cup, a bronze and amber pendant, some amber beads, and two gold bosses. The settlement was situated on a gently sloping tract of land bordering the harbour, on the north side of the Head. The inhabitants lived in huts composed of wattle and daub, with clay and gravel floors. There was evidence of working in gold, silver, bronze, iron, glass, and Kimmeridge shale. The presence of loom-weights and spindle-whorls showed that the art of weaving was known. Coins also appear to have been minted to a large extent, over 4,000 gold, silver, and bronze examples having been found, as well as metal in the crude state. The greater part of the coins was British, with a sprinkling of Gaulish and Channel Islands examples; many of them were new types. A large number was of a type that has only once been found before, and in the same locality. These were all in mint condition, and appeared to have never been in circulation. About 100 Roman coins were found in connexion with these British examples. The latest of these belonged to the reign of Antoninus Pius, in the middle of the second century A.D. That British coins should have been minted in the second century A.D. is of extreme interest, as it shows that the inhabitants of this part of the island, at any rate, had been little affected by the Roman occupation that began nearly a hundred years before.

Many small objects were also met with, including a bracelet of thick twisted gold wire, part of a gold torc, many brooches and other articles of different metals, also glass beads and bracelets of different colours.

The occupation of the site must have begun at an early period, as a large number of flints was discovered, most of them belonging to the Neolithic period. The latest objects found may be placed in the fourth century A.D.

It has been very difficult to fill the gap between the end of the Bronze Age and the period immediately preceding the

Roman period in this island. The excavations at Hengistbury have added considerably to our knowledge in this respect.

This period has been divided into two sections on the Continent, which have been named after sites where a large number of objects have been found, viz. Hallstatt, in the Austrian Tyrol (800 to 400 B.C.), and La Tène in Switzerland (400 B.C. to the Roman period). At Hengistbury a complete series of pottery, including the Hallstatt and La Tène periods, has been found. Many of the Hengistbury types have direct parallels in such places as the Armorican peninsula, the valley of the Aisne, Bavaria, and the south-west of France and the Pyrenees. Their prototypes may, in many instances, be traced back to the Illyro-Italic people, who inhabited the north of Italy and the lands north of the Adriatic. The Hengistbury examples include some fine specimens of the pedestal and cordoned urns, as well as pottery decorated with running scrolls, the Greek fret and wave patterns.

The paper will be printed in *Reports*.

Mr. REGINALD SMITH said the meeting had listened to a business-like account of a remarkable enterprise, and hoped that it would be worthily published. The Society was deeply indebted to Sir George Meyrick and the other contributors to the fund for the exploration of Hengistbury, and much good fortune as well as hard work had fallen to the share of Mr. Bushe-Fox. The exhibits were creditable to all concerned, and represented a period which might at last be said to be proved in England. One of the dark periods in British prehistory was that between the end of the Bronze Age and the Early Iron Age of La Tène; and Hengistbury had done much to make the transition clear. There was no time to describe the flints in any detail, but he thought some were earlier than the bulk of surface-finds. The occurrence of flints in the body of a grave-mound only implied that they had been lying on or near the surface when the barrow was raised; and erroneous conclusions might be drawn, for instance, from the flints found in Yorkshire barrows. The concentration of the flints in certain spots, in association with Bronze Age or later remains, proved not that they were all contemporary, but that ancient workshop sites had been disturbed; otherwise flints ought to have been found in all the excavated sites. It was a pity that the excavations had thrown no new light on the date of the double dykes which cut off the promontory fort. Pitt-Rivers had failed to prove by excavation the exact date of somewhat similar defences at Flamborough, but disposed of their traditional attribution to the Danes.

Professor Boyd Dawkins agreed with the last speaker as to flints occurring in the barrows and even on Roman sites; they could not be regarded as contemporary with either. The isolation of the headland reminded him of Glastonbury, where the British lake-village was cut off from the mainland by a deep foss and high bank. It would be interesting to know whether any of the dwellings explored were round or square in plan. He knew of no square buildings of that date in the country; and the nearest approach to that plan was at Glastonbury, where some seemed to have been pulled down to make way for circular huts. At Tre'r Ceiri it was possible the square plan was later than the British hut-circles. The paper had been one of the old-fashioned kind with a large proportion of original information and a minimum of theory.

The President bore witness to the high scientific interest of the paper, which followed the true comparative method and revealed a close study of the Hallstatt forms. With such a wide outlook the author had been able to establish the interesting fact that Hengistbury illustrated the history of Britain over a whole millennium, from the seventh or eighth century B.C. to the third century after Christ. That had not hitherto been possible, but the exploration of the site had shown a connexion between the late Bronze Age and Hallstatt forms of Britain, Bavaria, S. France, and the Pyrenees. The period named after La Tène, which began in Britain about the fourth century B.C. but lasted longer there than elsewhere, generally went under the name of Late-Celtic, and he was particularly gratified to find his own views as to the cordons and pedestals of Aylesford confirmed by later discoveries. New forms had come to light that found their closest analogies in the painted pottery of the Venetian region. A piece of enamel showed a further connexion with Mont Beuvray (the ancient Bibracte), Saône-et-Loire, France, and the art was evidently practised at Hengistbury. The Glastonbury parallels illustrated the transitions to Roman Britain. The coin finds were of special interest, Roman silver and British copper extending over about three centuries, most of the latter series being derived from the well-known Macedonian prototype; but there were others that were not British and indicated the ancient lines of commerce. Some forms were derived from coins of Seleucus, one probably came from the Cenomani, and others showed a connexion with the Pyrenees right across France. He himself had traced coins of the Greek emporia of N.E. Spain to the dolphin type of Syracuse. The latest native coinage was rather pathetic, being cast in the last state of degradation but still showing the British spirit of the West struggling against foreign influence. Gold was replaced by baser metal, and the last stage was copper, which was not even struck, but the old style persisted down to the second century.

Mr. BUSHE-FOX replied that the presence of rabbits in large numbers made stratification impossible, and the shape of the dwellings could not be accurately determined, but seemed to be oval rather than square or circular.

Thanks were ordered to be returned for these communications.

THURSDAY, 11th JUNE, 1914.

PHILIP NORMAN, Esq., LL.D., Vice-President, in the Chair.

The following gifts were announced, and thanks for the same ordered to be returned to the donors:

From the Author :—Notes on the history of the parish of North Wraxhall, co. Wilts. By Professor W. J. Lewis, F.R.S. 8vo. London, 1913.

From the Author :—An account of the Boynton family and the family seat at Burton Agnes. By Rev. C. V. Collier, F.S.A. 4to. Middlesbrough, 1914.

From the Author :—Some notes on a new Hittite inscription found at Carchemish. By R. Campbell Thompson, F.S.A. 8vo. n.p. n.d.

From Professor Haverfield, LL.D., F.S.A.:—
　　1. Old houses in Oxford. By F. E. Howard, Rev. H. E. Salter, and C. M. Toynbee. 8vo. Oxford, 1914.
　　2. An account of the Roman remains in the parish of Corbridge-on-Tyne. By Professor Haverfield. 4to. Newcastle-on-Tyne, 1914.

From Madame Hymans :—Portrait medal of the late M. Henri Hymans, Hon. F.S.A.

Lt.-Colonel G. B. CROFT LYONS, F.S.A., exhibited a glass quarry with the arms of Manning of Down, Kent.

L. A. LAWRENCE, Esq., F.S.A., exhibited part of a set of seventeenth-century counters, engraved with the Cries of London.

F. W. COCK, Esq., M.D., F.S.A., exhibited three pairs of iron ember-tongs.

WILSON CREWDSON, Esq., M.A., F.S.A., exhibited a portion of an alabaster carving representing the Adoration of the Three

Kings. The exhibit consisted of the figures of the Kings only, those of our Lady and Child having been on a separate panel. The figures are headless, but as holes for pins are visible, the heads were apparently carved separately. The alabaster is very delicately executed with a wealth of detail, and is probably of

ALABASTER CARVING OF THE ADORATION OF THE KINGS. ($\frac{1}{3}$)

Flemish or French workmanship of the last quarter of the fifteenth century. It is 11 in. high by 10 in. broad.

The front king kneels and presents an ornamental coffer containing coins. The lid, which he is opening, is mutilated, and the hands are gone. He wears a long cloak, and his right boot is fastened by a buckle: his left foot is hidden by the cloak. On the ground at his feet rests a cap, turned up with fur and surrounded by a coronet.

The second king stands immediately behind and rather to the back of the kneeling figure, and carries a covered horn-shaped vessel, round which is twisted a strap or belt ornamented with quatrefoils. The left arm is broken off below the elbow, but from the position of the arm it seems likely that the figure was represented as removing his cap, while the bend in the right leg indicates that the figure was represented in the act of kneeling. He wears a long cloak, fastened at the neck with a tasselled cord and caught up in his right hand to show the skirt of the tunic which is cut into points and fringed. He wears long hose.

The third king is standing, and holds a covered cup in his hands. He wears a long cloak fastened on the right shoulder by two buttons. It is caught up in front to show the lower part of the breastplate and a skirt of mail. He, too, wears long hose.

The figures are free standing, and the cloaks fall behind in long graceful folds. Below the base is a hole for the pin by which the carving was fixed.

This being an evening appointed for the election of Fellows no paper was read.

The ballot opened at 8.45 p.m. and closed at 9.30 p.m., when the following were declared elected Fellows of the Society:

> Thomas Henry Harvey, Esq., J.P.
> John Edwin Couchman, Esq.
> Thurstan Collins Peter, Esq.
> William Henry Ward, Esq., M.A.
> Willoughby Gardner, Esq., F.L.S., F.R.G.S.
> William Mangles I'Anson, Esq.
> Frederick William Morton Palmer, Esq., M.A., M.D., B.C.
> John Alexander Herbert, Esq., B.A.

Thursday, 18th June, 1914.

Sir ARTHUR JOHN EVANS, Knt., M.A. D.Litt., F.R.S., President, in the Chair.

The following gifts were announced, and thanks for the same ordered to be returned to the donors:

From H. W. Lewer, Esq., F.S.A. :—The naval history of Great Britain. By William James. 6 vols. 8vo. London, 1837.

From the Author, R. Stewart-Brown, Esq., F.S.A. :—
  1. Notes on Childwall. 8vo. Liverpool, 1914.
  2. Notes on the Chester Hand or Glove. 8vo. Chester, 1914.

From G. F. Hill, Esq. :—A collection of sketches, tracings, rubbings, and photographs of early datings, etc., in 'Arabic' numerals, mounted in a scrap-book.

From Henry Yates Thompson, Esq., F.S.A.:—Illustrations from one hundred manuscripts in the library of Henry Yates Thompson, consisting of 82 plates illustrating 16 MSS. of English origin from the twelfth to the fifteenth centuries. fol. London, 1914.

A special vote of thanks was passed to Mr. Yates Thompson for his gift to the Library.

The following were admitted Fellows:
John Alexander Herbert, Esq., B.A.
William Henry Ward, Esq., M.A.

MERVYN MACARTNEY, Esq., F.S.A., read the following paper on some investigations into the soil in and around St. Paul's Cathedral, and comparison with data in *Parentalia*:

"In writing this paper I have had two objects in view: first, to put on record the results of exploration and excavation in and around St. Paul's, during the time I have been surveyor to that building; secondly, to examine the truth of some of the statements in *Parentalia*.

This book has been generally regarded as a trustworthy guide as to the operations connected with the rebuilding of the cathedral. It was prepared by Wren's grandson from papers and information supplied by Sir Christopher Wren's son, the younger Christopher, and published about 1750. Stephen Wren (the grandson) was born in the year 1722, a year previous to Sir Christopher Wren's death. It is evident therefore that the compiler had to trust to his father for most of his facts, and corroboration of these was difficult, as most of the men engaged on the building are likely to have died before Sir Christopher.

It is safe to assume that there were few, if any, men living who could speak from personal knowledge of the events connected with the rebuilding, when Stephen Wren wrote the *Parentalia*. The book, therefore, cannot be taken as absolutely reliable.

For the sake of reference I have divided my paper into three sections: 1, The Architectural; 2, the Geological; 3, the Antiquarian.

1. Under the Architectural head, those discoveries which appertain more or less directly to remains of the old cathedral and the foundations of the present building will be considered.

2. Under the Geological division I propose to enumerate the results obtained from bore-holes, trial-pits, etc.

3. Under the Antiquarian division, the objects that have been discovered in the shafts and excavations in and around the cathedral and the remains of the old cathedral will be touched upon.

1. The well-known account of the erection of the north-east

angle seems to me untrustworthy. Let me quote the extract
from *Parentalia*[1] :

'In the Progress of the Works of the Foundations, the Sur-
veyer met with one unexpected Difficulty ; he began to lay the
Foundations from the West-end, and had proceeded successfully
through the Dome to the East-end, where the Brick-earth Bottom
was yet very good ; but as he went on to the North-east Corner,
which was the last, and where nothing was expected to interrupt,
he fell, in prosecuting the Design, upon a Pit, where all the Pot-
earth had been robb'd by the Potters of old Time : Here were
discovered Quantities of Urns, broken Vessels, and Pottery-ware
of divers Sorts and Shapes. . . .

'It was no little Perplexity to fall into this Pit at last : He
wanted but six or seven Feet to compleat the Design, and this
fell in the very Angle North-east ; he knew very well, that under
the Layer of Pot-earth, there was no other good Ground to be
found till he came to the Low-water mark of the Thames, at
least forty Feet lower. . . .

'His endeavours were to build for Eternity. He therefore
sunk a Pit of about eighteen Feet square, wharfing up the Sand
with Timber, till he came forty Feet lower into Water and Sea-
shells, . . . he bored through this Beach till he came to the
original Clay ; being then satisfied, he began from the Beach a
square Peer of solid good Masonry, ten Feet square, till he came
within fifteen Feet of the present Ground, then he turned a short
Arch under Ground to the former Foundation, which was broken
off by the untoward Accident of the Pit.'

In the first place, Wren did not begin to rebuild from the
west. He was instructed in 1675 to make a 'new Quire', 'with
the present stock of money', and no man with such a command
would begin at the other end of a building, 600 ft. long, en-
cumbered as it was with enormous piles of masonry, some of
them reaching to the height of 200 ft.

Moreover, we have the cathedral account books, and no mention is made there of the west end till 1689, nor of any pit except
the well in the middle of the building under the dome, whereas
great care is taken to specify the work in laying the foundations
on the north and east sides, at which places mention is made of
excavations 24 ft. deep.

Furthermore, when examining the condition of the foundations
for the London County Council I exposed the footings at the
points marked on figs. 1 and 2. The shafts were sunk as close
to this north-east corner as was safe, and in both cases, on reaching the last course of footings, I drove an iron crowbar as far
under the pier as I could, without encountering any solid mass.

[1] London, 1750, p. 286.

I am obliged, therefore, to regard this statement from *Parentalia* with suspicion, though I do not say that it is absolutely impossible. The exploration of the footings in the east end lead one to conclude that it was on this side that Wren experienced the greatest difficulty, though from the Conyers MS. (to which I will refer again) the north must also have occasioned him

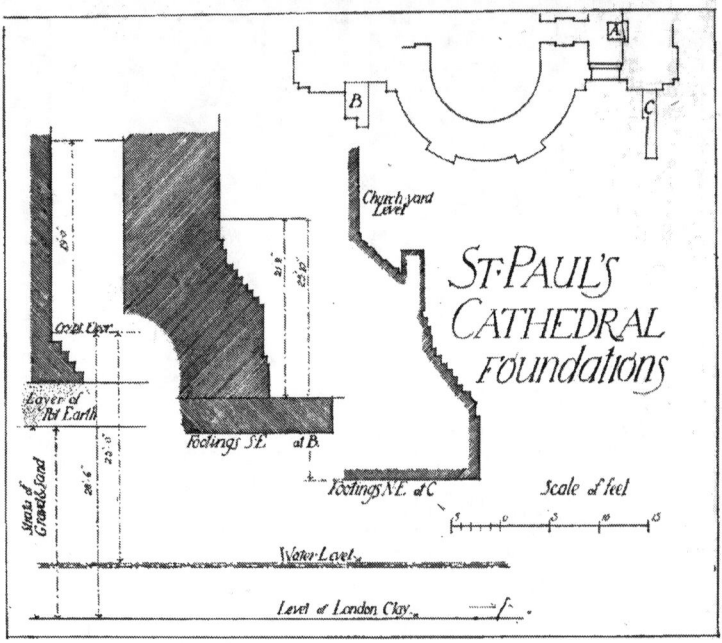

Fig. 1. ST. PAUL'S CATHEDRAL : SECTIONS OF FOUNDATIONS.

trouble. The cathedral accounts specifically mention an excavation 50 ft. long, 20 ft. wide, and 24 ft. deep in this place.

2. I now proceed to the second part of my subject, the geological. It has been my fortune, good or bad, to have sunk a considerable number of bore-holes since I have been surveyor. Nine borings, 6 in. in diameter (fig. 3), have been taken down to the London Clay, in and around the building. which have imparted much information as to the water-levels. It must be remembered, however, that the readings given below were not taken simultaneously, and that the water-level varies with weather conditions and the seasons of the year.

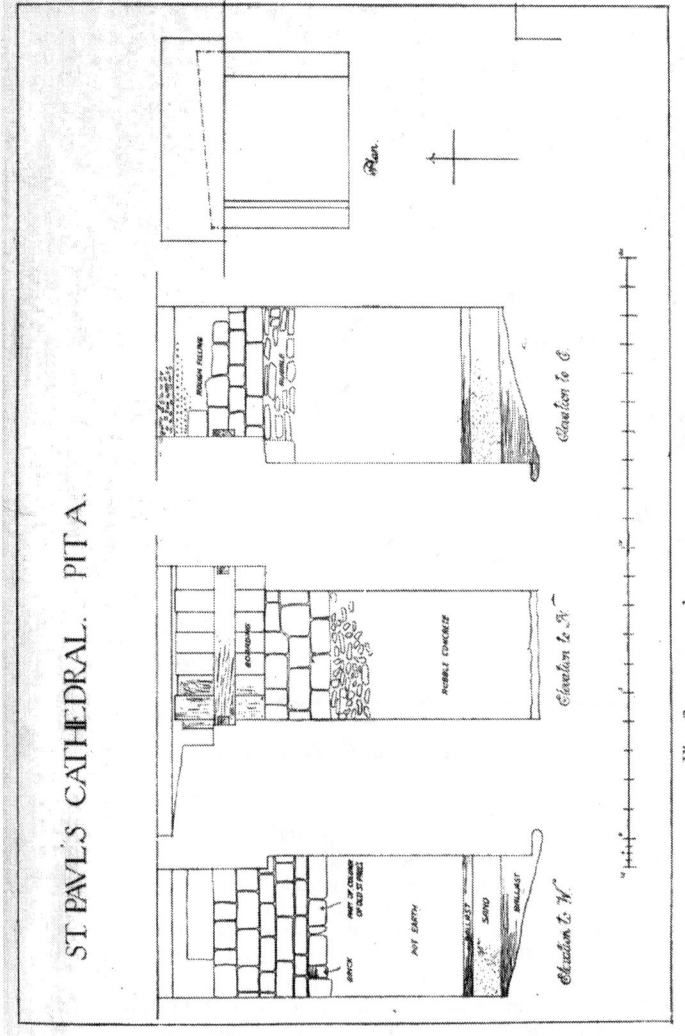

Fig. 2. ST. PAUL'S CATHEDRAL: PLAN AND SECTIONS OF PIT A.

Bore-hole No. 1.   Water-level is 20·9 feet above Ordnance Datum.

,,	2.	,,	23·0	,,	,,
,,	3.	,,	20·10	,,	,,
,,	4.	,,	21·0	,,	,,
,,	5. (*Daily Mail*)	,,	22·59	,,	,,
,,	6.⎫	,,	22·0	,,	,,
,,	7.⎬ L.C.C.	,,	20·5	,,	,,
,,	8.⎭	,,	23·75	,,	,,
,,	9. at G.P.O.	,,	26·43	,,	,,

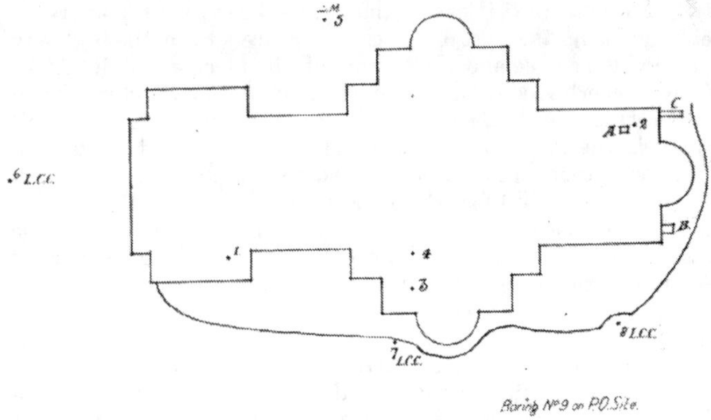

Fig. 3. POSITION OF BORINGS, ST. PAUL'S CATHEDRAL.

These figures show that there is a gradient south and west, and that the water-level is on the average 9·65 ft. above high-water mark, not, as stated in *Parentalia*, on the low-water level, which is 6 ft. below Ordnance Datum. Here is a definite statement which is manifestly inaccurate; for it is known that the level of the water in the soil has fallen in recent years. As an instance, the 4 ft. drain, built by Wren himself, which runs round the building, to keep the foundations free from water, is now quite dry.

It is unfortunate that Stephen Wren's facts cannot be depended on, as otherwise it might have been possible to make certain valuable deductions from his statements.

Nearly all the nine borings show similar strata. There is the débris; then pot-earth; then sand, and gravel, then both together, and lastly clay. In the débris are two layers of interments, medieval and Roman.

Here I must break through the dividing line of my sections and quote extracts from a contemporary diarist, an apothecary of Cheapside, by name Conyers, whom I have already mentioned. He confirms some of the *Parentalia* statements and gives some interesting particulars about the discoveries when the excavations were made, as to the Roman occupation. He writes as follows,[1] in a hand extremely difficult to decipher:

'1675, Aug. 20.   Memorandum that this month at severall dayes the labourers at the east end of St. Pauls London can tell one the north side of the church as the church is now altered by the care and direc[ti]ons of the Learned Sir Christopher Wren etc. this being the part of the church nearest to by the high way and Pauls Schoole and under part of the place where St. Paulls Cross formerly stood and a new cutt for foundacion the chirch being made wider much then formerly, the widening, the widnes all towards the North or the booksellers as you go to and from Cheapside there they was forced to digg in som places neare 5 or 6 and twenty or 30 foot deep for sound ground and there makeing the foundacion new all one that side vizt. ye north side of the east end of St. Paulls it doth appeare that in the highest part of sound ground the ground hath been raised at the least 15 or 16 foote and now it appeares allso that by 2 layers of corpes the one layer 6 or 7 foot deep and the other neare 10 or 12 foot deep the ground hath been there raised twise since they used to burye in that chirch yard and about 12 feet deep there was a layer of white matter which might bee chalke and hewings of stone when the chirch was built by William the Conquerors favorite Lanfrank Bishop of London.   Now a little below this veine of white chalke (that lay all along paralel the east end of St. Paulls) there appeared here and there flint pavement which was the pavement of yards for Lanfrank is said to purchase houses of citizens then to add to the chir[ch]yard of St. Paul which chirch was then layed in a larger foundacion then then ever before.   Now below the said flint pavements as the ground ceased to be black earth and came to be more of the yellow sand collour there was found a sort of Redd earthen Pottsheards the Pott as redd and firme as sealing wax', having inscriptions on them.   Coins of 'Romulus and Rhemus', Constantine, and Claudius, 'som glass and potts like broken urnes which were curiously layed one the outside with like Thorne pricks of rose trees and in the manner of raised work this upon potts of murry collour and here and there greyhounds and staggs and hares all in rais'd work, other of these were Cinamon collour urne fashion and were as guilded with gould, but vaded som of strang fashiond Juggs the sides bent in so as to be six square and these raisd worke upon them and curiously pinched. ... Many of these

[1] Sloane MS. 958, f. 105.

potts of the finer sort are lite and thinn and these workes raised or indented were instead of collours,' etc., etc. (figs. 4 and 5).

I must digress once more here to give the views of the compilers of *Parentalia* on this subject. It is stated that ' the Graves of several Ages and Fashions in strata, or Layers of Earth one above another, particularly at the North side of Paul's, manifestly shew'd a great Antiquity from the British and Roman Times, by the Means whereof the Ground had been raised ; but upon searching for the natural Ground below these Graves, the Surveyor observed that the Foundation of the old Church stood upon a layer of very close and hard Pot-earth, and concluded that the same Ground which had born so weighty a Building, might reasonably be trusted again '.

3. Now I approach the third section of my subject, the archaeological. According to Conyers, large quantities of bones of animals were found on the site of St. Paul's Churchyard, and great stores of crockery. *Parentalia* bears out these statements, but quotes Wren as an opponent to the theory that St. Paul's was the site of a temple to Diana. Remains of an altar to that deity were discovered near St. Vedast, Foster Lane, and I see nothing impossible in the popular superstition.

In my own excavation to the north-west, remains of graves at different levels were found, of the kind shown in fig. 6. Piers of rough masonry were also found which evidently belonged to the previous cathedral. The excavation for the foundations of Paul's Cross (fig. 7) revealed numerous remains of bones, the upper layer laid uniformly east to west, the lower without any apparent order. Some pieces of earthenware were found, but nothing of exceptional value—or at any rate nothing has come into my hands, with the exception of the few articles found in excavations in Paternoster Row which were presented to the cathedral by our Fellow Mr. Bagster.

But I understand that Mr. Philip Norman has been fortunate enough to secure some most interesting finds which he will describe at some future date. Perhaps he may be able to settle this *vexata quaestio* of Diana's Temple."

Mr. SOMERS CLARKE had for more than forty years been doubtful whether Wren began at the west end, and was at length convinced that the church was started at the east end. Wren was overwhelmed with material and was obliged to get rid of the surplus at the west end when the building was nearing completion. The flow of water towards the river was so rapid that it could be seen passing under the cathedral, and the gravel through which it flowed was very light.

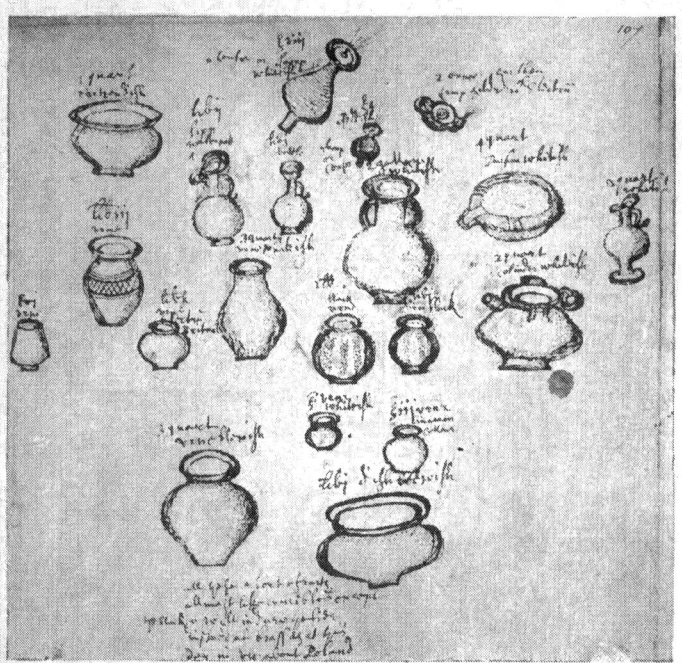

Fig. 4.   POTTERY FROM SITE OF ST. PAUL'S CATHEDRAL : FROM CONYERS' MS.;
SLOANE 958.

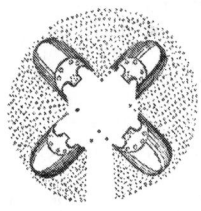

Fig 5.   POTTERY KILN AND CLUSTER OF FOUR KILNS FOUND IN LONDON IN
1675 : FROM CONYERS' MS. ; SLOANE 958.

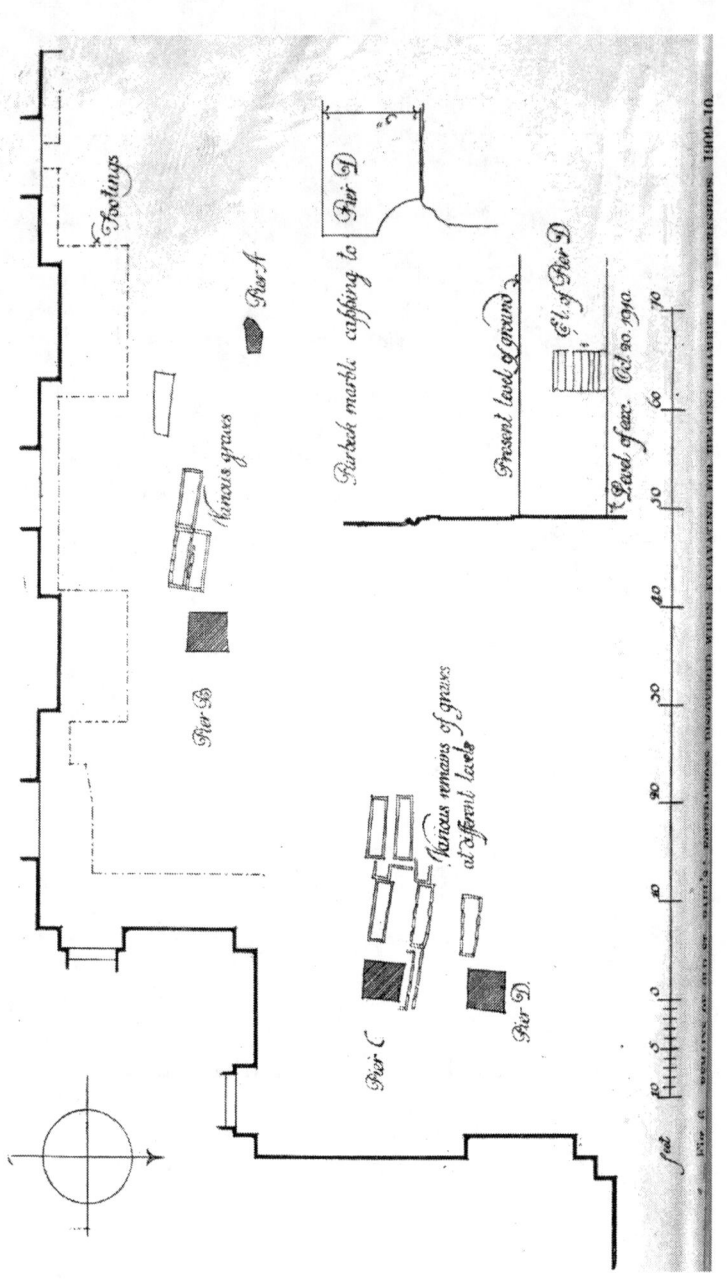

Footings

Pier A

Various graves

Pier B

Various remains of graves
at different levels

Pier C

Pier D

Perfect marble capping to Pier D

Present level of ground

El. of Pier D

Level of exc. Oct 20. 1901

feet

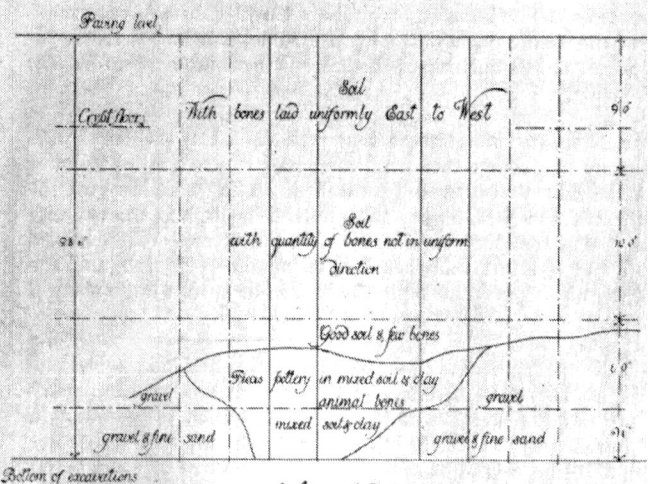

Paving level.

Crypt floor   With bones laid uniformly East to West   9'6"

Soil

with quantity of bones not in uniform direction

Good soil & few bones

Twas pottery in mixed soil & clay

gravel   *animal bones*   *gravel*

gravel & fine sand   *mixed soil & clay*   *gravel & fine sand*

Bottom of excavations

Section A-B

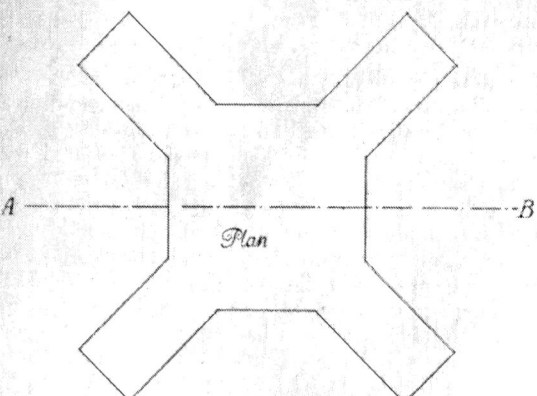

A - - - - - - - - - - - - - - - - B

Plan

Fig. 7.   EXCAVATION AND PLAN AT PAUL'S CROSS.

Mr. WEAVER had in 1909 exhibited the heirloom copy of *Parentalia*.[1] The book was brought out by Stephen Wren, grandson of the architect, assisted by Mr. Ames, a former Secretary of the Society; but nothing could prevent its being a scrap-heap of documents.

Mr. NORMAN thought the foundations of the cathedral were obviously in a dangerous condition; and it was a relief to know that the fabric was carefully watched. The water-level on the north side was 5 ft. higher than on the south, and the running sand had a tendency to slip towards the river. Wren looked ahead but did not take his foundations deep enough, and the problem at the present time was to anchor such a huge mass of masonry.

Mr. REGINALD SMITH thought that justice had not been done to the apothecary Conyers, who was no artist but a careful observer; and his sketches of the kiln and Roman vases found in the churchyard were easily intelligible to the modern archaeologist. Mention might have been made of the row of wells found at the north-east angle, which had been taken as evidence of a Roman road[2] running to Newgate across Paternoster Row.

REGINALD A. SMITH, Esq., F.S.A., read a paper on Irish brooches of five centuries, which will be printed in *Archaeologia*.

No systematic attempt had hitherto been made to date the large series of Irish penannular brooches, which had been assigned to widely different periods. There was a considerable variety in their form, and they were seldom found associated with each other or with datable objects; but the study of a large number, in the light of finds at Rogart and Croy in Scotland, and at Ardagh in Ireland, had brought to light a chronological sequence covering the greatest period of Irish art. The penannular brooch assumed its Irish form in the sixth century, and reached its highest development in the eighth, reflecting the glory of the Book of Kells. Notable specimens had been found in Scotland, and a few were preserved from England, but were probably made, like the enamelled bowls, by Irish craftsmen. Viking loot discovered in Norway included the brooch, which contrasts with the typical Viking type common in the tenth century. This was an adaptation of the Irish pattern under oriental influence, and the contemporary 'thistle' brooch marked the commercial route by way of Scandinavia. The type survived to the present day

---

[1] *Proceedings*, xxii, 524.
[2] The true Watling Street: *V. C. H. London*, i, 33. For the wells, see *Parentalia*, p. 272.

in Algeria and Northern India, and a modification of it was common in Scotland through the middle ages, but the series under discussion terminated with the tenth century. The typological method could here be controlled to some extent by historical data; and even approximate dates for the various forms assumed by the brooch might be of service in other branches of archaeology, and serve as a basis for future discussion.

Mr. LYON THOMSON said the author had assumed a good deal of knowledge on the part of his audience, and one or two points remained a little obscure. When the hoop was closed, the brooch could only have been worn by sewing it on the costume. The series represented was of extraordinary interest, as it showed among other things the development of metal-work. The splayed ends were produced by hammering, but later came the art of brazing metals. The Viking brooches were all hammered and riveted together. The use of wire was also an important point, and it seemed to him impossible for any one to produce such lengths of wire without an acquaintance with modern processes.

Mr. CRACE thought a broad distinction existed between the models with open and closed hoops, and considered the change a radical one, the original form having been lost sight of during an interval.

Lord CRAWFORD remarked that the flanged pin was broad, and it was more probably passed through a button-hole than through the cloth.

The PRESIDENT thought the meeting had enjoyed a beautiful study in the evolution of form and ornament. The chronological succession proposed in the paper should on the whole be accepted. There were certain fixed points, the simple form of the penannular brooch being, for instance, known from quite early Roman times, as at Hod Hill. In the fourth or fifth century it seemed to have crossed to Ireland, and its later development was well illustrated by the Croy and Cuerdale finds. Other evidence of date was afforded by the illuminated manuscripts, such as Lindisfarne and Kells, and the still earlier *Book of Durrow*. These constituted a solid basis for the classification proposed, and it was interesting to see the Celtic spiral supplemented by the Teutonic animal-motive, the result being a credit to Irish taste. In the discussion stress had been laid on the joined terminals, which made the penannular brooch annular. That form was adopted in the eighth century, and he suggested might be regarded as late Irish as opposed to the Viking form. Another interesting point just mentioned in the paper was the survival of the penannular brooch in widely distant parts of the world ; and it was curious to see how a British form passed right across to the Arabs, North India, and modern Algeria. It was an interesting commentary on Viking activity in many regions that linked up the east and the west. In the Cuerdale hoard there was strong oriental influence, but there was also a counter current that took Irish forms to the extreme east and south, and even to the remotest parts of Siberia.

Mr. SMITH, in replying, could not accept any hiatus in the penannular series described, as enough examples were extant to form a complete chain of evolution from the sixth to the tenth century; and the true penannular persisted throughout, though exceptional specimens, mostly heavy and elaborate, had the terminals joined. In the latter case the pin was detached at the head by means of a bolt at the back, the mechanism suggesting that the brooch was not often removed from the costume.

Thanks were ordered to be returned for these communications.

THURSDAY, 25th JUNE, 1914.

Sir ARTHUR JOHN EVANS, Knt., M.A., D.Litt., F.R.S., President, in the Chair.

The following gifts were announced, and thanks for the same ordered to be returned to the donors :

From Mill Stephenson, Esq., B.A., F.S.A. :—
1. A descriptive and historical account of the Russell monuments in the Bedford Chapel at Chenies. By George Scharf, F.S.A. 4to. London, 1892.
2. Chenies Church and Monuments. By Adeline Marie, Duchess of Bedford. Small 4to. London, 1901.

From the Author :—Aspects of death in art and epigram. Second edition. By F. Parkes Weber, F.S.A. 8vo. London, 1914.

From the Author :—Hertfordshire maps. A descriptive catalogue of the maps of the county, 1579-1900. Supplement. By Sir Herbert George Fordham. 4to. Hertford, 1914.

From Ralph Griffin, Esq., F.S.A. :—A survey and record of Woolwich and West Kent. Edited by Rev. C. H. Grinling. 8vo. Woolwich, 1909.

From Ralph Griffin, Esq., F.S.A., and T. Fairman Ordish, Esq., F.S.A.:— ' Le Livre enchaîné,' ou Livre des Fontaines de Rouen, manuscrit de la Bibliothèque de Rouen, 1524-1525. Par Jacques Le Lieur. Texte et planches. fol. Rouen, 1911.

From J. D. Crace, Esq., F.S.A. : —
    Palestine Exploration Fund—1. Quarterly Statement, October, 1896,
       to April, 1914.
    2. Annual for 1911, and 1912–13.

Sir ARTHUR EVANS, President, exhibited some matrices of seals
and signet rings from the collection of the late Sir John Evans.

MAURICE ROSENHEIM, Esq., F.S.A., exhibited a collection of
signet rings and seal matrices.

C. L. KINGSFORD, Esq., M.A., F.S.A., read a paper on ancient
deeds and seals belonging to Lord De L'Isle and Dudley, which
will be printed in *Archaeologia*.

The true Sydney descent was from a family settled at La
Sydenye, in Alford, near Guildford, as early as the reign of
Edward I. Through the acquisition of lands in Surrey and
Sussex the family had risen to a good position early in the
fifteenth century. William Sydney, of Kingsham, Sussex, was
the first to use a seal with armorial bearings on a deed, dated
15 August, 1451. He was three times married. His son Nicholas
by his third wife inherited an estate at West Preston, in Sussex,
and married Anne, daughter of Sir William Brandon, and aunt
of Charles Brandon, afterwards Duke of Suffolk. By her he had
a son William (1487–1554), who was knighted at Flodden, was
chamberlain to Edward VI as Prince of Wales, and had grants
of Robertsbridge Abbey in 1539 and of Penshurst in 1552. His
son Sir Henry Sydney (1529–86) was the Deputy of Ireland,
and his grandson the famous Sir Philip. As one of the coheirs
of the young Dukes of Suffolk, who died in 1551, Sir Henry acquired the lands of Tatteshall College. The early deeds, now in
the possession of Lord De L'Isle and Dudley, for the most part
related to Penshurst, Tatteshall, and Robertsbridge.

In 1580 the notorious Robert Cooke constructed a pedigree of
the Sydney family, tracing their descent to a supposed William
de Sidnei, who was described as chamberlain to Henry II. This
pedigree was supported by four alleged deeds, which are manifest
forgeries, though three of them have genuine seals, one being a
fine specimen of the seal of Henry II as Duke of Normandy.

The Penshurst deeds were of interest for the history of the
house, and also for some good heraldic seals: William de
Pulteney,1356; Sir Nicholas de Loveyn, 1370; Sir John Colpeper,
1370; John Platyn, 1375; Sir Robert Belknap, 1380; Richard
Chamberlayn, 1480.

The Tatteshall deeds related chiefly to the College founded by
Ralph, Lord Cromwell, but include some early seals, notably
Walter Bek, *c.* 1210, and Maude de Cromwell, 1400.

The deeds (over 600) of Robertsbridge Abbey had numerous seals of early date in fine preservation; about 400 deeds were of earlier date than 1300. Many were older than 1200. At the Abbey the deeds were carefully kept with an interesting system of press-marks.

Sir HERCULES READ said the exhibit of medieval seals was of special interest as showing that there was an English school of seal-engraving that was hardly surpassed by any other. His official responsibilities were confined to the matrices, which presented special difficulties in the absence of documents. The author had been led by the character of a counterseal to assign a later date to the corresponding seal than was otherwise indicated; but there was no necessary relation between the seal and counterseal and they might be of widely different dates. He had noticed in the series exhibited two seals on one document that were not of the same date. He recollected that the Robertsbridge seals had been described by Mr. Perceval years ago, and published in *Archaeologia*.[1]

Sir WILLIAM HOPE had been fortunate in seeing the exhibits some years before, and thought the most interesting question was whether four of the documents were genuine or not. The writing shown on the screen could not possibly date from the twelfth century, and was a clumsy imitation of later date, the work no doubt of the notorious Robert Cooke. The seal was certainly genuine and belonged to the individual concerned, having been appended to that particular piece of parchment in the twelfth century; but any one could see that the original writing had been scraped out, some traces of it being still left between the lines. The introduction of the Sydney pheon was another point of interest, and Lord Dillon had connected it with the broad arrow of Henry VIII. The first of the name only had W, but if it were written W the transition to the pheon would have been a simple matter, and the latter had been used by the Sydneys since 1451. He hoped for more details with regard to the keeping of deeds and the use of press-marks. Documents he had examined at Rochester had notes on the back for that purpose. In the fine series of matrices exhibited by the President there were several simple seals such as were used by persons of humble origin not able to afford seals of more expensive material than lead, jet, or wood.

Matrices bearing medieval gems were worthy of special study, and some were of real importance. The great twelfth-century seal of Waltham Abbey had a gem nearly 3 in. long with fine

[1] xlv, 427.

heads upon it. There were impressions in the Record Office, but
at a later date it was cracked right across and encased in a larger
matrix, the Society possessing an original impression in the extra
condition. The result was one of the most beautiful seals of
medieval times. It was possible to make a cast of any original
impression, and he undertook to produce copies indistinguishable
from the original. Unless it was assumed that Cooke made a cast,
a genuine impression must have been removed from a charter by
introducing a heated blade between the faces ; but it seemed
impossible to do that and leave the seal as it was.

Mr. O. Barron had derived much pleasure from the exhibition,
and thought the photographer should be congratulated as well as
Mr. Kingsford, who had well chosen his seals from a definite and
early period. Every one had noticed the foreign example when
it was thrown on the screen, and the fine English series showed
the development of heraldry in a most interesting manner. The
charges were at first crude, and led up to the Etchingham seal.
Heraldry rose up in this way both in England and France during
the twelfth century, and then a clumsy and inartistic rendering
of the charges was noticeable. The theory was perfect from the
start, but the development spoken of perhaps took place in the
mind of a particular man. The current flowed freely between
France, England, and Flanders, and the development went on for
about a hundred years. Then there was a change, as sudden as
the start of heraldry. By 1300 all the great barons had new
seals with the charges engraved, and as a rule magnates about
that time had seals of the new style. In the fourteenth century
the humblest citizen was able to order a seal such as could not
have been procured at all a century earlier. Carelessness as to
the number of bars on a shield had been alleged, but those were
not bars in the true sense. An indefinite number of lines across
the shield went under the name of burelly, and in early heraldry
any number of bars above three was an indefinite number.

Mr. Jenkinson said forgeries of still earlier date were common
in the Record Office. If a forgery could be so well executed,
then ideas on other points might have to be revised. He had
never seen an erasure which allowed such perfection of writing
on the surface subsequently ; and no amount of pumice-stone
could have prepared such a surface. The possibility of the seal
being a cast had also to be considered. The nature of the tag
was peculiar, and he had seen no instance of a tag twisted in that
way among a good many charters of Henry II. The wax of the
impression seemed to him curious : the red material was beeswax
coloured, and a seal of the sixteenth century would be of different

wax, so that a forger would have had to make a strange wax, with a spotted result. Very little was known as to press-marks of medieval muniments, and further work on the subject would be an interesting addition to archivistics.

Lord CRAWFORD remarked that the presumed forgery was scarcely 4 inches deep. If the seal were genuine, the parchment was also genuine and not a palimpsest; but there was often a blank space above the seal that might be utilized for later writing.

Mr. BAILDON was inclined to agree with Mr. Jenkinson, that the parchment was not of the date it purported to be. Notwithstanding the authority of the seals, the wax could have been moulded by Cooke with the aid of plaster of Paris; and he felt sure he could turn out a still more plausible charter. He had seen a palimpsest which still bore traces of the erased document, and had the new writing dated a year or two after the death of the person concerned. Gem seals occurred in considerable numbers, but he had never seen one with more than one gem, and three in one matrix must be extraordinarily rare.

The PRESIDENT thought the paper, interesting in itself, had given rise to a useful discussion, and was himself inclined to accept Lord Crawford's explanation of the forged document as the simplest brought forward. The extraordinary series of twelfth-century seals showed the great proficiency of engravers in England during the middle ages. In the beginning of the thirteenth century English work could compare with any on the Continent. The seals with mounted knights reminded him that they belonged to those parts of the world which were moulded by the Normans, and those very horsemen recurred with the same details on coins of the Normans in Sicily. In England the coinage lagged behind seal-engraving. Old engraved gems were still used at that time, and their adoption affected the actual engraving of the matrix, the engraver endeavouring to copy something good and classical, and twelfth-century work was often closely copied from classical originals. The same result was achieved on a grander scale in Italy and at as early a date. The Society would do well to prepare a corpus of the best examples of such seal-impressions from documents. There was a greater continuity of history in England than elsewhere; and with assistance from many quarters, the result might give a new impression as to the state of medieval art in England.

Mr. KINGSFORD replied that there was no red wax with specks about 1100. As to the traces of former writing on the suspected charter, he considered that the existing writing had set off in folding, though some of the marks might be imperfect erasures. For facilities afforded in the preparation of the paper he was much indebted to Lord De L'Isle and the Royal Historical Manuscripts Commission.

H. CLIFFORD SMITH, Esq., M.A., F.S.A., exhibited the 'Danny Unicorn Jewel', on which he read the following note:

"This remarkable pendent charm of Elizabethan date, which I have entitled the 'Danny Unicorn Jewel', is exhibited by the kindness of its owner, Colonel W. H. Campion, of Danny, Sussex. The jewel is formed of a half-section of a narwhal's tusk, set in enamelled gold and forming a semicircular pendant. The gold mount on the top is decorated with scrolls of arabesque foliage on a ground of black champlevé enamel. On an arch in the centre of the top is a rosette. Attached to this and to a lion's mask at either end are three gold chains united above by a ring, from which the jewel is suspended. The front has a band of black enamel, and a circular boss with a pattern of interlacing strapwork in blue and white enamel filled in with foliage on a black ground. The goldwork of the back, which is partly missing, is decorated with strapwork in pale blue enamel of two shades. Round the bottom runs a gold band with a rosette in the centre having the remains of a ring from which was probably hung a pendent pearl.

The jewel has been preserved for years at Danny, the Elizabethan home of the Campions in Sussex. There is no further record of its history.

Height, 1¼ in. (with chain 3½ in.); width, 2⅜ in.; depth, 9/16 in.

The long spiral horn, which was none other than the tusk of the narwhal (*Monodon monoceros*) of the Arctic seas, was for centuries foisted upon the credulous as the horn of the fabled unicorn. Being esteemed of enormous value in early times the horn was seldom preserved entire, save in the treasuries of princes or of the Church. More generally, as in the present case, it was cut up, and the precious fragments sumptuously mounted were worn as ornaments to ward off evil or bring good luck. They were also used to neutralize or detect the presence of poison in food or drinks. For when, suspended by its chain of gold, it was plunged into a poisoned dish, the horn was supposed to sweat and change colour. The persistence of the belief in its power may be judged by the fact that in the Court ceremonial of France as late as 1789 the unicorn's horn was still used for testing the royal food for poison. The horn was evidently esteemed of value also as a medicinal amulet, for the surface of the tusk at the back of this jewel can be seen to have been partially scraped away, the powder mixed with water having been probably taken internally as a medicine.

A semicircular pendant of precisely the same design, formed evidently of a unicorn's horn in black enamelled setting, is shown on a portrait, dated 1580, of Robert Bristow, ascribed to Zuccaro, in the possession of Sir Thomas Neave at Dagnam Park, Essex.

The black enamel with which the goldwork of the pendant is enriched offers an interesting comparison with similar black enamel-work upon other Elizabethan jewels, notably the *Memento Mori* charm from Tor Abbey, Devonshire, in the Victoria and Albert Museum, and the small pendent gold case containing the last prayer of Edward VI, the property of Lord Fitzhardinge, preserved among the Hunsdon heirlooms at Berkeley Castle.[1] Another similar example is the gold enamelled prayer-book belonging to the Earl of Romney.

The following lines from a contemporary play, Chapman's *Bussy d'Amboise*, published in 1607 (Act I, Scene i), are of especial interest in connexion with the jewel now exhibited:

> ' An angrie Unicorne in his full carier
> Charge with too quicke an eie a Jeweller,
> That watcht him for the Treasure of his browe;
> And ere he could get shelter of a tree,
> Naile him with his rich Antler to the Earth.' "

Mr. CLIFFORD SMITH also exhibited a tapestry cushion-cover woven in coloured wools and silks and enriched with silver and silver-gilt thread—English (probably Warwickshire) work of the second half of the sixteenth century.

"This fine tapestry panel, woven with twenty warps to the inch, measures 1 ft. 7 in. in height, and 1 ft. 6½ in. in width. The border, 3 in. wide all round, is decorated with apples, pears, plums, pomegranates, and apple and pear blossom, the fruit being arranged in the corners in baskets. On each side is a terminal figure; the remainder of the border being ornamented with oval medallions united by strapwork and containing six lion masks and two female busts. The centre of the panel is occupied by a shield with the arms of Sacheverell: quarterly of six. 1. Silver, on a saltire azure five water-bougets gold (Sacheverell). 2. Silver, a lion rampant sable crowned gold, with a mullet for difference (Morley). 3. Gules, a pale lozengy silver (Statham). 4. Azure, a lion rampant silver (?). 5. Gules, a duck silver ducally gorged gold (Snitterton). 6. Silver, three hares playing bagpipes gules (Hopwell). Across the chief is

---

[1] H. Clifford Smith, *Jewellery*, plates 44 and 35.

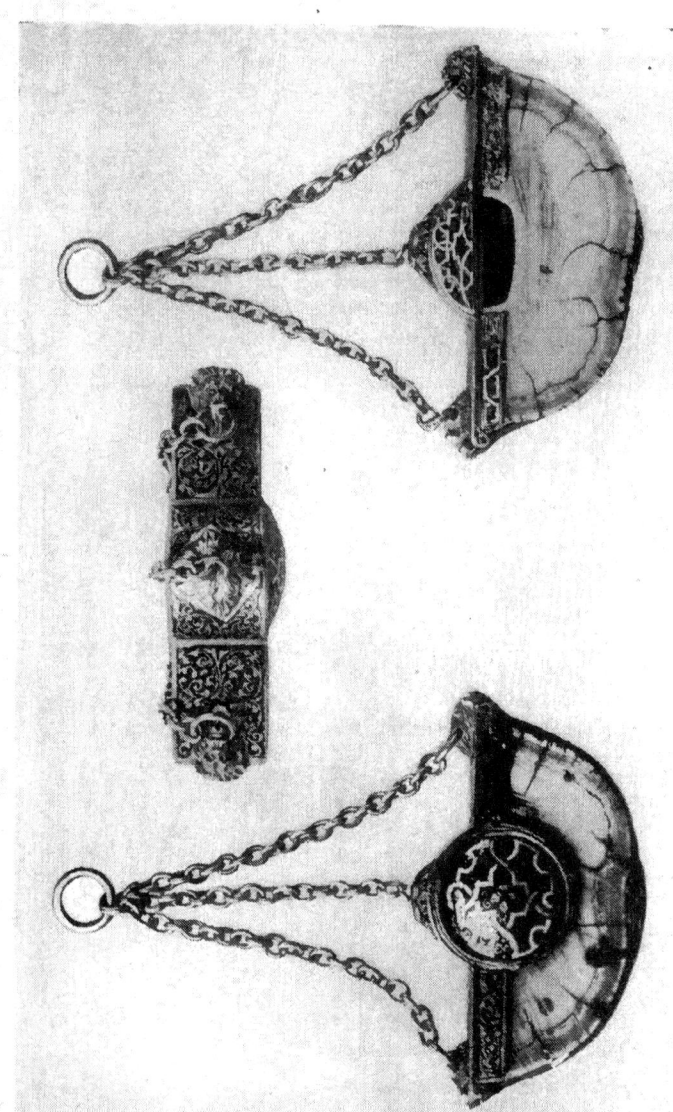

THE DANNY UNICORN JEWEL, FRONT, TOP, AND BACK VIEWS. $(\frac{1}{1})$

a label of three points.[1] Below the shield are the initials H. S. P.,
i. e. Henry Sacheverell *Primogenitus* (?), probably Henry Sacheverell (died 1581), the eldest son of Ralph Sacheverell of Rearsby,

SIXTEENTH-CENTURY ENGLISH TAPESTRY CUSHION-COVER.   ($\frac{1}{4}$)

Leicestershire. The field around the shield is decorated with a
variety of flowers: larkspur, foxglove, pansy, rose, marigold, pink,
cornflower, daisy, strawberry, picotee, daffodil, lily of the valley,

[1] One-third of this, worked in a lighter-coloured wool, is now apparently
silver.

and cuckoo flower. On either side of the shield is a coloured popinjay. The flowers, it is interesting to note, are the same as those mentioned in Shakespeare,[1] in whose time and country the tapestry was probably woven. There are besides, apart from the arms, other features which prove this panel to be of English work : the design of the lion masks, which is characteristically Elizabethan ; the crisp colouring ; and especially the presence of a yellow dye, more permanent than that employed by the Flemish weavers.

This rare and remarkable specimen of English weaving was formerly at Wollas Hall, the seat of the Hanford family, situated on the borders of Worcestershire and Gloucestershire ; and was produced, in all probability, at the factory first set up and endowed about 1550 by William Sheldon in Warwickshire. In addition to the five tapestry maps, two in the Bodleian Library and three in York Museum, which are known to have come from the Sheldon looms, other specimens, presumably from the same source, have been brought to light during the last few years. These, the panels of the four seasons at Hatfield, the panel with the arms of the Earl of Pembroke (d. 1570) in the Victoria and Albert Museum, and the hangings from an old house in Worcestershire now the property of Mr. Henry Howard, of Stone House near Kidderminster, are described by Mr. A. F. Kendrick in the second annual volume of the Walpole Society (1912-13), p. 89. Further examples are the hanging belonging to Mr. M. G. Knight at Chawton Manor, Hampshire, executed in 1564 for the family of Lewkenor ;[2] and a smaller panel at Hatfield with the arms of Cecil impaling Cooke, being those of William Cecil, first Lord Burghley, and Mildred Cooke, whom he married in 1545, as his second wife, and who died in 1589."

HAROLD CRASKE, Esq., exhibited a Late-Celtic cinerary urn found at Letchworth Garden-city, Herts., and the following note on the exhibit was subsequently communicated by Mr. REGINALD SMITH :

"The cordoned urn with pedestal foot, of which a photograph is reproduced (fig. 1), was found a few inches below the surface by workmen digging gravel in 1913 at Letchworth, near Hitchin, and belongs to the First Garden City, Ltd. It was accidentally damaged at the time of its discovery, but is fortunately complete except for a hole near the foot and about half the foot itself. It is 15 in. high with a maximum diameter of 9·3 in., and the outside measurement across the mouth is 8·5 in. The occurrence

---

[1] H. N. Ellacombe, *The Plant Lore and Garden Craft of Shakespeare* ; C. Roach Smith, *Rural Life of Shakespeare* (2nd ed., 1874).

[2] W. Austen Leigh, *Chawton Manor*, p. 146.

Fig. 1. LATE-CELTIC URN FROM LETCHWORTH GARDEN CITY, HERTS. (ABOUT $\frac{1}{3}$)

of human bones suggests that this was an interment after cremation.

Similar finds in the neighbouring town of Hitchin have been published by the Society (*Proceedings*, xiii, 16) and seem to be related to the Welwyn group (*Archaeologia*, lxiii, pl. III); but the Letchworth urn may be not exactly contemporary with either. Its slender form is significant, and its cordons are well turned, while the high shoulder is a feature that links it with the older series of La Tène objects in this country. The ware is of the usual brown colour, fairly soft, and wheel-made, the body in

Fig. 2. BASE OF URN : LETCHWORTH GARDEN CITY. (½)

two pieces joined about the middle, and the foot applied afterwards.

The view here given of the broken base (fig. 2) shows the peculiar construction of the pedestal, which is common in the pre-Roman period ; and the concavity of the foot is a rough criterion of date. The Marne specimens dating from the period known as La Tène I have the foot hollow,[1] and the floor of the urn seems gradually to sink till it is practically level with the foot-rim, as in several of the Aylesford examples.

The bronze object (fig. 3) found with the urn may be regarded as a link to connect two straps, and is not unprecedented. One somewhat smaller (1·4 in. long) with two joined rings in the centre was found in the Glastonbury Lake-village and is described as a harness-ornament ;[2] and another figured on the

[1] *Iron Age Guide* (Brit. Mus.), p. 66, fig. 57.
[2] Bulleid and Gray, *Glastonbury Lake-village*, i, 229, pl. xliv, E 262. Other examples quoted on p. 228.

same plate (E 190) has three columns joined in the middle and
a free column at either end, 'suggesting a junction between
strap-ends'. The present example has in the openwork centre
a device that occurs in various forms on objects of Late-Celtic
art; it is an irregular trigram with two dots on the front, plain
at the back. A symmetrical example is published from Dowalton
Loch crannog, Wigtownshire.[1] There are two projections on
the front of the swelling hoop that are much rubbed and cannot

Fig. 3. BRONZE CONNECTING-LINK OF BELT. ($\frac{1}{1}$)

be more precisely described. The extreme length is 1·8 in., and
height 1·6 in.

This is not only an addition to a very small class of Late-
Celtic bronzes, but the association of the bronze and the cinerary
urn is important from the chronological point of view; and
a few more discoveries of the kind would render possible a more
precise division of the four centuries immediately preceding the
Roman conquest."

ALEX. O. CURLE, Esq., F.S.A., Local Secretary, communicated
the following report on archaeological discoveries in Scotland
during the session 1913–14 :

" A considerable amount of research has been conducted in
Scotland during the past year and important results have been
obtained.

In certain districts of Scotland, especially on the lower moor-
lands, hut circles are numerous, but hitherto very little exploration has been done on this class of structure, and evidence of

---

[1] *Cat. Edinb. Mus. Antiq.*, 254, HU 62.

their period of erection has been scanty. Last autumn, Mr. J. G. A. Baird, F.S.A.Scot., of Muirkirk, in Ayrshire, excavated two hut circles on that estate. The first, situated at an elevation of about 900 ft. above sea-level, measured some 18 ft. in diameter and was represented by a low ring of turf and stones. In the interior, on the removal of the surface soil, a paved hearth was exposed, 6 ft. in from the entrance, adjacent to which lay the fragments of an urn of Bronze-Age pottery, but insufficient in quantity to afford indication of the exact form of the vessel. The second circle, at an elevation of 700 ft., was of larger dimensions, measuring some 34 ft. by 38 ft. internally, and near its centre was found a circular pit, 4½ ft. deep and 7 ft. wide, from the bottom of which was recovered almost the whole of a vessel of the same period having the shape of a beaker of late type decorated with impressed markings, but not, however, in the characteristic style of a vessel of that class.

Mr. A. H. Bishop, F.S.A.Scot., conducted an exhaustive examination of shell mounds in the Island of Oronsay, from which he obtained multiple-barbed harpoons, a number of round-ended, chisel-like objects of bone and stone, and a necklace of small pierced cowrie shells. From a careful examination of the stratification, and observation of the levels, the explorer concluded that the site had been occupied during the period of the formation of the 25-30 foot beach in Scotland, by a people whose culture filled the gap between the Palaeolithic and Neolithic phases.

The writer himself explored a small vitrified fort overlooking the estuary of the Urr in the Stewartry of Kirkcudbright. Before excavation vitrifaction was only observable at one or two places, and that in very small quantities; the cutting of a rampart, however, on one flank, revealed within a vallum of loose earth and stone, some 14 ft. wide, a built wall 18 in. thick and 3 ft. high, firmly coagulated with vitrified matter from top to bottom. The rampart followed the contour of the hill at the edge of a steep slope, and the wall occurred within it at a regular distance of 3 ft. 6 in. from the outer face, thus acting as a revetment to hold the rampart in position. Seeing that vitrifaction occurred at no other part of the rampart, and was complete throughout the wall, the writer concluded that in this instance at least vitrifaction was a structural process and could not have been produced with such regularity by the occurrence of watch-fires. Further, the evidence showed that the wall must have been built and vitrified previous to the completion of the rampart. In the interior of the fort there was discovered the site of a foundry in which objects of Celtic art had been cast in bronze from moulds of baked clay. Numerous fragments of these moulds were found, for casting penannular brooches, crosses, and plaques showing interlacing designs, also for pins and carding combs. In the interlaced patterns it is noteworthy that the bands forming the interlacements are in many cases incised with a double line, a characteristic usually claimed for the Italian and continental patterns as opposed to the Celtic. A number of small pieces of glass beakers were also found, showing some analogy to Anglo-Saxon glasses and to certain beakers found in the Island of Björko, near Stockholm. A ninth-century date is suggested for these finds.

The more important objects added to the National Museum of Scotland during the past year are as follows: two pairs of oval, bowl-shaped Viking brooches of bronze. In one pair the brooches are formed of single plates enriched with clearly expressed zoomorphic ornament. They were found in a grave in the Island of Oronsay, associated with a pair of iron shears, a bronze pin with a movable ring head, and a short cylindrical object of bone, 2⅜ in. in length, perforated longitudinally and transversely. The second pair came from a grave in sand-hills in Caithness. The brooches in this latter case are formed with a pierced shell over a gilded convex oval plate, and the zoomorphic character of the design is more debased than in the foregoing examples. The associated relics in this grave were a bronze pin, very similar to the last, a horse's bit of iron, and a buckle which had been coated with tin. From Dumfriesshire there was acquired a Viking sword with a triangular segmented pommel and curving guards, similar to a sword in the British Museum found with a pair of oval bowl-shaped brooches at Santon, Norfolk. A bronze sword-blade of rapier form, 18.2 in. in length, found many years ago with five or six smaller blades in the ditch of a circular earthwork at Drumcoltran in the Stewartry of Kirkcudbright, was presented. There were obtained an urn of food-vessel type, and portions of a beaker urn, found associated in a short cist at Edington Mill, Chirnside, in the county of Berwick. Though no cairn now exists at the spot, there was evidence of the cist having been formerly within such an erection, which indicates the likelihood of a secondary interment having taken place when the food-vessel was placed in the cist.

Detailed accounts of the above-mentioned excavations, and more particular descriptions of the objects acquired by the National Museum, will appear in the next (forty-eighth) volume of the *Proceedings of the Society of Antiquaries of Scotland*.

That Society has begun this summer excavations on a fortified hill of considerable extent in East Lothian, known in former times as Dunpender, but now popularly as Traprain Law.

Already, on the sites examined, evidence of three different occupations has been revealed, the earliest of which was contemporaneous with one of the earlier Roman expeditions into Scotland. A number of Late-Celtic relics have been found in association with pieces of Samian ware, which will be particularized in a subsequent report.

The volume published this year by the Ancient Monuments Commission (Scotland) deals with the Stewartry of Kirkcudbright, and contains *inter alia* descriptions and plans of several Neolithic chambered cairns, also illustrations of the numerous examples of cup-and-ring markings to be found on rocks in that region."

George MacDonald, Esq., LL.D., communicated the following report as Local Secretary for Scotland:

"During 1913–14 the Glasgow Archaeological Society has made considerable progress with the systematic excavation of the fort at Balmuildy, which had obviously been one of the most important of the 'stations' on the Antonine Wall. Although the site has been sadly plundered since Gordon and others wrote of it so enthusiastically in the early part of the eighteenth century, it has proved possible to recover a very complete plan of the original structure, which had evidently been subjected, on at least one occasion, to extensive alterations. When the results are fully worked out, they ought to be of much interest, and to throw a clearer light on the history of the Limes. At present the indications seem to point to three well-marked 'periods'. Among the individual buildings the best preserved are two sets of baths, one within the walls of the fort and the other in an annexe outside. So far there is no trace of an Agricolan occupation. Pottery, coins, and inscriptions appear to be all of the second century. The finds include some interesting fragments of sculpture.

Elsewhere on the line of the Wall operations conducted by myself on a very much smaller scale have yielded a certain amount of valuable information. Their immediate object was to determine as nearly as possible the exact course followed by the Limes in those places where no marks of its presence are now left upon the surface. Sometimes this can be done by uncovering the stone foundation that supported the great rampart. More frequently the foundation has long since been torn up, and there is nothing for it but to search for the ditch. The longest continuous stretch dealt with in this way last year consisted of two miles at the western extremity. Earlier surveys, carried out as they were without any help from the spade, had been compelled to leave the space almost entirely blank. Now it has been filled in from end to end. A highly satisfactory confirmation of the soundness of the methods employed was forthcoming when the banks of the Clyde were reached. The exact position of the terminal fort, hitherto unknown, was revealed and some remains of the ramparts brought to light. Nine or ten miles farther east a singularly troublesome gap at Cadder has been successfully bridged; and here again a buried fort has been located and its original dimensions approximately ascertained. Towards the Forth the problem is even more severe, although not by any means hopeless Good beginnings have been made to the west of Polmont and also at Kinniel. A year hence it may be possible to report substantial progress In the meantime it is worth noting that something has been done towards determining the outline of the fort at Mumrills, first discovered three years ago. It had been defended by a rampart of earth, resting on a stone foundation and supported at either side by a bank of clay It is remarkable that a homogeneous work like the Antonine Limes should present examples of the *Erd-*, the *Rasen-*, and the *Steinkastell*. Further, the great rampart itself is less homogeneous that has been usually supposed. To the west of Falkirk it seems to be everywhere built of turf. On the other hand, wherever I have cut into it to the east of that town, I have failed to find the slightest sign of caespiticious construction , it has been of earth and clay precisely like the rampart that surrounded the fort of Mumrills.

At Cadder the labour for the investigations I have been describing was generously provided by Captain Stirling of Keir. The expense incurred at other points has been defrayed out of a research grant from the Carnegie Trust for the Universities of Scotland. With the help of the same grant, Professor Haverfield and I examined a large fortified enclosure in the north of Aberdeenshire, near the head-waters of the Ythan. Although we were not fortunate enough to find any datable objects, the nature of the defences was sufficiently characteristic to leave no doubt in our minds as to their Roman origin. The rampart had been laid upon a base of clay, the ditch was V-shaped, and the gates had been strengthened by traverses. The camp—for it was rather a camp than a fort—had covered an area of 120 acres, and must have been capable of accommodating a considerable number of men, perhaps as many as 15,000. In all probability it should be associated either with the last of Agricola's campaigns or with the punitive expedition of Severus. It would be interesting if further work enabled a definite decision to be come to. The camp at Ythan Wells, it should be added, does not stand alone. It is the most northerly of a series that Roy shows extending through Strathmore between the Grampians and the sea."

F. W. BULL, Esq., F.S.A., communicated the following report
on Romano-British finds at Kettering:

"On 18th April, 1912, I read a few additional notes on these
finds to the Society.[1] The workings on the Kettering Parish
boundary have since then been proceeded with. For a time
finds of a similar nature to those already described were made,
but few, if any, have found their way to the collection now
deposited at the Kettering Public Library. Most of them have
unfortunately been sold to any collector who came along. For
the last few months, however, practically no items of interest
have been discovered, and it may probably now be assumed that
the limit of the area of occupation in a northerly direction has
been reached.

A find has however been made, in another part of the parish
altogether, in the shape of an urn of rough light brown ware
filled with earth and burnt bones. It is 7 in. high and tapers
from about 5 in. across the top to 3 in. at the base. It has
no distinctive marks, but Mr. Reginald Smith puts it about
the second century. The urn was found by itself about 2 ft.
below the surface of a field in the southern part of the parish
numbered 59 on the Ordnance Survey (1900, 2nd edition) and
adjoining the Long Spinney. The site has been from time to
time worked for sand but no other finds are recorded. The field
lies to the south of the road leading to Barton Seagrave, where,
not more than about half a mile distant, some interesting Anglo-
Saxon finds now in the British Museum were made many years
since."

E. C. R. ARMSTRONG, Esq., F.S.A., subsequently communicated
the following report as Local Secretary for Ireland:

"The period 1913-14 has not been an eventful one for Irish
archaeology. The various subjects of interest may be divided
as follows:

1. *Excavation.*   (*a*) Lochpaire Crannog near Tuam, Co.
Galway. This was excavated in the summer of 1913. The
objects discovered were of the types usually found in Irish
crannogs, and presented no unusual features. They were late
in date. A full account of the work and the finds is published
in the *Proceedings of the Royal Irish Academy*, vol. xxxii, Sec. C,
p. 147.

(*b*) A rath on the townland of Knockshanawee (Cnoc Sean-
Mhaighe) near Crookstown, Co. Cork. This rath was examined
in October, 1913, with a view to discovering Ogham inscriptions
on the lintels, etc., of the Souterrain in the fort. Six inscrip-

---

[1] *Proceedings*, xxiv, 223.

tious of an interesting nature were discovered, and the inscribed
stones have been placed in the museum of University College,
Cork. A great deal of most unfortunate newspaper controversy was raised by the removal of these stones and the consequent falling-in of the chamber, but archaeologists will be
grateful for any excavations carried on in a proper manner, and
the removal of objects of interest to places where they will be
available for study. An account of the rath will be found in
the *Journal of the Cork Historical and Archaeological Society*,
vol. xvii, second series, p. 59, and an account of the Ogham
inscriptions in the *Proceedings of the Royal Irish Academy*,
vol. xxxii, Sec. C, p. 140.

2. *Finds.* (a) An interesting find of objects was made in
April, 1913, at Annesborough, between Lurgan and Loch
Neagh, Co. Armagh. The objects comprised a nearly complete
bronze torc, a fragment of another, three bronze bracelets, of
which only two were obtained, a bronze palstave, and a hinged
brooch of provincial Roman type. The find was acquired for
the Royal Irish Academy's collection in the National Museum.
Gold twisted torcs have often been found in Ireland, but there
is only one of bronze in the Academy's collection and its
provenance is considered doubtful, so it is interesting to get
a well-authenticated example. The brooch is also of importance
as having a recorded locality. As the objects of the find differ
considerably in date it is probable that they represent a founder's
hoard collected together for the purpose of remelting. The objects
together with a full account of the find are published in the *Proceedings of the Royal Irish Academy*, vol. xxxii, Sec. C, p. 171.

(b) A hoard of gold objects supposed to have been found in
the neighbourhood of Strangford Loch, Co. Down. Much
uncertainty surrounds the discovery of these ornaments, as they
were removed from Ireland and passed into the hands of a London
dealer who offered them to the British Museum, and it is owing
to the courtesy of the authorities of the Department of British
and Medieval Antiquities, who at once communicated with the
officials of the National Museum, that the objects were enabled
to be acquired for the Irish National Collection. They were
purchased at Count Plunkett's suggestion by the Rt. Hon.
Viscount Iveagh, K.P., F.S.A., and by him presented to the
National Museum. The portion of this hoard which is now in
Dublin consists of a gold twisted torc which has been enlarged
by attaching a twisted bar to the recurved ends, a model of
a shield, two pins, and five model axes with flanges and slight
stop ridges. The shield, one of the pins, and all the axes are
ornamented with spirals. Other portions of this find are extant,
the whereabouts of two of the gold axes being known and of

others suspected. It is much to be regretted that this find should have been dispersed, but we must be thankful that a portion of it at least is available for study. It is published in the *Proceedings of the Royal Irish Academy*, vol. xxxii, Sec. C, p. 176.

3. *Preservation of Irish Archaeological Monuments.* The obtaining of a Royal Commission on the Ancient Monuments of Ireland similar to those now at work in England, Scotland, and Wales has been exercising the minds of Irish archaeologists for several years, and efforts have been made by the Councils of the Royal Society of Antiquaries of Ireland and of the Royal Irish Academy to have a Commission appointed to deal with Ireland, but hitherto without success. On May 25th, 1914, the question was again brought before the Royal Irish Academy in the form of a full Report dealing with the matter historically and showing how the working of the Church Act, Ancient Monuments Protection Act, the Local Government Act, and the Land Act have affected the monuments and their preservation, and giving a selected list of twenty-five monuments that have been destroyed or seriously injured since the passing of the Land Act of 1903. The Report was ordered to be referred to the Council to consider what steps should be taken to urge upon the Government the necessity of preparing a survey of the ancient monuments of Ireland. The Report has been published in full in the Academy's *Abstract of Minutes*, 1913–14, and all who are interested in the preservation of Ireland's ancient monuments are recommended to read it. In connexion with this it may be mentioned that voluntary effort is doing something, the Honorary Secretary and Honorary Editor of the Galway Archaeological Society having made surveys of three parishes in the Barony of Dunkellin, which have been printed in the Journal of the Galway Archaeological and Historical Society. Dr. R. Cochrane has also published a list of the ancient and national monuments in the County of Cork, which has appeared in the Journal of the Cork Historical and Archaeological Society. Excellent as these efforts are it is quite out of the question to expect that individuals will be able to deal in a satisfactory manner with the 60,000 antiquities of various kinds that it is estimated now exist in Ireland, and which require to be properly surveyed and listed.

4. *General.* The retirement at the end of March, 1914, on a pension, of Mr. George Coffey, for many years Keeper of Irish Antiquities in the National Museum was a matter of regret to all students of Celtic antiquities, to whom his work was well known. His retirement was necessitated by continued ill health, and it is hoped that complete rest may do something to restore this. The Department of Agriculture and Technical Instruction

for Ireland appointed to the Keepership the writer of this notice, who had formerly acted as Mr. Coffey's assistant."

Thanks were ordered to be returned for these communications and exhibitions.

The Ordinary Meetings of the Society were then adjourned until Thursday, November 26.

INDEX

TO

PROCEEDINGS, SECOND SERIES, VOL. XXVI

THE COUNCIL OF THE
SOCIETY OF ANTIQUARIES OF LONDON

CUMBERLAND . . .	William Gershom Collingwood, Esq. M.A. F.S.A. *Lanehead, Coniston.*
DERBYSHIRE . . .	Rev. Frederick Charles Hipkins, M.A. F.S.A. *Bamford.*
DEVONSHIRE . . .	Robert Burnard, Esq. F.S.A. *Teignmouth.*
DORSET	J. E. Acland, Esq. F.S.A. *Dorchester.*
	Henry Colley March, Esq. M.D. F.S.A. *Portesham.*
DURHAM	Rev. Joseph Thomas Fowler, D.C.L. F.S.A. *Durham.*
	Rev. Henry Gee, D.D. F.S.A. *Durham.*
ESSEX	George Frederick Beaumont, Esq. F.S.A. *Coggeshall.*
	Henry Laver, Esq. F.S.A. *Colchester.*
GLOUCESTERSHIRE .	Rev. William Bazeley, M.A. *Matson Rectory, Gloucester.*
	John Emanuel Pritchard, Esq. F.S.A. *Bristol.*
HAMPSHIRE . . .	William Dale, Esq. F.S.A. *Southampton.*
	N. C. H. Nisbet, Esq. 45 *Jewry Street, Winchester.*
(ISLE OF WIGHT) .	Herbert Appold Grueber, Esq. F.S.A. *Bembridge.*
	Percy Goddard Stone, Esq. F.S.A. *Merston.*
HEREFORDSHIRE . .	Rev. E. Hermitage Day, D.D. F.S.A. *Belmont.*
	A. P. Maudslay, Esq. F.S.A. *Hereford.*
	Henry Thomas Weyman, Esq. F.S.A. *Ludlow.*
HERTFORDSHIRE . .	William John Hardy, Esq. M.A. F.S.A. *St. Albans.*
	William Minet, Esq. M.A. F.S.A. *Little Hadham.*
HUNTINGDONSHIRE .	Rev. William Mackreth Noble, B.A. *Wistow Rectory, Huntingdon.*
KENT	Leland Lewis Duncan, Esq. M.V.O. F.S.A. *Lewisham.*
	A. R. Goddard, Esq. B.A. *The Bungalow, Grotto Hill, Margate.*
	George Hubbard, Esq. F.S.A. *Eltham.*
	Rev. Grevile Mairis Livett, F.S.A. *Wateringbury.*
LANCASHIRE . . .	Col. J. W. R. Parker, C.B. F.S.A. *Clitheroe.*
LEICESTERSHIRE . .	William Jesse Freer, Esq. F.S.A. *Leicester.*
	Rev. Sidney Thorold Winckley, M.A. *Houghton Rectory, Leicester.*
LINCOLNSHIRE . .	Alfred Atkinson, Esq. *Brigg.*
	Rev. Arthur Frederick Sutton, *Brant Broughton Rectory, Newark.*
	Edward Mansel Sympson, Esq. M.A. M.D. F.S.A. *Lincoln.*
LONDON & MIDDLESEX	A. W. Clapham, Esq. F.S.A.
MONMOUTHSHIRE .	J. G. Wood, Esq. M.A. F.S.A.
NORFOLK	Leonard G. Bolingbroke, Esq. *The Close, Norwich.*
	Hamon le Strange, Esq. M.A. F.S.A. *Hunstanton Hall.*
NORTHAMPTONSHIRE .	John Alfred Gotch, Esq. F.S.A. *Kettering.*
	Christopher Alexander Markham, Esq. F.S.A. *Dallington.*
	Rev. Robert Meyricke Serjeantson, M.A. F.S.A. *Northampton.*
NORTHUMBERLAND .	Robert Blair, Esq. F.S.A. *South Shields.*
	William Henry Knowles, Esq. F.S.A. *Newcastle.*
NOTTINGHAMSHIRE .	Rev. A. du Boulay Hill, M.A. *East Bridgford.*
	George Harry Wallis, Esq. F.S.A. *Nottingham.*
OXFORDSHIRE . . .	Viscount Dillon, D.C.L. F.S.A. *Ditchley.*
	Francis John Haverfield, Esq. LL.D. F.S.A. *Oxford.*
RUTLAND	Rev. E. A. Irons, M.A. *North Luffenham, Stamford.*
SHROPSHIRE . . .	Rev. William Gilchrist Clark-Maxwell, M.A. F.S.A. *Bridgnorth.*
	Rev. William George Dimock Fletcher, M.A. F.S.A. *Oxon.*
SOMERSET	Rev. Edward Harbin Bates Harbin, M.A. *Newton Surmaville, Yeovil.*
STAFFORDSHIRE . .	Charles Lynam, Esq. F.S.A. *Stoke-upon-Trent.*
SUFFOLK	Rev. Edmund Farrer, F.S.A. *Hinderclay.*
SURREY	Rev. John Kestell Floyer, M.A. F.S.A. *Esher.*
	Marquess of Sligo, F.S.A. *Haslemere.*
	Thackeray Turner, Esq. F.S.A. *Godalming.*
SUSSEX	Edwin Henty, Esq. F.S.A. *Ferring, Worthing.*
	Robert Garraway Rice, Esq. F.S.A. *Pulborough.*
WARWICKSHIRE . .	G. A. Auden, Esq. M.D. F.S.A. *Birmingham.*
	Sir James Sawyer, F.S.A. *Birmingham.*
WESTMORLAND . .	John Flavel Curwen, Esq. F.S.A. *Kendal.*
WILTSHIRE	Harold Brakspear, Esq. F.S.A. *Corsham.*
	Rev. George Herbert Engleheart, M.A. F.S.A. *Dinton.*
	Rev. Edward Hungerford Goddard, M.A. *Clyffe, Swindon.*
WORCESTERSHIRE . .	William Pearce, Esq. F.S.A. *Pershore.*
	John William Willis-Bund, Esq. M.A. LL.B. F.S.A. *Worcester.*
YORKSHIRE	John Bilson, Esq. F.S.A. *Hull.*
	William Brown, Esq. F.S.A. *Thirsk.*
	Thomas Boynton, Esq. F.S.A. *Bridlington.*
	Edwin Kitson Clark, Esq. M.A. F.S.A. *Leeds.*
SCOTLAND	A. O. Curle, Esq. F.S.A. *Edinburgh.*
	G. MacDonald, Esq. LL.D. 17 *Learmonth Gardens, Edinburgh.*
IRELAND	E. C. R. Armstrong, Esq. F.S.A. *Dublin.*
	George Dames Burtchall, Esq. 44 *Morehampton Road, Dublin.*
	Sir Bertram Coghill Alan Windle, M.A. F.S.A. *Cork.*
WALES (NORTH) . .	Edward Neil Baynes, Esq. F.S.A.
WALES (SOUTH) . .	Henry Owen, Esq. D.C.L. F.S.A. *Poyston, Haverfordwest.*
ISLE OF MAN . . .	Rev. Ernest Bickersteth Savage, M.A. F.S.A. *Douglas.*
CHANNEL ISLANDS .	R. R. Marett, Esq. M.A. D.Sc. *Exeter College, Oxford.*
CYPRUS	George E. Jeffery, Esq. F.S.A. *Nicosia.*
EGYPT	H. R. Hall, Esq. M.A. F.S.A.

_{*} *These Local Secretaries are appointed for the quadrennial period beginning at the Anniversary 1913 and ending at the Anniversary 1917.*

PUBLICATIONS OF THE SOCIETY

N.B.—Fellows can purchase ONE copy of each publication, at the Society's apartments, at 25 per cent. off the prices quoted below.
Additional copies can be obtained from Mr. Bernard Quaritch, 11 Grafton Street, New Bond Street, W.

ARCHAEOLOGIA.

Vols. I—XXVII. (Stock sold off.)
Vols. XXVIII—XXXIV, each Volume in two parts. Price 15s. per Part.
Vols. XXXV—XLV, each Volume in two Parts. Price 21s. per Part. Vol. XLV, Part 2, out of print.
Vols. XLVI—XLVIII, each Volume in two Parts. Price 30s. per Part.

Volumes.	Parts.	Price per Part.	Volumes.	Parts.	Price per Part.
		£ s. d.			£ s. d.
XLIX.	1	1 11 6	LVI.	2	2 2 0
XLIX.	2	2 2 0	LVII.	1 & 2	2 2 0
L.	1 & 2	1 11 6	LVIII.	1	3 3 0
LI.	1 & 2	out of print	LVIII.	2	2 12 6
LII.	1	1 11 6	LIX.	1	2 12 6
LII.	2	3 3 0	LIX.	2	3 3 0
LIII.	1 & 2	2 2 0	LX.	1 & 2	3 3 0
LIV.	1	2 2 0	LXI.	1 & 2	3 3 0
LIV.	2	out of print	LXII.	1 & 2	3 3 0
LV.	1	2 2 0	LXIII.	complete	3 3 0
LV.	2	2 10 0	LXIV.	,,	3 3 0
LVI.	1	2 10 0	LXV.	,,	3 3 0

The complete Series of Vols. XXVIII—L may be had for 25 Guineas.
General Index to the Archaeologia, Vols. I—L. Price 2 Guineas.

VETUSTA MONUMENTA.

Vols. I—V. (Stock sold off.)
Vol. VI. Early portion. (Out of print.)
   CHAIR OF ST. PETER. Three Plates. Price 1s. 6d.
   ILLUMINATIONS IN IRISH MSS. Four Plates. Price 4s.
   THE EVANGELIA QUATUOR OF LINDAU. Two Plates. Price 1s.
Vol. VII.
   TOMB OF AN ARCHBISHOP AT CANTERBURY. Five Plates. Price 15s.
   ATCHIEVEMENTS OF EDWARD, PRINCE OF WALES, IN THE CATHEDRAL CHURCH OF CANTERBURY. Five Plates. Price 15s.
   ROYAL CUP OF THE KINGS OF FRANCE AND ENGLAND. Four Plates. Price 15s.
   OBITUARY ROLL OF JOHN ISLIP, ABBOT OF WESTMINSTER, ETC. Ten Plates. Price 21s.
AN INDEX TO THE 4TH, 5TH, AND 6TH VOLUMES. Fol. Price 7s. 6d. 8vo. Price 2s. 6d. TITLE-PAGE AND INDEX TO VOL. VI. Price 2s. 6d.

PROCEEDINGS.

FIRST SERIES, Vols. I—IV. Price 15s. per Volume ; or the set of four Volumes, £2 2s.
SECOND SERIES, Vols. I—XX. Price 10s. 6d. per Volume ; or the set of the first ten Volumes, £2 12s. 6d. The current parts of Vols. XXI, XXII, and XXIII and the complete Vols. XXIV, XXV, and XXVI, may also be had at 6s. each.

REPORTS OF THE RESEARCH COMMITTEE.

No. 1. Excavations at Wroxeter in 1912, by J. P. Bushe-Fox. Price 2s. 6d.

CATALOGUES.

PRINTED BROADSIDES IN THE POSSESSION OF THE SOCIETY, by
ROBERT LEMON, F.S.A. Price 10s. 6d.

PRINTED BOOKS IN THE LIBRARY OF THE SOCIETY OF ANTI-
QUARIES OF LONDON. *With Supplement.* London, 1887. Price 16s. 8d.

CODEX EXONIENSIS; a Collection of Anglo-Saxon Poetry. Edited by
BENJAMIN THORPE, F.S.A. 8vo. London, 1842. Price 10s. 6d.

LAƷAMON'S BRUT, or CHRONICLE OF BRITAIN; a POETICAL SEMI-
SAXON PARAPHRASE OF THE BRUT OF WACE. Edited by SIR FREDERIC
MADDEN, K.H. 3 vols. 8vo. 1847. Price £1 7s. *(Out of print.)*

LIBER QUOTIDIANUS CONTRAROTULATORIS GARDEROBÆ ANNO
28 EDWARDI PRIMI. 4to. London, 1787. Price in cloth, 5s.

ORDINANCES FOR THE GOVERNMENT OF THE ROYAL HOUSE-
HOLD. 4to. London, 1790. Price in cloth, 7s. 6d.

MAGNI ROTULI SCACCARII NORMANNIÆ. Edited by THOMAS
STAPLETON, F.S.A. 2 vols. 8vo. London, 1840-4. Price in cloth, 10s. 6d.

PREHISTORIC STONE MONUMENTS: CORNWALL. By REV. W. C.
LUKIS, M.A. F.S.A. Sm. Fol. London, 1885. Price in cloth, 10s.

ARCHAEOLOGICAL SURVEYS:
  (1) KENT. By GEORGE PAYNE, F.S.A.
  (2) HERTFORDSHIRE. By SIR JOHN EVANS, K.C.B. V.P.
  (3) CUMBERLAND AND WESTMORLAND. By CHANCELLOR FERGUSON,
      F.S.A.; and LANCASHIRE NORTH-OF-THE-SANDS. By H. S.
      COWPER, F.S.A.
  (4) LANCASHIRE. By WILLIAM HARRISON.
  (5) HEREFORDSHIRE. By REV. J. O. BEVAN, F.S.A., JAMES DAVIES,
      and F. HAVERFIELD, F.S.A.
  (6) NORTHANTS. By T. J. GEORGE. Price 5s. each.

YARD AND METRE SCALE FOR PHOTOGRAPHIC PURPOSES.
Price 6d., or 5s. per dozen, post free.

ILLUSTRATED CATALOGUE OF THE EXHIBITION OF ENGLISH
MEDIEVAL ALABASTER WORK. Price 15s. (no discount to Fellows).

HISTORICAL PRINTS.

1 Le Champ du Drap d'Or, or the Interview of Henry VIII and Francis I
   between Guines and Ardres, 1520. 21s. *(Out of print.)*
2. Encampment of the English Forces near Portsmouth, 1545. 8s. 8d. *(Out of print.)*
3. Embarkation of Henry VIII at Dover, 1520. 20s.
4. Procession of Edward VI from the Tower to Westminster. 20s.
5. Departure of Henry VIII from Calais, 1544. 10s. } or 16s. 8d. the
6. Encampment of Henry VIII at Marquison, 1544. 4s. 8d. set of three.
7. Siege of Boulogne by Henry VIII, 1544. 4s. 8d.
8. Plan of London, temp. Elizabeth. 13s. 4d. *(Out of print.)*
9. Roman pavement at Stunsfield, Oxon. *(Out of print.)* } 8s. the set.
10. Two views of Mr. Lethieullier's Mummy. *(Out of print.)*
11. Henry VII and his Queen; Henry VIII and Jane Seymour. 6s. 8d.
12. Procession of Elizabeth to Blackfriars. 6s. 8d. } or 20s. the set of four.
13. Cenotaph of Lord Darnley, etc. 6s. 8d.
14. Battle of Carberry Hill. 6s. 8d.
15. Three Children of Christian II, King of Denmark. 6s. 8d.
16. Charles Brandon, Duke of Suffolk, and Mary, Queen of
    France. 6s. 8d. } or 20s. the set of five.
17. Frances, Duchess of Suffolk, and Adrian Stokes her second
    husband. 6s. 8d.
18. Lady Jane Grey. 6s. 8d. [6s. 8d.
19. Edward VI Granting the Palace of Bridewell for a Hospital.
20. Charles I and Henrietta Maria. 10s.
21. Plan of Whitehall. 5s. 4d. *(Out of Print.)*
22. View of the Charity Children in the Strand, 7 July, 1713. 2 sheets. 4s. 8d.
23. Portrait of Sir John Hawkwood. 2s.
24. Four Views of Stanton Harcourt, Oxon. 9s. 4d.